THE STAGE

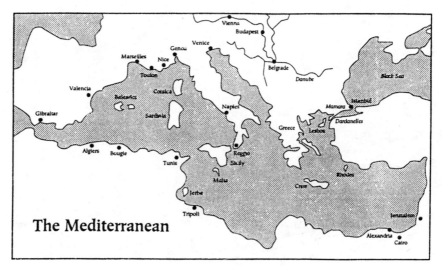

The Mediterranean

THE PLAYERS

(active period)

Barbarosa, *Turkish Viceroy, Grand Admiral* 1518-1546
  Aruj, *his brother*
  Ochiali, *his friend*
  Dragut, *his friend*
  La Bella, *his love*

Charles, *Holy Roman Emperor, King of Spain* 1519-1558

Francis, *King of France* 1515-1547

Suleiman, *Sultan of Turkey* 1520-1566

Andrea Doria, *Soldier of fortune, Genoan Admiral* . . . 1510-1550

The Rowed War Galley

A cast of thousands

Barbarosa

THE SWORD OF ISLAM

Galley War in the Mediterranean

An Adventure — A Life

BARBAROS HAYREDDIN PASHA
Galley Pirate
King
Viceroy
Grand Admiral

RODNEY S. QUINN
Gorham, Maine
2005

Design and photos by author.

Note for Librarians: A cataloguing record for this book is available from Library and Archives
Canada at www.collectionscanada.ca/amicus/index-e.html
ISBN 1-4120-7054-6

*Printed on paper with minimum 30% recycled fibre. Trafford's print shop
runs on "green energy" from solar, wind and other environmentally-friendly power sources.*

Offices in Canada, USA, Ireland and UK
This book was published *on-demand* in cooperation with Trafford Publishing. On-demand
publishing is a unique process and service of making a book available for retail sale to the
public taking advantage of on-demand manufacturing and Internet marketing. On-demand
publishing includes promotions, retail sales, manufacturing, order fulfilment, accounting and
collecting royalties on behalf of the author.

Book sales for North America and international:
Trafford Publishing, 6E–2333 Government St.,
Victoria, BC v8t 4p4 CANADA
phone 250 383 6864 (toll-free 1 888 232 4444)
fax 250 383 6804; email to orders@trafford.com
Book sales in Europe:
Trafford Publishing (uk) Limited, 9 Park End Street, 2nd Floor
Oxford, UK ox1 1hh UNITED KINGDOM
phone 44 (0)1865 722 113 (local rate 0845 230 9601)
facsimile 44 (0)1865 722 868; info.uk@trafford.com
Order online at:
trafford.com/05-1965

10 9 8 7 6 5 4 3

The worldly hope men set their Hearts upon
Turns ashes — or it prospers; and then,
Like snow upon the Desert's dusty face
Lighting a little hour or two — is gone.

— Omar Khayyam

This book chronicles the life of a 16th Century Turkish Admiral who, through fifty years of adventure, rose from an obscure birth to one of the most powerful offices on earth. He was bibber of wine, a renown devotee of women, and a vain man. He was also a classical scholar, a student of music, a linguist of the first order, a marine architect of note, an administrator of world class skills, the supreme master of galley warfare, and a warrior of exceptional personal courage who survived forty years of sea battles unharmed, to die in bed in a wealthy old age, his hand held by a new wife of twenty.

His story also serves as a canvas on which to paint one of the world's great — but too little known — Empires during its heyday, and it brings alive a critical period of the age-old war between Islam and Christianity.

In a few instances the chronology is manipulated or characters are created in order to give coherence or to fill gaps in the historical record, Each is clearly identified. Otherwise, the people in this book all lived and the adventures all happened.

The accuracy of this story is the
accuracy of most history.

BARBAROSA
Two Views

As seen by Turks

As seen by Christians

CONTENTS

ISLAMIC JUSTICE

A PROLOGUE, A PRELUDE

GLOSSARY

SELECTED BIBLIOGRAPHY

ILLUSTRATIONS

This book is dedicated to Melba,
who midwifed it.

THANKS

To Lucy McCauley, a Cambridge author of talent
and heart, the Honorable James Mitchell, Maine's
best wordsmith and one of it's better judges, and
Dick Spencer and Dan Warren, honest lawyers.

ISLAMIC JUSTICE

As he made his way across battle rubble to the fort-center, he exchanged banter in several languages with resting soldiers and their enthusiasm marked his passage like the wake of a ship.

Although unarmed, he was a striking presence, one that well repaid the time he had taken to change his clothing. Deferring to the unseasonal warmth of the spring afternoon, rather than armor, he now wore light silken trousers and a soft shirt open at the neck over which a brocade vest and decorative jeweled belt reaffirmed the sun's brightness. Soft leather slippers replaced iron-shod boots, and on his head an oversized turban flaunted the Egret plumes and glass tube of a Turkish Pasha.

Not quite six feet, his exceptionally wide shoulders announced the strength of a wrestler. Although he suffered a slight salting of gray in his auburn beard and the first indications of mid-life corpulence, his catlike movements and vigor were those of a man in his thirties. In fact, he was fifty. And not anxious to show it.

Once he crossed the central square to station himself on a low platform, an artist might think the scene staged. A buttery-soft spring day. A riot of color. Charred wreckage and dead or wounded fighting-men framed by bright hibiscus, oleander, and lush palms. A limpid harbor shared sunlit diamonds with the rich blue Mediterranean.

Battle devastation was embarrassed by the backdrop of beauty.

In the parade square, a mixed group of his warriors formed an audience. Algiers was the western hub of the Turkish Empire and the colorful collection of fighting men represented opulent Muslim diversity — their clothings a rainbow; their arms a cornucopia of 16th century warfare.

On the left, resplendent in brilliant battle jackets and boxy turbans, stood two companies of light-haired Slavs and taller-than-average Greeks, members of a special Turkish infantry known as Janissaries. A company of Egyptian Mameluke pikemen reclined at the far end of the square, Their scarlet capes and turbans contrasting with desert Berbers in white flowing robes. Dark-skinned Moorish cavalrymen minus their mounts were gathered on the right, high boots glistening, capes tied back to reveal lethal Turkish short bows.

In the center of the square, with body armor dulled with blood and grime, stood the losers: forty seven stocky, narrow headed, bearded Spaniards.

After greeting his officers waiting on the platform, he stepped forward, and turned to nearby guards, and in Arabic ordered, "Bring Don Martin de Vargas to me."

The officer of the Guard, honored with a personal command from his King, shouted in ringing Spanish, "Captain of prisoners to stand forth in respect before Barbarosa Hayreddin Pasha, King of Algiers and Viceroy of the Ottoman West!"

Hearing the command, a tall, thin Spaniard wearing body plates, bareheaded and so begrimed as to be almost unrecognizable as an officer, stepped forward. "I am Don Martin de Vargas, Captain of the garrison. Because I was rendered senseless by a near strike of one of your cursed stones, my flag was struck and I find myself your prisoner."

Obviously intending disrespect, he did not offer to bow.

The two took measure of one another, Barbarosa with a methodical appraisal; the Captain with a deliberate eye contact — known to be offensive to a Muslim. Although he had lost the fort, Spain was certain to ransom him. This motley collection of pirates would not injure him and risk the gold his ransom would bring.

He believed.

The meeting between the two had been a long time in the making. A Spanish fort on a small island known as the Penon had controlled the harbor of Algiers for decades. Although Algiers had become a main base for the largest pirate fleet ever assembled and, even though it was the center for a North African kingdom accepted as a protectorate of the Ottoman Empire, its ship traffic had to operate from a nearby beach. Barbarosa had no siege guns and his ship's guns were too light to reduce the fort. In frustration, a year earlier he had attempted to take the fort by stealth, using two young Morisco[1] boys as spies, only to have the Spaniards uncover the plot and hang the youths from fort walls in plain view of the city.

This was an embarrassment sufficient to justify an appeal to Turkey for heavy siege guns.

His request was granted, and six stone-firing pedreros of the type known in Europe as murlaccios arrived from Istanbul the following spring. These primitive cannons were objects of awe. Ten hands thick at the breech walls, they weighed twelve tons and easily threw two hundred and fifty pound stones across the harbor. Emplaced within days, they began the methodical destruction of a fortress wall, block by block. For guns hardly more accurate than mortars, they did well.

Three weeks of battering killed or maimed half the garrison and breached the wall sufficiently to permit an assault. Even so, when the attack came, the few surviving Spaniards courageously resisted for two full days — surrendering only when fewer than a quarter remained standing.

Turks respected valor on the part of their enemies and frequently recruited brave opponents into their own service. Entry into the Islamic brotherhood was easily made; only a pledge was required. Barbarosa had come to make such an offer to the Captain of the garrison.

The Spanish Captain, now silent, but continuing to insult the Muslim King with his eyes, stood motionless, head rigidly erect as though offended. Barbarosa studied him for a moment, then came to a decision. Honoring his prisoner by using Spanish, he said, "Don Martin, has peleado noblemente, ningun soldado podria haber hecho mas. Estoy impressionado por tu valor" — "You have fought nobly, no soldier could have done more. I am impressed by your bravery and steadfastness."

The Don nodded slightly. He didn't speak.

Barbarosa continued, "A warrior of your courage is rare. I should like to offer you a place of honor in my service."

Observers later credited the Don with residual battle excitement; the man could well have been out of his mind. Obviously under tight self-control, he clenched his jaws, swallowed in spite of himself and locked his hands behind his back to prevent any visible trembling — all the

---

1. Moriscos — Muslim refugees from Spain.

while assaulting his captor with his insolent glare.

His effrontery was deliberate.

Barbarosa's green eyes turned cold under heavy brows, but he pressed on, "I will make you a Captain and give you command of my guard. You need only swear loyalty and accept The Law...."

De Vargas had closed his eyes for a moment; he now opened them and, with released breath, bathed the square in vitriol. "I spit in your face. There is no greater shame for me. The religion of Mohammed is a vile, corrupt perversion. Whores despise you."

Among the mixture of Muslim soldiers, only the Moriscos understood Spanish, but the Castilian sibilants hissing across the quiet square needed no translation. An angry murmur swelled; postures stiffened, grips on swords and pikes tightened.

Unheeding, the Spaniard continued to drive a sword into his own heart. "The whore-masters before whom your mother knelt cannot decide which of them cast off the seed she swallowed to produce you!"

With well chosen accuracy, he had pierced the two tenderest parts of the psyche of any True Believer — his religion and his mother.

Restrained by a raised hand, the murmur died. A silent square waited. Without taking his eyes from the Spaniard, Barbarosa held his hand out. Without instruction, an officer standing behind him laid a heavy Turkish scimitar on his open palm. Barbarosa secured a battle grip on the glittering sword and, showing no emotion beyond a slight facial darkening, studied his prisoner for a moment.

Suddenly, with the speed of a striking cobra and the total body involvement of a gladiator, he brought the heavy sword around and down in an overhand blur.

The Spaniard's scorn decayed into fear and he attempted to ward off the scimitar with his forearm. The blade severed the arm and struck the juncture of shoulder and neck, slicing well into his chest cavity, bending body armor for a half dozen inches. The victim's involuntary attempt to avoid death toppled his body backward where it convulsively fountained its life fluid into the sand. Because his metal breastplate slowed the scimitar, the body was still joined, one arm and part of the chest remaining with the bearded head; the other shoulder joined to the rest of the body. The remnant of the arm which had betrayed fear became an accent piece to the scene.

From the grasp of the sword to the Spaniard's death was only an instant, but it encompassed an entire drama — the unspoken understanding of the officer who placed the sword in the outstretched hand, the lightning speed and extraordinary strength of a single blow, the severed body parts spouting blood, the ashen fear of the nearby prisoners, the surge of emotion among the closely packed Muslim fighting men — all in a silence washed by the light, flower-fragrant breeze.

The Muslim soldiers understood that Barbarosa — not only a King in his own right, but a champion of Islam recognized throughout the Ottoman Empire as a "Defender of the Faith" — would avenge blasphemy of The Prophet. And it went without saying that any man would demand payment of a life for insult to his mother.

To them the execution was well deserved, a proper decision of a great warrior. Would the King's legendary temper now extend to the prisoners?

The square remained as quiet as a mosque before prayer; the air charged with a blood lust that would be given life with the slightest signal.

But there was none.

Instead, Barbarosa motioned a guard and handed him the sword. "Have this blade cleaned and sharpened." Turning to the officer who had given the sword, he continued in Turkish, "Dragut, old friend, don't punish his men. Extend them the decencies due brave fighters."

Then he spoke to the square, this time in Arabic, "Tolerance and mercy are limited and must not be wasted on the undeserving. For them Prophet requires justice."

Brushing in distaste the blood that had spattered his clothing, he turned and walked alone to the shore where his eight-oared gig waited.[1]

---

1. Islamic and Christian historians, who ordinarily see Barbarosa's actions from different points of view, generally agree on the execution of de Vargas.

A PROLOGUE, A PRELUDE

Religion in the 16th century was the cement that held together the political, and social structures of both Islamic and Christian worlds. It pervaded every aspect of existence; its zeal underlay all actions.

In the third century, the conservative soldiers who ruled Rome found Christian laws and rules useful and, as an "official" religion, the Roman Catholic Church eventually expanded to assume many of the functions of Imperial Rome. In the process, it became not only an economic colossus — the greatest land-owner in Europe — but, by the 16th century, corrupt to the core; honeycombed with rot.

In the Arabian deserts, seven hundred years after Christ, the revelations of a camel trader named Mohammed were interpreted by his followers into a comprehensive, detailed code of behavior that made Islamic government and religion essentially inseparable — as well as aggressively expansionist.[1]

Conflict between the two religions was inevitable.

With remarkable early vigor, in less than two centuries Muslim armies washed across Arabia, Asia-Minor, Africa, and Spain in a religious and martial tidal wave. Once established however, Islamic leadership fell prey to dynastic and theological quarrels, and in the following two centuries the Christian Crusades retook most of the "Holy Lands."

The door of aggression was to revolve again as Muslim converts from the steppes of Asia took up the gauntlet for Islam. By the end of the 15th century these fierce, fleet horsemen had retaken Crusader holdings in Asia, as well as conquering Greece, the Balkans, and much of the Black

---

1. A code so detailed that it contained specified positions for urination, defecation, and sexual intercourse

Sea littoral. They also stuffed Constantinople, the thousand year capitol of Christianity, into their saddle bags.

Crowning this renewed advance of Islam, a young and brilliant Turkish Sultan took aim at Central Europe, promising to say his prayers in France and to stable his horse in Rome. By 1530 his armies had thundered hundreds of miles up the Danube, and digested not only Hungary, but much of the old Holy Roman Empire. European kings trembled before the Turkish hordes. Christian prayers rose like a winter fog.

And were answered at Vienna. There, at the gateway to Austria and the interior of Europe, Turkey was repulsed.

On land, Vienna demonstrated that Turkish armies had reached the limits of 16th century logistics, and at sea an Islamic challenge seemed out of the question. Maritime strengths and skills in the Mediterranean — where war was fought with the rowed galley — were overwhelmingly Christian.

Spain was the richest and most powerful; its great ships and strong sailors world-dominant. Venice laid rightful claim to the title "Bride of the Sea;" its galley-building the best in the world, its galley fleet the largest. Genoa's banking wealth could afford to hire the best of ships and men. The Pope, every Italian city-state, the Knights of Rhodes all supported up-to-date galley fleets.

Land-oriented Turkey, on the other hand, had only a beggar's ration of ships and seaman; fewer than any single Christian power.

And here is our story. In one short generation, the unique Ottoman system of government was to call on brilliant leaders, create great galley fleets from whole cloth and, with these, conquer the Mediterranean.

.

Our adventure opens with a young boy on Lesbos, a Greek Island belonging to Turkey, the year after Columbus discovered America.

1

A Beginning

1493

Winter had yielded its throne to spring.

Anointed with animal offerings, freshly turned earth competed with the rich tang of tars and oils belonging to wooden ships. Roses overlaid an erotic fragrance on springtime hillsides. The vibrant Aegean sun, a King of light, poured warmth into the stone of the ancient quay, gave life to the crowded harbor, and brought glints from the auburn of the boy's curly hair.

He apparently spent much of his time in the open, for the fire of the sun had bronzed his skin and dimmed his curls. Unusually stocky, with shoulders finishing the apprenticeship of childhood, his young frame promised a strength that only a few would possess, a characteristic that, together with a quick, pleasant, smile, compensated for his rather heavy features. Like most of the working waterfront, he was barefoot and clothed simply in a well worn shirt and patched trousers that boasted only a rope belt. However, he sported a pair of rolled silken scarves, one at his neck and one on his brow, much as a sailor dandy on shore leave — a vanity that identified him as Greek, a native.

As love belonged to the Goddess Sappho, this boy was the product of Lesbos, her island.

The harbor nestled comfortably beside and below the stone walls of the ancient town, little changed since the days of antiquity. Surrounding the waterfront, accented by brilliant spring blossoms, were wall upon wall of white houses marching up hills green with spring , their tile roofs a patchwork of color highlighting silver gray olive groves.

Thirty years earlier, Mehmed the Conqueror had added Lesbos to the

Turkish collection of Aegean islands, and Mytilene, as the harbor was
known, reflected the energy of the young and vigorous Ottoman Empire. Lean ships and strong men were preparing to assert their annual
domination of the sea.[1]

A curious ear could distinguish a half dozen languages common to
the Mediterranean world, and religion, frequently identified by the clothing of adherents, was similarly varied. Most Muslims, whose faith required them to touch their foreheads to the ground in prayer five times
daily — and to whom head covering was a necessary dignity — typically
wore turbans. Many of them observed the popular superstition that
Mohammed would be reborn to a man by wearing voluminous, drop-
centered pantaloons secured at the ankle, thus preventing injury to the
infant in the event the birth were to catch one unaware. Arabs generally
added the robe-like Jellaba as an outer garmet.

Greeks, Magyars, and lean mountain men from the Balkans who retained Byzantine Christianity through the tolerance of their Turkish
masters could generally be identified by their colorful blouses and rakish
straw hats. Roman Christianity was represented with the full-sleeved
shirts, bloused pants and knee length stockings common to central Europe. Jews with their distinctive skull caps and hair locks were sprinkled
throughout, especially in the market area.

There were a few Turkish officials. Generally stocky, rather dark men,
most wore mustaches; none wore beards. All flaunted impressive turbans, green striped pantaloons and, in the case of soldiers, crossed chest
belts supporting long, murderous scimitars.

The vessels in the crowded harbor, like the men, came from every
port in the eastern Mediterranean and, like the men, varied richly. The
smallest were Arab coastal craft known as feluccas, light enough to be
rowed by only a few men if the wind failed their single sail. At the high
end of the scale were the "round" ships — up to two hundred feet in
length and displacing four hundred tons or more — square rigged sailing vessels ranging from stubby caravelles and blocky coasters to high
pooped three and four deckers.

Somewhat smaller, but impressive, were the "long" ships, or galleys
— craft designed to be rowed. Each of them had at least one large mast

1.   16th century Mediterranean ships did not go to sea in winter. Venice, the major
     maritime state, forbade travel between mid-November and late January.

A water-taxi.

A war galley.

Galley Types – *16th century*

and one small foremast for lateen sails,[1] but their striking characteristic was oars — each ship bristled with them. The smaller rowing ships, called galleots, were more or less miniatures of their large brothers, with fewer oars and smaller sails.

With one hundred and eighty oars, wearing a vicious red iron bow ram, its black hull maintaining a lethal dignity, a war galley rested at anchor in the outer harbor. About one hundred and fifty feet long, the craft was so slender there was barely room for a narrow central walkway to divide six rowers, three on a side on each oar bench. With gunwales only an arm span above the water, only the most skilled seamanship would keep this nautical javelin afloat in a heavy sea.

The boy was interested in one of the smaller rowing ships, a relatively wide cargo galleot that had managed to obtain docking space. He stood and moved to meet the dark-eyed, middle aged man who stepped ashore. Like the boy, the man was dressed plainly. His lack of beard, round felt hat, and fierce mustaches announced him a Turk. He turned attentively as the youth approached and, when the boy inquired, admitted to being the captain.

The boy went straight to a business proposal. "My father, who makes pottery, has given me leave to make my own shipping contract. I'm told that you sail from Constantinople and, if you'll enter with me on shares, I wish to ship with you." The short speech was made without pause; he intended to complete it before his listener could lose interest.

Although he was dealing with a person whose age and appearance allowed some skepticism about any status as a genuine trader, the Turk answered graciously, "It is true, I trade between here and the great city of Istanbul." Then he enlarged on his courtesy, "What shares do you propose and of what quality is your pottery?"

"I will provide the goods, and I ask two shares for me, one for the Captain and crew, and one for the owner of the ship. The quality of my father's pottery is respected."

Now curious, the Turk said, "Since I am not only the Captain but have the misfortune to own this ship, those shares would be attractive. But, I am curious as to why you don't send such heavy merchandise in a round ship? They have more room than my small craft and carry cargo more cheaply."

---

1.   A triangular sail, with its apex pointing forward which could be swiveled 45 degrees or, for an opposite tack, have its boom lifted over the mast.

The boy answered honestly, as though truth was the medium of exchange to be expected among men. "I thought that you might accept a better price, or at least be more interested in my proposal. Also, once at sea, those tubs may have no wind for weeks. Even without wind, your ship should reach the Golden Horn in not much more than a week."[1]

The direct answer impressed the Turk enough to keep him talking. "Where may your goods be seen?"

"At the place of my father, Yakub," replied the would-be merchant prince, "The building with the yellow wall on Albehar hill."

Now the Turk was surprised. "I know of Yakub the potter. He was at one time a Captain of the Sultan's Janissaries, and I know something of his son, Aruj. Since Aruj has his own ship and is apparently your brother, why don't you form shares and sail with him?"

The boy answered, "His voyages involve more risk than simple trade." Honesty made him add, "Mostly, however, I don't sail with him because he won't take me before I'm seventeen. He also insists that I learn the language of Italy first — for he has no one on his crew with that language."

"Your brother is spoken well of."

Neither mentioned that the brother was a pirate. Sitting just below the entrance to the Dardanelles and the water route to Asia, "The Nest" — as Lesbos had been traditionally known — was ideally situated for small rowing ships that could strike and escape to cover within hours. In recent years, pirates had restricted their activities to Christian ships and had reached the status of respected entrepreneurs.

The Captain went on, "Italian can be useful on a ship such as your brother's. You are Greek, but your Turkish is as good as mine. If you will forgive my curiosity — do you have a talent for languages?"

"Yes." A simple statement of fact. No hint of un-Islamic pride. "I have Greek at home. I am at work on Italian, and I have a friend that will teach me the language of the Southern Franks when I am fifteen."

Already feeling a vague approval of this confident boy, the Turk said, "I have long respected your father. I should be honored to meet him. Perhaps you could arrange my introduction before we consider business further. May I know your name?"

The boy salaamed courteously. "Khizr, the fourth son of Yakub."

---

1.   Istanbul harbor was known as the Golden Horn.

The Captain returned the salaam with a slight, good-natured bow. "I would suspect that your name honors a Persian poet. I am named for Osman, the leader who freed us from the misrule of our Seljuk cousins, and the man for whom my people are called Osmanli."

The boy knew little of the origin of Turkey, and none of his own name. Out of things to say for a moment, he led the way briskly along the busy dock area with its small eating places and outdoor market, past the three Greek taverns the town afforded, and up a steep street which led past the House of Joy. The lady in charge of the establishment, a striking woman with a proud mustache, was enjoying a quiet maintenance hour in the morning sun with some of her employees. She nodded respectfully. One particularly attractive resident, brushing waist-length yellow hair, spoke directly to Khizr. "Good morning, my red-haired young friend." To Osman, she added, "Good morning to you, sir." As she spoke, her raised arms exposed an alabaster neck and most of an outstanding pair of firm breasts.

The boy answered, "Mademoiselle, I have the honor to accompany Osman reis" — using the formal title for a ship's captain[1] — "who brings his own ship from Constantinople."

With a warm smile she acknowledged the polite Frankish title awarded her by the boy. She offered the Captain a welcome to the city. Her speech was without guile; she seemed a woman of good manners and training. The Captain was impressed by her manner and he complimented her light hair, telling her that such hair was rare in Istanbul and treasured by his countrymen. He also seemed to appreciate, but did not mention, her magnificent breasts.

Courtesies completed, the potential business partners, so different in age and status, continued on their errand. As the House of Joy dropped out of sight and individual homes joined the small street, their stone path featured occasional tile or marble at gateways and was alive with bougainvillea, gardenias, and several kinds of lilies and azaleas.

The Captain commented on the display of spring beauty, but the boy still had the beautiful courtesan in mind. Sounding like a man of the world, he confided, "She insists on waiting until I'm in my fifteenth year, and she isn't yet twenty herself."

His listener nodded. "She apparently is Christian. The greatest Chris-

---

1.   Reis – same form singular or plural.

tian Emperor, Justinian, married a prostitute named Theodora — a woman who enjoyed and exhausted a dozen men an evening — and she was loved by the people. Her bravery once saved Constantinople from internal riots and war."

"This woman is also Christian. Her father was a Frank sailor who came here as a trader."

Thinking back over their conversation, a coincidence struck the Captain. The young man had said he would have an instructor in French when he was fifteen. Now he was announcing that he would become eligible for the woman's favors at the same age. The captain raised his eyebrows as he asked, "Will this lady be your teacher for the Frank language?"

No boasting, no innuendoes. "Yes."

The Captain resisted a comment on the variety of skills the lady might possess. Khizr was silent for a moment but his natural curiosity soon overcame him. "What are the prostitutes in Constantinople like?"

Amused at the boy's serious manner, the Turk answered, "Crude, generally. And not only the women. A taste for young boys is a curse of many of my countrymen. There are houses of boys younger than you where their bottoms are announced by the size of the wooden pegs on which they sit."[1]

Pederasty was nothing new to the boy. After all, the use of male children had been developed to a fine art by his Greek ancestors — and love of fellow man was common among the Arabs on the Mytilene waterfront. He was far more interested in Constantinople, the capitol of the Roman Empire for centuries, recently become the seat of Ottoman power. Like all Turkish subjects, he thought of that great city as the center of the world.

"It's said that there are fountains of water for everyone in Constantinople."

The Turk nodded. "The Prophet requires that water be given to all men."

By now their way had leveled and joined a wider paved stone road which afforded passage for animals and carts. Enjoying the walk and pleased to continue the boy's education, the Turk asked, "Do you know much of the City's history?"

---

1.   So-called "peg houses" were still in existence in 20th century Istanbul.

"Please tell me of it."

Pausing to pluck a spray of blossoms, the Captain began a recitation of the most famous victory in Turkish history — the capture of Constantinople forty years previously.

"Mehmed The Conqueror's efforts to extend the privilege of Turkish rule to the people of Rum[1] were seriously hampered by the fortress of Constantinople, and he resolved to occupy it. He ordered monster siege guns that required eighty oxen to move, guns that could throw a stone of fifteen hundred pounds. At the same time thousands of men dug a trench over which galleys were dragged to attack the unprotected Christian rear. While his ships failed to do much harm, the cannons destroyed some walls and the Janissaries stormed through a gate carelessly left open.

"Mehmed saved many Byzantine structures. The greatest Christian church, Hagia Sophia, was unharmed. Mehmed rode his horse into the center of the magnificent structure, struck a pillar with his sword and declared it a Mosque. That move must have been approved by God, for it is said that the marble pillar grew a flowered vine in the scar of his sword strike."

The older man paused and glanced sideways to see if the boy accepted the popular myth.

He apparently did. "My father served Mehmed, and considers him the greatest Sultan. He told me that some Greeks were traitors and were executed."

The Turk was equivocal. "True. Mehmed executed some Greeks, but there is more to the story."

They were passing a small stone wall marking the passage to a private path, and Khizr broke into the Turk's train of thought, "Excuse me, let me interrupt for a moment. This path and garden belong to a school in which my next oldest brother, Elias, studies to be an Imam. I thought it might interest you."[2]

Osman nodded, "Your father should be proud of his family. A budding Iman, a brave sea Captain, and a son destined to be the leading merchant of Mytilene. Are there others?"

"Yes, another brother, Isaac, who is a carpenter and who sails with Aruj." He added somewhat shyly. "And I have two sisters. They, like my

---

1.   "Rum" = "Rome". Eastern Europe, subsequently known as European Turkey.

2.   Muslim religious scholar and prayer leader. Islam has no priests.

Hagia Sophia. Built 1000 years before St Peter's in Rome, and fully as impressive in architecture and beauty. Converted to a Mosque by Mehmed (note four minarets). Today it is one of Istanbul's famous museums.

mother, are followers of the prophet Jesus."

It was certain that as the son of a Turkish Janissary, the boy himself would be well schooled in Islam; nevertheless he appeared unconcerned with the Christianity practiced in his home — as well as with the Muslim custom that accounted women no more worthy of discussion than domestic animals.

The Captain returned to the subject of Mehmed the Conqueror. "As a slave of the Sultan since childhood, your father's admiration is easy to understand. But one must see not only the building, one must know the stones and mortar. Mehmed was a violent man of strange urges, exceedingly cruel, and life had no value to him.[1] Let me tell you the rest of the story about the Greek officials, and you will have a more balanced impression of him.

---

1.   Mehmed also had a unique sense of humor. He once told several thousand Serbians they were to retain their heads — then he cut them in two.

"Greek Christians feared Rome more than they did Islam and were willing to cooperate with a Muslim ruler. The Sultan made Lucas Notarus, a prominent Byzantine official, governor of the city, and permitted him to retain his own household. One evening somewhat later, during a banquet, Mehmed decided to test his new governor's loyalty. Lucas had a son about your age sufficiently good-looking to arouse desire, and the Sultan decided he wanted the boy in his bed. He sent a messenger to the home of Lucas commanding delivery of the boy.

"Lucas refused, and the messenger returned empty handed.

"In a rage, Mehmed ordered the mutes who served as his bodyguards to bring the heads of the father and son to him, and that the father be made to witness the execution of the son. For good measure, he ordered the death of any other male in the home. As it happened, there was a school-mate of young Lucas visiting that evening and the three heads were brought to Mehmed and placed on the banquet table as decorations, where they remained for the rest of the evening."

Amazed, Khizr blanched and his eyes widened. He hesitated a moment, and then said softly, "My father never mentioned this story. Is it really true?"

"Aye. And after that night's festivities were concluded, the Sultan decided that many of the Byzantine governing officials were not sufficiently loyal to him, and he had them killed." Almost as an afterthought, he added, "Other stories could be told about The Conqueror, especially where his sexual pleasures were concerned, for he not only preferred boy children, he derived pleasure from inflicting pain."

Khizr could accept stories of sexual peccadilloes, but the tale of the executions strained belief. His first impulse was to reject it out of hand, but he restricted himself to being non-committal. "Efendi, you tell me history of which I have never heard."

"When you see Istanbul, you may think it worth the price of a few victims. Most do." As two shawled women passed and greeted Khizr, the Turk added, "You seem to be well known; everyone greets you."

"When my father retired and was given land here in Mytilene, he married my mother, who was a widow of a Byzantine priest with no children of her own. She came from a local family, and everyone seems to be my cousin." He added, "My father has never taken another wife, although he is still vigorous."

"Since your father was a Janissary, he must have been a child slave taken by the Sultan's agents. Do you know where he was taken?"

"Yes, from the Peloponnesus when he was eight."

"Then you are fully Greek. Some of Turkey's greatest leaders were born Greek. Does your father speak of his own family?"

"No, he knows them not. The only family he ever knew was the Janissary Corps."

"Does it trouble you that your mother and sisters are Christian?" The older man risked discourtesy.

Khizr didn't mind. "No. My father permits others descended of Abraham to believe as they wish. He expects nothing from them if they are not of the Faith."

"Aye. The Prophet indulged the practices of other Men of The Book."

When they reached the small factory, Khizr made introductions to a tall, wiry, gray haired man, whose formal turban, erect carriage and lack of beard proclaimed a military background — a respected person in any part of the Ottoman Empire.

Osman deferred. "Efendi, I am honored to be brought to you. When the Banner of God was raised over Constantinople, the Janissaries were my greatest heroes. My keenest disappointment was that as a Turk, I could never become one myself."

Yakub nodded appreciatively, "It is a pleasure to be remembered. My days with my kettlemates were the best of my life."

After courtesies and an explanation of Khizr's business proposal, Yakub escorted a tour of the factory and offered the inevitable tea, poured Turkish style over hard sugar in small cups. After a few moments of small talk, he extended an invitation, "Osman reis, will you honor my family by sharing food with us?"

Mohammed propounded law which did much to lift women from their near-animal existence in tribal life, but in the centuries since His death, observance of the law had weakened. In the holy lands of Islam the idea that a woman might meet a strange male visitor would be considered outrageous, if not actually unlawful. Observance of such probition relaxed with the distance between Mytilene and Mecca. Nevertheless, this was an unusual family.

The family dwelling, a sprawling, unpretentious single story structure adjoining the factory, was built in the rural Greek style of living areas

Mehmed II – The Conqeror. 1451-1481. (two views). In contrast with his treatment of civil authorities, Mehmed reinvigorated the leaderless Greek Orthodox Church by personally honoring and installing the monk Gennadius (George Scholarius) as Patriach "with all the privileges that Patriachs before you enjoyed", and by guaranteeing freedom for the Church to manage its own religious and secular affairs.

surrounding a courtyard. Spring flowers were blooming in carefully tended boxes and there were manicured shrubs on both sides of the paved stone yard. The table, with simple utensils placed on embroidered blue linen, was set out under a lath roof, itself woven with vines for shade. Small flowers were vased on the table; everything was spotlessly clean.

The attractive scene was accented by two dogs lazing with their heads between their paws, tails wagging as they reviewed visitors. These animals seemed accustomed to the privilege of human affection, another unusual touch. Other than as beasts of burden, most Muslims had little use for animals.

Khizr's wholesome mother appeared to be in her late thirties. Her silvering black hair neatly tied in a practical bun, she wore a simple, ankle length cotton dress and no shawl. Even had she been Muslim, her dress was not unusual, for Purdah was not worn in rural areas where all women had to work.

She welcomed the visitor in heavily accented Turkish, and Osman was at first disconcerted, for her arms were uncovered and she looked directly at him. She asked for permission to present Khizr's sisters. "It is not often my daughters get to meet someone from The City, and after you have eaten, they would like to try their Turkish with you for a few minutes."

Later, the girls were a further revelation — well mannered, and although shy, obviously educated. He was sure that they could even read and write.

The partnership agreement was signed that afternoon.

⸱⸴

For the next four years, although Yakub's small business prospered, he insisted that Khizr follow a rigorous program of learning, consequently there was less and less time for the young man to trade pottery. Yakub himself had begun his own education as a small child conscripted for Janissary service, and Khizr was the involuntary beneficiary of Yakub's belief that youth was not to be wasted.

The training varied from formal to informal, from tutor to tutor. The most exciting part of the curriculum had to do with arms and was conducted by Yakub himself. As a member of the elite Janissary guards for thirty years, he was an instructor of unmatched skills and knowledge.

Exceptionally strong and well coordinated, by his sixteenth birthday Khizr was skilled in the pike, superior to all but experienced bowmen with the cross bow, and well ahead of local competition with both short and long swords. However, his short bow performance was barely passable. He had the strength the two hundred pound pull required, but did not have the year of constant practice the murderous weapon demanded.[1] The strength promised by his young body had been delivered. Even professional wrestlers could rarely take him off his feet. He was urged to study wrestling, but he thought of it as low class entertainment in comparison with the more noble arms, and his vanity, although unspoken, found the contact of oiled bodies in the dirt distasteful.

Beyond arms, he was given to a Greek Christian scholar for mathematics and what passed for history — and to his brother's Islamic school for philosophy and rhetoric.

There were occasional youthful diversions, such as physicking a neighbor's donkeys — an experiment that resulted both an expenditure of energy and a new skill for Khizr. Once the prank came to Yakub's at-

---

1.   Properly termed "Curved Recomposite Bow", it was the fiercest weapon of the day.

tention, the prankster paid the hire of three donkeys out of his own savings two hours every day for two months while he occupied himself with collecting "donkey apples" for fertilizer.

For a half-day all of one winter, he worked as a carpenter at a harbor ship-way, holding, hauling, hoisting at the pleasure of an exacting, unpleasant Russian carpenter. Come spring, he escaped that duty with unbounded relief, but the skills to which he was exposed were to be helpful in future years.

In his fifteenth year, unknown to his father, he voluntarily entered training with his instructor in the French language. The courtesan was an excellent teacher. Caring, affectionate, she was lover, mother, sister, and skilled erotic tutor. When maturity beckoned the growing youth to distant interests, she helped him grow out of his infatuation with a minimum of pain. She also convinced him not to enroll in the college of waterfront girls, thus foregoing the genital irritations common to that University — but more importantly, the armor of her affection and gentle nature protected him from the callous ignorance typical of young Muslim males, to whom females were either shrouded virgins or simple playthings.

Pronounced fluent in French and passable in Italian,[1] immediately after his seventeenth birthday he went to sea with Aruj where, with hardly an interruption, he was to remain for the best part of fifty years.

In one season he sailed over most of the Aegean, learned the basic tactics for seaborne attack, participated in two shore raids on small villages, was taught the basics of command, and honed nautical skills that were practically bred into the bones of every Mytilene youth — discovering in himself an aptitude for navigation and weather forecasting.

Piracy could be profitable. Seaborne trade was rich and varied. From Italy came fruits and oils. From the East came fragrances and beauty pastes more valuable than gold. Spices from Asia could make a ship owner rich in one voyage. Venice alone imported and exported millions of ducats worth of goods each year officially, while Venetian shippers operating without a license — and thus without soldiers or insurance for which they would have to pay — accounted unofficially for perhaps twice as much.

---

1.   In his lifetime he spoke eight major languages perfectly, and could make himself understood in six or eight more dialects.

Yet, with all these riches at sea, Khizr came ashore in his eighteenth year.[1]

---

1.   Khizr's family, life on Lesbos, and the story of Mehmed are accurate.

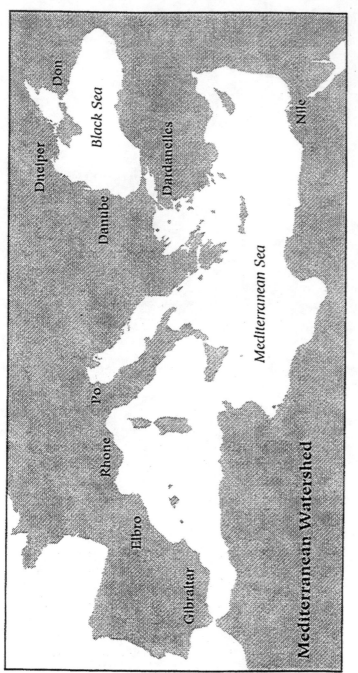

Mediterranean Watershed

Don

Dnelper

Black Sea

Danube

Dardanelles

Nile

Mediterranean Sea

Po

Rhone

Elbro

Gibraltar

Originally part of the Atlantic Ocean, as North Africa was slowly raised by continental plates buckling upward, the Mediterranean was separated into a closed sea and, since the river inflows frm Africa and Western Europe were insufficient to maintain sea level, the basin became mostly desert. Then, some six million years ago convulsions ruptured the moutain barrier, and a colossal flood filled the basin to its present boundaries.

2

EDUCATION

1498

By the time Khizr was eighteen Yakub had two ships of his own and the pottery business needed an agent in Istanbul. Among the men of the family Aruj's course was already set, Isaac was fulfilling his talents as a ship's carpenter, and Elias was a religious student. Khizr was the logical choice — and there was little trouble convincing him. No healthy young man with funds at his disposal would be averse to a sojourn in the world's greatest city.

Yakub, aware of his youngest son's exceptional intelligence, and respecting the Islamic obligation to see that such talent was developed, arranged to have Khizr accepted in the Galata Saray school in Istanbul, one of the new medresses founded by the Sultan and maintained by Sherifs. In keeping with Islamic strictures any Muslim student who could benefit was welcome. The Sherifs asked Khizr for a hand-decorated map of Lesbos and a poem of praise of Mohammed written in Arabic. They were as impressed with his product as they were with the discovery that he not only spoke his native Greek and Turkish, but was fluent in Italian and French.

Thus, the next year, at the first sign of good sailing weather, Khizr found himself a supernumerary on Aruj's galleot, making the eastward passage to Istanbul through the Sea of Marmara. A favoring breeze idled the oarsmen, filled the lateen and invited the vertical oar blades lashed outboard to become wings. Aruj, a red haired giant famous for his strength and his joy in battle, was conning the galleot with one of the new hinged stern tillers that permitted the steersman either to stand or to sit. He and a lookout were the only active members of the company.

Khizr took this chance to continue his education. From his reclining position on the steering deck he turned toward his brother and asked, "Aruj, what do you know about eunuchs?"

In Aruj's case, the impatience or annoyance to be expected of an obsessively masculine and unusually aggressive older brother where a young brother's questioning was concerned had long since yielded to respect — almost awe — for the depth and range of Khizr's mind. He felt a secret pleasure in being asked, but it was not something he chose to admit readily. From his seat on a coil of rope, comfortable and relaxed against a stout equipment box, he grumbled about another "asking fit".

Khizr only smiled, and after a moment Aruj grudgingly accepted the task. "I know enough. Mostly to think that all Egyptians qualify. Why do you want to know about them?"

"I'm curious. Since I'm now bound for The City, I don't want to be a peasant in these matters."

Aruj studied the maturing young man, who even to the most insensitive observer would appear anything but a peasant. "We've only been at sea three days. Are you already planning a raid on the Sultan's stable of riding mares? Do you need to know how to get past the harem guards?"

Again no answer. Only a younger brother waiting patiently. So Aruj capitulated. "All right, scholar, where shall we start, and shall we include Isaac in this school?"

They both knew that the quiet, good-natured carpenter had little interest in questions other than those he could answer with his skilled hands. Khizr answered, "Our brother is busy carving braces for the rambade[1] and probably wouldn't consider the interruption worthwhile." He rolled on to his back where he could study the few cotton clouds defying gravity in their blue space, and opened the discussion, "I want to know exactly how eunuchs are made and what they are able to do in sex. But first I want to know why so many are powerful officials?"

Aruj shifted his shoulders into a more comfortable position against the box, took a look at the sail to make sure he was spilling no wind, and explained, "As to why they rise to power — first of all, don't forget that mutilation does not affect their minds. Dogs do not lose their scent, oxen are stronger than bulls, and some of the fastest horses are geldings. Those

---

1.   Rambade. Raised deck on forepart of galleys used to launch boarding attacks. Later also mounted cannons.

A present day Galata Saray School in Istanbul

eunuchs who are assigned to important positions may be cruel, or self-ish, or womanish, but they are never fools. It is also said that many of them, like women, have a sixth sense about other men, and can judge truth or loyalty on very slender evidence.

"Beyond that, they never have families and they don't waste time on many of the distractions common to men." As the spring sun poured over him, he leaned back, adjusted his loin cloth with an affectionate hand and reflected, "Think of the time a man wastes on the eternal mystery between a woman's legs!"

Relaxed in the afternoon sunshine, he chewed reflectively on a ship's biscuit for a moment, then went on, "Now for the last, and perhaps the most important reason: Inasmuch as eunuchs have been removed from their families while young, they have no one to protect them except their owner. Consequently, the loyalty normally extended to family is transferred to the master. Eunuchs are frequently in a position to serve a master personally and are often in his presence. From there it is but a small step to be given duties in which they can demonstrate complete loyalty. The smart ones soon become trusted with power."

Khizr noted, "It is said that some of them are strong, even warriors — but I have never seen any."

"You have heard correctly. When one thinks of a eunuch, one thinks of a hairless, narrow chested, wide-assed, flabby, high voiced flower. But that's not always true. Specially selected Assyrian warriors and some famous Greek athletes had this unfortunate operation. In order to remain strong, a eunuch can't be cut while still a child, only after becoming a man. Done that way, eunuchs may develop as strong as the best of men.

"And more than that", he smirked, "If these men lose only their walnuts and are permitted to retain their members, many can still perform the dance of the two-backed beast. Any farmer who has waited too long to cut a lamb or calf — they call it 'cutting proud' — can tell you that the animal will keep mounting the females with enjoyment by both. So it is with men. Take off the balls late and leave on the member, and some eunuchs are able to give services women demand. The Anatolians refer to them as stags. They are rare and expensive, but sought after in some harems.[1]

"At your age, with a more or less permanent bone in your pants, you may think that a king can actually use a hundred women, but it is not so. Many harem women go unused and their fires burn high. As the Koran teaches us, women possess the true desire for sex and must be carefully controlled. Harem women live with eunuch slaves night and day, and if a slave they can trust has a hard member and no seed will be planted, you can guess the result as well as I." He concluded, "Anything is possible where sex is concerned, especially when the women are powerful or the master is lost to opium."

The massive Aruj, whose hair, unfettered by a turban, glinted in the sun six and a half feet above his sandals, stood and stretched. He motioned Khizr to take the tiller, and observed, "Osmanli harem women rid themselves of all the hair on their bodies, including their honeypots, and some eunuchs are trained as barbers. How would you like that kind of work?"

He stepped to the lee rail, and after answering nature's call, returned to his steering station and offered his views on the current Ottoman Sultan. "For a Turk, Bayazid is said to be quite straightforward. He doesn't care for boys, has no exhibitions performed, and never takes more than one woman at a time. I believe that his harem is rarely over a hundred, a small collection by most standards. If the women don't bear children, he

---

1.   Roman writers such as Juvenal state that 'performing black eunuchs' were a popular toy for rich Roman ladies.

gives them away when they reach twenty five.

He leaned closer and, with a nod, indicated the bull-like man teaching sword thrusts on the rambade deck. "My Master at Arms, Pragos, used to be a Janissary like our father. When he retired to Lesbos two years ago, he was given one of the Sultan's harem slaves as wife — a woman who is widely agreed to be beautiful."

Khizr had heard the story of Pragos and his wife. He shifted the subject to Christianity. "Do Christian kings have eunuchs?"

Aruj shook his head. "Christians don't have harems. They steal their pleasure from other men's wives. But they do have eunuchs for boy singers. If a boy of common family shows singing talent, priests remove his little chestnuts before his voice changes. Then they make him sing in Christian mosques and theaters for pay. The priests don't use the boys for sex very much, just for singing. The word for those singing children is 'castrata' — you can add that to your Italian!"

Khizr offered, "We use boys for prostitutes."

"If I were a tender young boy, I could stand a few hard rams up my naughty — as those who follow the practice refer to that small hole — rather than lose my balls for life!"

"Are there eunuchs in Istanbul who are prostitutes?"

"Yes. About half the price of boys, for they generally don't have any equipment, a preference of customers who like to suck or fondle."

Then he went on in a different tangent, "I'm glad to see that your tastes run to women. You were such a serious boy and you always insisted on dressing like a bridegroom, so I wondered. But as you came of age, I stopped worrying, because you were spending most of your money on that light-haired beauty in the House of Joy. I could never figure out why she didn't leave the island for the riches of The City."

Khizr didn't offer to explain that the support of the courtesan's parents and lame brother had kept her on Lesbos; he didn't want to talk about his first love and teacher of erotica. In the mind of the roistering Aruj, such shyness was a mild peculiarity to be outgrown, but although women were to be a major preoccupation, Khizr's reticence about personal intimacies would remain a lifetime habit.

Cramped, the scholar rose to his feet, stretched himself, and started forward along the narrow passage between benches, hardly wide enough for two men to clear. "I'm going to the water cask. Can I bring you some?"

"Yes, no wine until we eat."[1]

Khizr stopped midships where the benches had been cleared and several of the crew were occupying themselves in time honored ways of idle sailors — carving small wooden pieces for sale in the market, working decorative rope designs, and comparing the sexual benefits of various ports. He spoke respectfully to the sailing master, a prematurely gray and taciturn man splicing ropes with speed and skill, aloof from the bawdy conversation, and he greeted the Master at Arms, earlier identified as Pragos, whose sword practice was ending with the afternoon sun.

Chief Eunuch in 16th century Ottoman court.

Taking a cup of water from the cask lashed to the small forward mast, he drank slowly, facing aft to watch the sparkling sea given life by the failing sun. As the soft velvet of a spring evening prepared to envelop his small world, inhaling deeply, he swore to himself he could taste pine fragrance in the breeze that only a few hours ago had kissed the forests of Anatolia on its way to do the crew's work. A light burst of laughter from the tale-spinners brought him back to reality, and he looked for Isaac. The dying day was making it impractical to continue carpentry, and when he could catch his brother's eye, Khizr motioned an invitation to come aft.

He took the water to Aruj who welcomed it with praise. "By the Beard of the Prophet, fresh water is good to have." He gave a mock toast and drained the cup. "When those wooden casks turn green in the summer, I swear I can taste frog piss." Then he welcomed Isaac. "Our young brother here has been learning about eunuchs. We would have asked you to join us earlier, but we thought you would rather keep massaging wood."

"True. I have little interest in those creatures."

---

1. The Islamic proscription of wine was largely ignored by seamen — especially pirates of Greek ancestry.

Aruj turned to Khizr, "Well, let's get on with it. What's next?"

"I want to know how the surgery is performed."

Aruj made an exaggerated face at the reserved, somewhat prudish Isaac, and said to Khizr, "Very well. Most of what I have comes from a crew member who rowed with me years ago. He had been all over the western sea and at one time had traded in African slaves. Lazy and a poor rower, but expert with the short knife. Farouk the Egyptian. You remember him, don't you, Isaac?"

With typical brevity, Isaac agreed, " I remember him, but never cared for the man."

"Nor I. But he had traveled in parts of the world unknown to me, and he praised Africa as a land where one can pass the gentle winters fishing, sleeping, and satisfying young women. According to him True Believers are welcome in many African ports, and his stories of fat merchant ships in the Western Sea left me hungry." For a moment Aruj was lost in reverie, dreaming of a sleepy land where strength and ambition might yield a kingdom.

"The surgery," Khizr finally prompted.

Aruj returned to the present. "Very well. Traders bring boys out of Abyssinia and central Africa where they are purchased from their own chiefs. Since the Koran forbids mutilation of men, the surgery must be done in small towns enroute before the caravans reach any city. The traders prefer to cut only the balls because the death rate is not so high, but few buyers will accept eunuchs with the pleasure member, so both dingler and danglers are removed.

"For the removal, tight bandages are tied on the upper part of each leg and around the lower belly. A man's best friend is rich with blood. With its head cut off, one can bleed to death. The offending equipment — balls and good friend alike — are struck off together, and hot oil is used to stop bleeding. The next step is to insert a plug in the piss hole and close it up with camel dung and bandages. The creature is walked around for an hour or two, then buried in dung for three days."

Isaac's discomfort was evident. He got up and moved toward the lee rail "God forbid! Don't they give anything for the pain?"

"The man said no. Opium is too expensive. The pain, by the way, probably gets worse in the following days, when they cannot pass water. They are not allowed to drink, but the body will produce water by itself."

Khizr listened, wide-eyed in spite of himself.

"Their bandages and plug are removed on the third day. It is the critical time, for if they cannot piss, or their wound has reddened and they have fever, they are as good as dead. But if they can piss — and he told tales of stupendous streams squirting forth — the affair is a success, and the market now has a new eunuch."

Isaac was finished. Without a word he went forward, and neither brother commented on his squeamishness. The giant Aruj, in whom battle produced joyous laughter, whose satisfaction was greatest when his oversize scimitar split an enemy, a Captain who had no hesitation in bastinadoing a man to death — was blissfully unconcerned with Isaac's sensibilities. The studious Khizr was similarly unmoved, but in his case an inquiring mind did not tolerate distractions. Inspired by the imagery, and thinking about 'performing stags', he pressed on, "What about those who lose only their balls?"

"According to Farouk the best method is to take the little olives out through slits cut in the bag, or to crush them right in the bag with a wooden mallet — Isaac left us too soon; he could have found a new use for his tools — but most buyers won't have the creatures if they still have a bag. Who's to know that balls wouldn't grow again? So, the bag is simply cut off."

Aruj fell silent and abruptly came to his feet. Even in casual circumstances, he was aware of the slightest change in sea or ship, and the forward lookout was shading his eyes. Motioning Khizr to take the tiller, he leaped on to the catwalk, and in a half dozen running steps reached the small mainmast. With an agility becoming an acrobat, he skinned up the mast twelve feet or so to stand on the lower boom holding the sail. His sudden movement caught every one's attention.

Information was not long in coming. "May a mad fakir mount the Doge of Venice — there's a galley, and he's seen us. He's changing course to intercept us. I can't tell much about his hull shape from here, but for a trader he seems curious."

By its length he knew it was a full galley, outclassing his small ship four or five times. He would not know for some time whether it was friend or enemy, but only the most expensive goods warranted the speed and expense of a long ship, and Turks were not traders. The odds against it being friendly were poor.

A galley could overtake their small galleot within hours; there was no time to waste. Without orders, the men rapidly took up positions on the rowing benches. They would have to reverse course and would be headed almost directly into the wind. Khizr ran to pull in the lines holding the lower boom of the lateen while the shipmaster freed the upper boom. The sail collapsed, and working together rapidly, they furled the cloth, unstepped the mast and lashed it and the booms for storage.

While the sail was being secured, the starboard rowers stood and fell back as one, while the port oars were held rigidly in the water. Four strokes and the ship had reversed itself, and all twenty oars picked up the rhythm commanded by the tambour.[1] After a somewhat ragged first few strokes the men quickly reached the maximum count of fifteen per minute — peering aft each time they stood with their oars, making their own estimates of the threat represented by the stranger's flashing oars.

Aruj spoke, "Some may call the Marmara the White Sea, but at night it's as dark as any sea in the world, and if we can keep distance from that lump of turtle shit until nightfall he'll never see us again. When does the moon rise?"

"Tonight the moon will be more than half, but it won't rise for nearly three hours."

"We'll need that three hours."

Their safety equation had become the amount of daylight remaining against the distance between the two ships. The setting sun flashing on the larger ship's oars announced its gain each minute and little was said for another hour while everyone made his own mental calculations. Except for the tambour thump, the grunting of the men as they strained back on each stroke, the creaking of the oars in the leather ports and their splash each time they took the water, silence was their escort.

Quiet himself, and as cool as though he were entering home port and studying the welcome on the docks, Aruj calmly turned to Khizr, "Your education on eunuchs and harem sex is now over. Let's see how much you retain of last year's sea lessons. What kind of ship is that? And whose is it?"

As the detail of proximity slowly qualified the appraisal of distance, Khizr studied, then estimated, "It's a heavy galley; but it's moving well, so if it has any cargo, it's probably spices and scents. I can't tell the flag,

---

1.   Single headed drum.

but my guess would be that he's from the Black Sea and has cleared the Bosporus. If I'm right, he is either Genoan or Venetian and would have paid duty at Istanbul. He'll have soldiers aboard to protect cargo."

Aruj calmly agreed, "I'll bet a virgin she-slave against a sick donkey he's Venetian. Treaty or no treaty, with soldiers to board us, they would cut every throat, sink us, and deny ever having seen us."

He made a slight tiller adjustment and asked, "What's its size?"

"If its a typical Venetian, its about 400 botte."[1]

"How far away is he?"

"Less than two miles."

"How soon can he board us?"

"Touch and go — about dark."

"Bombards?"

"He appears to have three." And without being asked, added, "He can fire them in an hour."

Within that hour the large galley had gained to within three hundred yards of its quarry, but the small galleot was becoming indistinct in the dusk, and would soon be lost. Three flashes winked from the stranger's bow, but even the intended recipients of the stone balls had to smile at the optimism of gunners who thought they could hit anything from such a distance. One ball hit the water not more than a hundred yards ahead of its own muzzle, the other two were little better. The Venetian, if that was in fact his origin, ceased rowing to steady his ship for a final try — a delay giving birth to distance that would take an hour to regain.

And he didn't have that hour.

With the sun melting, the eastern sky rapidly spread its dark blanket across the sea, and night descended like a benediction, a blessing. Nothing could be distinguished more than a few hundred feet away, and with sails furled, the galleot's black hull blended completely into the night.

Aruj offered his own version of a prayer of thanks, "I wish that flea-infested relative of a sick ape red-assed monkeys for sons." He shouted cheerfully to the men, "Keep rowing, you crotch lice — and I'll buy each man a night's wine in The City."

Once certain of his own invisibility, Aruj turned north for an hour, and then east again to add sail to oars. By the time the half moon ven-

---

1.   Cretan wine barrel, about 500 kilograms, 1100 pounds. In this case the ship was about 250 tons. Ton, a British term that has become an international standard, was also taken from a large barrel of wine — a "tun."

tured into the heavens, the horizon was undisturbed; their escape was complete. Aruj called to Khizr, "The polestar is easy to see now. I'll send a man to spell you on the tiller; the rest can use some sleep. Pray for the good wind to continue. We'll be in the Golden Horn by daylight."

He was exactly correct. They rowed past Seraglio point and into the harbor of Istanbul just as the morning sun blinded them from the east.

K hizr needed only a day to locate a small house within easy walk of the market and the waterfront. The Galata Saray school was itself on the waterfront, nearly next door. The school had a small population and taught only advanced students, the most numerous of whom were cadets specially selected out of Janissary military training for duty in palace administration and government.[1] With his flair for languages, Khizr was soon popular with his classmates, and although sharia, the basic law of Islam, blindered the classes of logic and history, in the school he discovered the world of mathematics, and he formed the view he was to have in later years of international conflict and war as shifting tides of national self interest rather than as purely religious affairs. He also learned that the Persian language was a necessary qualification for an educated Turk, and set about adding it to his personal collection.

Outside school, a composite mixture of city wonders dazzled his island eyes and warmed his youthful urges.

With the exception of the fortified island of Rhodes, during the previous century Turkey had retaken every significant Crusader conquest and had ventured into Europe. When Mehmed the Conqueror seized Constantinople in1453 — the strength and glory of Christianity — he removed the only possible base for a Christian counterattack, thus legitimizing Ottoman control of Greece, the southern Balkans, and most of the western littoral of the Black Sea.

This fortunately placed city had a huge and fertile food-producing area immediately adjacent and was easily defensible. It was also the gateway controlling trade between Europe and Asia, an asset which fertilized city wealth from the traffic of two continents. Mehmed's policies, reaffirmed by his son Bayazid, who assumed the throne in 1481, provided

---

1.   These trainees normally attended the main religious university — eight colleges located at the palace mosque. They were rarely permitted outside palace grounds.

The Harbor of Constantinople – shortly after becoming known as Istanbul.

subsidies for traders — an honored Islamic profession[1] — and offered free land to all. Christians and Jews were specifically included in the welcome and were permitted to govern their own religious activities. In fifty years, the newly named Istanbul had reestablished its luster as the touchstone between Europe and Asia — as well as becoming the heart of a new world power.

Where the Sultan lived, there lived the Empire. The magnificent palace, the treasured mosques, the universities, the wealth and art, the hospices, the market center, the public baths, the slave markets and centers of illicit pleasure, the mixtures of cultures and religions, the spectacles and ceremonies, the multitude of officials, soldiers, foreign dignitaries and esoteric visitors, combined to create an Oriental fantasy — a city greater than any in the world.

Awe suffused Khizr's first letter to his father.

"You wouldn't recognize The City since your time here in the Sultan's guard. Building is going on everywhere, all city streets are paved, and the Golden Horn is so busy that ships have to wait for days. The Sultan's

---

1.   The Prophet said, "Merchants are the couriers of the world and the trusted servants of God... In the day of judgment, the merchant will take rank with martyrs of the faith."

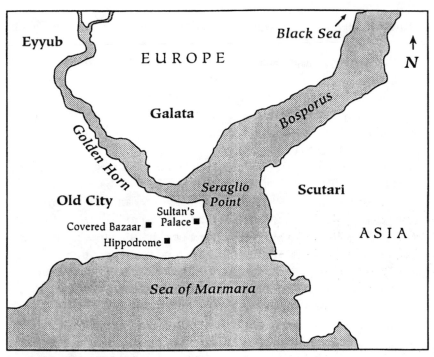

Istanbul in Barbarosa's time.

settlement policies of free land and loans for anyone have produced a flood of people. Byzantine Christians are fleeing from their brothers in Rome, and the Jews are being driven from Spain. Less than half the city is Muslim."

From the meddress library, he sent home a copy of a city census which showed 41,110 Muslim and 45,143 non-Muslim families.[1]

In early visits to the now retired Osman, Khizr had asked for a description of the capitol. He was told, "The city straddles the Bosporus with one foot in Asia and one in Europe. The section in Asia is Scutari where mostly Turks live. On the European side there is the palace, the hippodrome, and many mosques in what is called the 'Old City.' The foreign market with the riches and marvels of the world is in the section called Galata, where you live."

---

1.   The census was reported in 1491. Istanbul's rate of growth resulted in nearly a million people by the end of the 16th century, making it the largest city in the world. (London in the same century never exceeded about 200,000).

Khizr wanted to know where the section of the city known as Eyyub was.

Osman pulled at his mustache, "I wondered how long before you would ask. It is just north of the Old City and is full of prostitutes, gambling, and opium. If you aren't careful you can get your head broken there. There you may learn something about the throwing of dice, but I doubt that you'll find any companion as attractive as the yellow-haired lady you introduced me to in Mytilene five years ago"

Getting no response from Khizr, he continued his description of the rest of the city. "Each of the four divisions of The City has its own Mulla to settle disputes and issue orders. Questions they cannot answer, or decisions that need higher authority, reach the Supreme Divan, the highest leaders of the Empire. This group meets weekly in a large room at the Palace. Anyone may attend. You will see some foreigners there — they have a great curiosity about it. As a rule, Bayazid himself presides."[1]

"Khizr asked about the police. " The tubes and feathers on the turbans of the police are the same as those worn by Janissaries."

"They are Janissaries — the Sultan's soldier slaves performing city police work. Everyone is safe, especially women and children, anywhere, anytime. Janissaries arrest lawbreakers if they catch them in the act or if an oath is sworn against them. If no one seeks protection, whatever men choose to do without harm to others is of little interest to them. The Koran forbids the houses you will see in Eyyub where the fruits of a man's loins are harvested, but if you behave with dignity, you will not be bothered. The women are either slaves or there by choice.

"We Turks take a common sense approach to these problems. For example, wine has always been smuggled into the city, and its use is more or less open. The Divan concluded that the best way to handle the problem was to lay a tax on the traffic. In that way, we have not interfered with the practices of other religions, and the trade can be kept under control. The same is true of kef."[2]

"Tell me about the guilds." Khizr's question went to the heart of city life. "The public reports list over five hundred of them. They seem to be organized for every kind of activity, fishermen, butchers, gold smiths,

---

1. Later, when Suleiman became Sultan, he abandoned the time consuming practice, and had a wall grill installed from which he could listen unseen — which tended to keep the judges on their toes.

2. Asian hemp, marijuana.

Samples of Janissary Dress Head-gear. While head-covering of some type was an Islamic requirement, ornate headgear was originally developed by the ostentatious, decadent, Greek Byzantine court — and was adopted (along with many other customs) by the Turks. They, in turn, raised the practice to obscene heights as symbols of power, position — or simply love of display. Dozens of styles for all officials, limited only by the wearer's imagination and status, could be seen on nearly any occasion.

stamp men who certify the silver content in coins, tailors, tanners, shoemakers, prostitutes — the list is endless. I even noticed icemen. Where does ice come from in the summer?"

"You are observant; these organizations are perhaps the key to governing a large city such as this. Guilds have regulated life in European cities for many years and we borrowed the system. Later this year you will see a festival and parade in which every guild is represented; it will involve probably fifteen thousand people and will take most of the day to pass. Even the beauties from Eyyub will be there. I'm sure they will wave to you!"

As an afterthought he added, "Ice, by the way, comes from the mountains in northern Anatolia. It keeps all summer packed in sawdust."

Outside of school, Khizr's city life broadened him rapidly. He acquired enough knowledge to appraise craftsmen — from stone masons to goldsmiths, from shipwrights to gunsmiths. Daily, everywhere, he practiced languages. He did gamble occasionally in the pleasure pits of the city, as much as a challenge to his own powers of concentration as anything else, and it was during one of these evening tours that he cemented a youthful friendship.

Boaz, the brightest of the palace students and exactly Khizr's age, was born a Jew in Albania, a Turkish possession. When he was eight, Turkey and Venice signed a treaty realigning the Balkans which gave the part of Albania in which he lived to Venice. Under Islamic Turkey, Jews had enjoyed freedom to worship and trade, but with the hate and intolerance of Christian rule imminent, life for a Jew would be hopeless. The boy's mother was dead, the ill father knew himself to be dying, and there were no close relatives. He chose the option of offering his son to the service of the Sultan.

An annual or bi-annual conscription, known as a Devirsme, was conducted throughout Turkish Eastern European possessions such as Greece and Albania, drafting from two to four thousand of the brightest and healthiest eight to twelve year old non-Muslim boys — generally Christian — for training in the elite Janissary infantry Corps. In time, these children became devout Muslims and were lost to their countries and families, but they acquired great opportunity to advance themselves.

From among the Janissary trainees, two to four hundred of the most intelligent and attractive youths were periodically chosen (frequently by the Sultan himself) for further special education in court duties and government administration. These men would eventually govern Turkey at all levels, including the highest posts in the empire.[1] Osman had explained the devirsme system to Khizr. "Ottoman Sultans aim to avoid the growth of powerful families. By making the government non-Turkish, and by keeping power from passing father to son, the Sultan keeps the reins of power firmly tied to his own pommel."

Boaz's father had assured him, "It is by merit that men rise in the Sultan's service. Authority is assigned only to the competent. Honors, high posts and judgeships are the rewards of great ability and good service. There is neither discrimination nor favor. If you are accepted in the devirsme, you will have the opportunity to rise to any level. I pray for you a power that can help you make the world a better place for the Chosen of God. Do well, and my sin will be forgiven."

---

1.   In the 70 years from 1460 to 1530, nine of ten Ottoman Grand Viziers (Prime Ministers) were of devirsme origin.

Brilliance marked Boaz and he had been selected as one of the top forty cadets each year to be chosen as a page in the royal seraglio. There was no higher honor for a devirsme slave. Khizr, an island boy, was impressed by him, and curious about his name. "Were you given the name Boaz when you entered arms training?"

"No, there was an oversight in my case. Boaz was given me by my father. The Sultan has permitted me to choose my own when I move to the Palace."

They both had a flair for mathematics and both enjoyed dice as exercises in probability. The game of barbudi[1] was their favorite. Bets were placed against each throw and different number combinations required different odds. In their evenings, the two paired off and, jokingly referring to themselves as the barbudi twins, spoke nothing but Persian to one another as they risked small amounts. The burly, muscled Khizr and the almost fragile Boaz were a study in contrasts: One was cheerful and outgoing, large, fair, beardless, immaculate and stylish in his clothing. The other was reserved — even shy — slender, dark with a beginning beard, and subdued, drab clothing.

In the fourth or fifth of their expeditions, trouble erupted. A fat, dirty Georgian mule-driver, somewhat the worse for drink, accused Boaz of reneging on a bet. "You mule dung — if you're going to play with men, then act like a man! That was my bet you covered, and you lost. Pay me before I pull off your turban and stuff it down your throat." He reached across the betting board and his greasy hand fastened on the young man's jacket.

Boaz tore himself loose and stepped back, "You dirty mule fucker, keep your hands off me!" and he made the error of drawing his knife.

Lightly for a man of his obscene bulk, the Russian vaulted the low table and laughed, "Ho, ho, you look like the donkey who swallowed the camel's prick. I'll give you something to swallow!" While still in the air his heavy boot struck the knife aside and grazed Boaz's head hard enough to knock him off his feet and stun him. With Boaz on the floor and groggy, the mule driver, his huge belly swinging before him, advanced with intent to injure.

In the next minute, Khizr made a friend for life.

Stepping between the two, he grasped both wrists of the attacker, and

---

1.   Two six sided dice, quite similar to modern craps.

as the man attempted to free himself, applied a twisting motion so powerful that it turned the victim's wrists white and forced him to his knees. For several seconds the only sounds were fierce imprecations and growled obscenities from the mass of kneeling flesh. In a desperate attempt to free himself, the Slav lurched sideways, aiming a kick at Khizr's crotch. Khizr deflected the kick with his hip, released one of the man's arms, and with a lightning move used both hands to bend the other imprisoned arm against his knee.

That brought the insults to a halt and entertained the audience with a Russian scream. Khizr had broken the man's arm much as one would have snapped a piece of kindling. The fight was over. Only the victim's moans disturbed the audience. Khizr looked with disgust at the dirt the drover's boot had left on his clean trousers. He stepped up to the man's head, clenched jaws and whitened knuckles predicting more damage, but, after a moment, restrained himself. With a deep breath he turned and helped the still disoriented Boaz to his feet.

Placing a gold coin on the gaming table and moving Boaz slowly towards the exit, he addressed the crowd, "This mule driver has taken too much wine. This gold will pay for his arm." He looked down at his own stained clothing and added, "May a camel piss on his shoes and a mule shit in his breakfast. Tell the drunken fool that I shall take the cost of these clothes from his manure filled belly if I ever see him again!"

To Boaz, still recovering his wits, Khizr appeared larger than life, a strange combination of caution and explosive danger. Beardless and young, his presence was strangely dominating. Intent, calm, with no uncertainty in his voice or manner, Khizr surveyed the room. No one wanted to come within range of those quick and unbelievably strong hands. The pair were allowed freedom to leave.

Once outside and well away from the scene, Boaz felt Khizr's arm, "By the Beard of the Prophet, you are strong. You bent his arm as though it was a short bow. Are you made of steel?"

Khizr was embarrassed, "No, no. I practice daily to challenge my older brother in arm wrestling. He could tear off that man's arm and hit him in the face with it. Anyway, the break was not wholly the result of strength. It was the way I twisted the bone against my knee. The lower arm has two bones, one larger than the other, and they resent being twisted in a spiral against one another. I will show you the trick one day."

All of the students were aware of Khizr's concern with his appearance, and Boaz apologized, "I'm sorry about your trousers." Then he had to know one more thing. "Why did you leave the gold?"

"A struggle is not always decided by what is right or wrong. I don't relish explaining the matter to the patrols, and as a potential Grand Vizier, you might also be embarrassed. If the man accepts the money — and I have no doubt that he will — he accepts our peace and there should be no further trouble. Our best course from here on is to play in different games in different establishments."

Boaz paused, then smiled. "A friend is a garden planted with care and watered with love."[1]

---

1.   Little detail is known of Khizr's early days. Boaz is fictional.

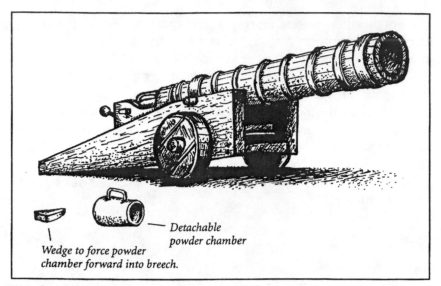

*Wedge to force powder
chamber forward into breech.*

*Detachable
powder chamber*

Bombard – Early stone firing cannon made of wrought-iron rods secured with encircling hoops. Range 100–200 yards, extremely inaccurate. Siege model shown. Shipboard guns were rarely over four feet in length, and carriages were shorter.

Stone Cannon Balls – after four centuries.

3

GALLEY SLAVE

1500

Just twenty five, Aruj was a mature man in his world, an audacious and successful captain. Turkish pirates who warred on Christians provided a respectable, if speculative, investment, and for the past three years, his venture had been financed by a consortium consisting of a Jewish merchant, three wealthy Turks, and the Sanjakbey of Anatolia, a royal prince named Kourkhoud, the eldest son of Sultan Bayazid.[1]

After delivering Khizr, Aruj made good his promise of a "night's wine in the city" for his crew, spent three days in annual negotiations with his consortium, and then set about buying replacement oars, crossbows, and two of the new arquebuses. Before departure, he invited Khizr to a demonstration of one of the muskets at a walkway overlooking the channel. After unloading the paraphernalia from a carrying box, he carefully measured powder, forced it down with a cloth plug, and tamped a lead ball firmly in place with a long rod. He spread powder on the flash pan, inserted the slow burning match into its holder and, making sure his two observers were clear of him, laid the six foot barrel of the weapon on the tall wooden aiming fork.

Aiming at a seagull on a stone wall, he steadied the weapon, pulled the ratchet that allowed the slow burning fuse to ignite the powder, and the bird became an explosion of feathers.

Khizr was impressed. "How far was that shot?"

"Exactly one hundred and twelve yards." Aruj bluffed smugly.

---

1.   Anatolia was Asian Turkey — roughly the land area of modern Turkey. Sanjakbey (Bey of a Sanjak) was the equivalent of Governor of a province.

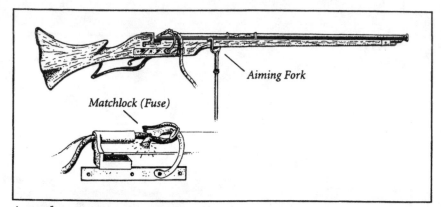

Arquebus — Early musket. Effective to about 100 yards. Awkward to load and fire. The famous German 16th century drill master, Maurice of Orange, published a drill for the arquebus that required 43 steps. Early muskets were fired from the center of the breast — which helps explain their light charge. Moved to shoulder at beginning of 16th century.

Khizr chose not to challenge such a miraculous measurement, but there was no doubt that accurate shooting would be valuable at sea. "Let me try one."

When the gulls had settled down, he came no closer than a puff of sandstone dust two yards away. "How much practice would a man need to duplicate that shot you made?"

"Depends on the man. Maybe twenty or thirty with a good eye and steady hand."

Together with all of its gear — aiming fork, ammunition, powder in water protective containers, wadding, cleaning supplies — each gun weighed over twenty pounds. Khizr questioned this drawback and criticized the complicated loading procedure.

"Doesn't matter on shipboard." Aruj responded. "We'll store the guns in sheep grease. No rust. We can drill a hole in the deck for the shaft of the aiming fork and can secure a small chest nearby to keep the fuses and powder dry. It will make a good project for Isaac. We'll make a marksman of him as well as a carpenter."

⌣

S upplies aboard and arms secured, Aruj and his men put back to sea. There was no wind and the Sea of Marmara was calm. Strong islanders, glad to work out city kinks, the men gladly rowed for two hours at a stretch. With a forty man crew, the ship had two rowing teams, and the galleot could keep underway steadily.[1] Two of the men were simple musicians, and the crew was enjoying a shepherd's flute duet that marched with the tambour as it signaled the oars.

A visual song of beauty, the sea was offering its best appearance. Under a canopy of royal blue, the ship, animated by diamond wavelets, seemed grateful, excited, to be headed toward adventure, carelessly tossing up a white wave the height of a man's knee on either side of its smooth black hull, flaxen brush strokes merging into a hundred-yard wake. The European shore painted a smoky gray border limiting their world to the north; otherwise they traveled alone in a soft, silent universe.

Talking to his shipmaster, Aruj mixed history with his plans. "This sea was known to the ancients as Propontis, the entrance to Prontis, the Black Sea — the beginning. I think of it in the other direction, for once we reach the Dardanelles, we'll have the current with us and less than sixty miles of easy travel to reach the Aegean." He went on in a more practical vein, "If the weather holds, I'll go south outside."

By "outside" he meant west around Lesbos, a fast route that typically offered a favorable wind — but one which put them hours from a safe harbor if the weather should turn.

At evening the skies deepening into night offered an especially brilliant early display of planets, then a carpet of stars, and finally, dimming the stars, a golden moon. The men continued their steady grind, any bantering long since ceased. The graceful waterbug continued its stride, stroke by stroke in a brilliant trail of phosphorescence. Even the minute sea creatures seemed to be celebrating their passage.

The next morning, as the celestial roof of their world paled for morning, the current that emptied the Mamara into the Aegean accelerated the galleot's progress. The occasional shepherd's fire along the shores of the Dardanelles began to move astern more rapidly and, shortly after the sun spoke a brilliant good morning, Gallipoli presented the passionate blue of the Aegean to the travelers. There, the heavier salt water of the Mediterranean — distinctly different from the comparatively fresh water of the Marmara — welcomed them as it lightened and raised their ship.

---

1.   A galley could maintain between two and three knots indefinitely — more with wind astern.

One of the crewmen asked the ship-master, "Bosun, they talk of a sea in Arabia that's so salty that nothing can sink. Is it true?"

"Aye. It's called the Dead Sea. I don't know about a ship, but a swimmer, if he can stand the salt, will not sink."

To the gratitude of the tired crew, as they turned south after passing the straits, a favoring breeze found them. They raised the sail, lashed the oars outboard, and let nature do their work. Each man welcomed a generous ration of hard biscuits soaked in wine, a bowl of cold barley, salt fish and vegetable cakes dripping olive oil — and a chance to sleep.

By noon, with their rapid progress, a course decision became necessary: inside or outside? While the wind was somewhat stronger than Aruj liked and the air somehow felt gray, the sky was cloudless. He decided to throw the dice of chance for continued good weather. He ordered a course change of two points starboard that would send them west of Lesbos.[1]

Any galley seaman with a bent for poetry could testify that a storm at sea could be an experience more exhilarating than a woman's embrace, more exciting than battle. In challenging the gods, a stream of nervous fear flows through a man; a dread so intense that it creates an unlikely exultation. To throw back one's head and stand in challenge to the insane concert of madness and destruction of a full storm at sea is to be lifted outside oneself.

Before the night was over, Aruj and his men were to experience the accuracy of such a description, for his weather dice turned up losers.

In early afternoon, with the wind swinging north and thus more astern, Aruj's decision to go outside seemed a wise one, for they moved easily and the sky, though hazy, remained clear of clouds. Four hours later, however, the sea had deepened into violet and the wind had lost its amiability. From the distant mountains of the Adriatic littoral, a five hundred mile mass of cold dry air, eight miles deep, sensed lower pressure to the south and east, and began a sudden surge over the upper Aegean, goading the sea into hostility.

Practically unknown in the spring of the year, and famous for giving little warning at any time, a bora — or mistral as Christians referred to it — struck.

By nightfall, they were entirely at the mercy of outraged seas, now

---

1.   A point is 11.25 degrees, one of 32 divisions of the compass — commonly used in giving steering orders.

taking on a grayish tint, that would have swamped their narrow craft in minutes if it had not run with them. In place of the lateen they had raised a small square of canvas which gave them steering headway, but even so, each wave demanded all the skill and strength of two men on the heavy stern rudder to keep the ship from broaching.

As the twenty and thirty foot waves — leviathans racing faster than a running horse — rumbled from astern to catapult them forward, their world was enclosed in walls of water. At their stations, encased in a stygian hell, the seated men could put a hand overside and touch each malevolent wave crest as it hissed under them. Within each man, the display of nature's power authored an ambivalence of feeling. There was fear. If their shallow craft were to broach they would drown in minutes. But at the same time there was exultation in conquering each wave, in each tiny dominance of the enemy. Excitement married fear; euphoria and fatigue shared a wedding bed as the men fought on into the night.

Unable to alter their course in any way, they were being driven southeast, directly toward the rocky shore of western Lesbos — a course which left them with two equally unattractive options: a nighttime crash on a rocky shore that would make kindling of their wooden vessel within minutes or capsizing by turning in any direction other than that directed by the storm.

Within the hour the choice loomed, unavoidable.

A mass darker than the sea, decorated with irregular horizontal streaks of white, beckoned them from dead ahead.

Land. Rocks.

Only minutes away.

Through the dark of the storm they could perceive the phosphorescence of waves higher than the ship's masthead, rearing in frustrated anger as they destroyed themselves against ledges guarding the face of hundred foot cliffs. Some men praised God. Others cursed the devil.

All knew they would die in minutes.

Aruj took the tiller from the two crewmen, motioned one to the oars and the other to the mast, pantomiming for him to spy what little could be seen in the dark — a last, desperate chance. The man leaped along the catwalk, and in seconds had fastened himself by one arm well up the short mast.

And then the Gods took notice.

The lookout's scream could be heard above the wind. He was frantically waving his free arm while being flung to the length of his anchoring arm with each pitch of the ship.

He had seen something on the port side.

Risky as it might be to turn the ship broadside, and not knowing what the man had seen, Aruj didn't hesitate. With a single sword blow, he cut the line holding the storm sail, allowing it to blow loose as he forced the ship hard to port. For a sickening moment the sail fragment fouled itself on the mast and the ship was nearly blown over on its starboard beam, but just before they went over, it ripped free.

Once broadside to the storm and recovered from the sickening roll, as the next wave raised the ship, two faint lights on a stone quay hinted at safety only ship lengths away, but even over that short distance, the chance of survival was slim. Now that they were broadside, oar blades were submerged in the trough and suspended in the air on the crest, giving them only a few seconds to set and pull on the face or back of each monster. The sailing master's skill in anticipating the timing of the rolling mountains would give them their only chance at life.

Every man on the ship except Aruj, who had the necessary strength and skill to handle the tiller alone, the lookout on the mast, and the deck master counting for stroke, was on the oar looms. When pulled, the oars thrust the galleot forward as though it were alive. Displaying the strength for which he was famous, and the courage that eventually made him a legend, his turban blown off, shirt in shreds, Aruj stood as a shrouded outline, a vague giant challenging the sea and the wind, demanding obedience and frantic effort each time the shipmaster's shrill whistle split the storm with its imperative.

"Pull, you donkeys! Pull out your guts, you sons of whores! Break your scrawny backs! Twenty strokes! Twenty strokes, you camel lice!"

It took courage to hold the new course, for the galleot started to fill. The first huge roller quartered on them and sent only a small amount of water aboard, but by the time the second one arrived, the ship was fully on a cross course, and the wave crest poured aboard. The third sea followed suit, and their survival had now been reduced to a race between a goal only imperfectly seen and the capacity of their shallow hull to hold the sea cascading over the men and benches.

Suddenly, they won.

Aruj's guess of twenty strokes proved close to the number they were permitted before foundering. With every rower sitting in water, they reached safety behind what turned out to be a stone jetty, a breakwater from which two boat lanterns had sent them an invitation to live a few more days. From there they could swim their foundering ship to the beach more easily than it could be rowed.

Another wave and they would have capsized.

They had threaded a needle in more ways than one. The pure happenstance of being blown on to shore precisely where a small harbor existed — a hundred yards would have put it out of sight — the luck of the lookout in seeing the protected lanterns, the instant decision of Aruj to gamble on a turn broadside in the hope of reaching a shelter he could not see, the timing skill of the shipmaster, and the disciplined strength of the rowers provided their hair-thin margin of safety.

They had reached Sigri, a small fishing village on the west coast of Lesbos, and the only harbor within thirty miles.

Ready hands helped the pirates draw the foundering galleot up the beach and pour the water from it as from a giant gourd. Welcomed as fellow seafarers — in two or three cases as island cousins — they were sheltered and dried, and hot food and rations of ouzo were pressed on them. Even companionship could not overcome the days of rowing and the effort to master the storm. They were asleep before the ouzo cooled.

The storm passed sooner than the night, disappearing as quickly as it had appeared , and they put to sea again early the next day with only a ground swell to remind them of its passing. God had willed that they should survive; there was no time to live in the past. By nightfall Lesbos was under the horizon.

They slept the next night in another Greek village on the island of Khios, a Genoan possession that paid a handsome annual rent to Turkey. Khios made its living by trading, and successful traders in the Mediterranean didn't ask questions. The inhabitants were more than willing to host potential sources of income.

The fifth night they passed the Island of Samos and, early in the evening of the sixth day, settled on an operating location on an uninhabited section of the mainland of Anatolia where a long channel between a short series of rocky islands and the wooded mainland narrowed to less than fifty yards. There they found a sandy cove with fresh water springs and

Black Sea

Istanbul

Greece

Mamara

Dardanelles

Lesbos

Anatolia
(Asian Turkey)

Khios

Samos

Vahti

Aegean Sea

Rhodes

Aruj's Voyage

Scale 1" = 70 mi.

heavy forest growth on the shore behind which they could wait unseen. A replaceable pine skid installed over the keel made the shallow, nearly flat bottomed galleot easy to haul ashore, and in only a few moments they had wolfed cold rations and embraced the sleep of fatigue.

The seventh day provided typical Aegean weather: calm, sunny and windless. Relaxed after the week's efforts, the men took their time as they lit breakfast fires and cooked enough barley and rice to last two days. Minor repairs and water casks occupied most of the morning and by noon they were ready to explore the vista around the wooded point to the south. They launched and set course to round the point.

At the beginning of the season, Aruj had not availed himself of the advice of astrologers for the voyage on which they were now engaged. Whether the turn of fate waiting for him was because he ignored the wisdom of stargazers, or because he failed to follow the example of the Creator who rested on the seventh day, this particular seventh day was to teach him a dramatic lesson.

Before the day was over, seven crew members, including Isaac and Pragos, would be dead and Aruj himself a galley slave.

Once afloat, the pirates aimed for a nearby break in the wooded ledges that would take them into an open bay beyond the wooded point. Moving smartly, their slender craft slid out beyond the dense forest that grew to the water's edge, coasted past the last tall rock, and came face to face with an apparition from the worst of pirate dreams.

Patiently resting on its oars, a monstrous gallease waited, bowmen stations manned, arquebuses resting on aiming forks, and gunners with lighted slow matches standing by bombards. On the silk and damask canopied after-deck passenger area, couches, chairs and tables had been secured for action, and spectators were crowded by the rail.

The hybrid ship, a greatly expanded galley designed both to sail and to row, was a nightmare in four decks of crimson. The Knights of Rhodes were known to mix a distinctive red in their hull tarring, and a singular eight-pointed Christian cross[1] decorated the breastplates and jerkins of the men, as well as the slack mainsail. To provide absolute certainty as to its identity, Pragos translated aloud the Latin which appeared in gold letters along the ship's hull: "Our Lady of the Conception".

The shock caused by the sight of the oaken apparition laid a patina of

---

1.   The Knight's cross was later to be famous as the "Maltese Cross".

silence over the pirates until they heard a salutation from the deck captain on the Christian ship. "Ship those oars and heave to, you heathen, or I'll sink you and feed you to the fish." The promise was in broken Turkish, but comprehension was in good supply.

Forty-two men could hardly fight three hundred trained soldiers, and they could not escape. The gallease was an ungainly rower and their light craft could accelerate and outrow it, but they could not hope to gain a safe distance before the guns gaping from Christian bulwarks could do their point blank work. Nor was swimming an option. A man in the water would be hostage to the crossbowmen ready with wound bows, or to arquebusiers resting their pieces on aiming forks, so close that the engravings on their elongated barrels were visible.

In a short moment, the fox had found a leopard.

To emphasize the command for surrender, a bombard on the Christian ship spoke a traditional warning, and the pirates could easily see the whitish stone ball as it whistled just over their heads to splash into the sea, throwing up a twenty foot geyser of water. With a shrug of fatalism Aruj ordered his rowers to ship their oars, and with a stroke of his sword cut down the green banner of Islam. While he would fight any man that lived, he would not foolishly sacrifice his ship and crew.

Then a misunderstanding occurred. Reckless with a belief in good deeds, with a stubborn refusal to accept misfortune, the ship's carpenter made the one gesture of hostility his galleot was to make that day. Isaac lit off one of the new arquebuses — and a soldier balancing on the gunwale of the larger ship did a parabola into the sea, shot cleanly through.

· Outraged, the Christian deck officer screamed at the gun crews on his lower gun deck, "Put some stone into those bastards!" He spoke French, but his shout needed no translation for the pirates.

Gunners set matches and four bombards fired.

Even at point blank range, only two guns scored hits, but those two were enough. Less dense than cast iron, but with a similar shock value, the stone balls radiated splinters and debris as they smashed through the oars and penetrated the elevated rambade deck. Between the two strikes, the granite globes insured that five of Aruj's oarsmen would never again raise a cup in the House of Joy, that Pragos would no longer enjoy the charms of his beautiful wife, and that Aruj had one less brother. The forty pound balls destroyed the men as easily as they ruptured timbers.

Rigid with fear, his men sat like statues, but Aruj threw his turban in the sea, tore his jacket off, and screamed in his native Greek, "We yield, you sons of common whores, does your shit scow need to sink us?"

Arquebusiers swung their weapons in his direction, but were waved down by the bosun.[1] He leaned over his rail, now not forty feet away, and advised Aruj in Turkish that while he didn't understand his heathen language, if he didn't show some courtesy, a hot iron up his fundament would teach him some manners. That graphic promise convinced Aruj that he would have to learn to appreciate the art of dissembling, and he subsided. He also refrained from informing the deck master that Greek, far from being heathen, was a Christian language long before any Roman Pope existed.

Everything else was anticlimactic. Voiced commands and whistled signals brought the great ship alongside its victim. The seven dead were unceremoniously heaved overside and the rest of the pirate crew brought aboard the gallease and temporarily ironed. A swarthy group of mercenaries boarded the galleot as a prize crew — the Knights themselves being above such common duty — and the galleot departed for the auction market.

Now that the brief excitement was over, the arrival of the prisoners on the larger ship caused little stir. Less than three dozen new slaves among the two hundred already chained on the lower deck was hardly significant. Aruj did cause some comment by his size and hair color, but mostly to suggest that he would be a great pacemaker on the long oar in the first starboard bank. The incident was hardly more than an interesting happenstance on a long cruise. For the passengers on the shaded after-deck, chess games and fencing practice commanded more interest.

The new men were chained to stanchions one deck below the cannons. Overhead hatches had been secured earlier when the ship prepared for battle, and while the pirates were aware that other men shared their quarters, they could barely see them in the dim light. For a while no conversation was needed, for the ship began to move under oars, and the symphony that was to press on their brains for the rest of their lives — the splash of water against the hull, the rattle of the tambour, heavy oar-looms rustling against leather sea shields, and the dull thud of two hundred men falling back on padded benches — penetrated their sad thoughts

---

1.   Bosun (boatswain) is a deck petty officer — sometimes termed "deckmaster."

more than any conversation.

Pirate life was primitive and dangerous. Hardship was a daily lot and injury or death were common. But like hopeful fishermen, they courted the magic, the excitement of a big strike. No less than hope of riches, freedom made pirate life worth living — the sky above them, the fragrance of the sea mixed with fir and balsam from the shore, and the sparkle of the morning sun on the blue waves.

Now, in an instant, they had become a class of animal to be kept only for the work their bodies could produce.

A monumental chagrin and regret overwhelmed Aruj. No longer investing in fertile dreams, he was now harvesting sterile reality. Through his own carelessness he had lost his ship, his brother, and six friends. He had condemned to a life of misery thirty-four men who had looked to him for protection. Granted that a meeting between two such mismatched ships would be a rare occurrence at any time and that the location where they were captured would be thought impossible for a ship as large as Our Lady of the Conception, the catastrophe was still of his own making.

As he discovered within a day or so, the galleas had been charting the nearby coast and had spotted the smoke from the breakfast fires. The large craft could not enter the narrow passage past the ledges on the wooded point, but since no ship was its equal and its cannons completely covered the entrance, they had simply waited in safe water for whatever the hideaway would produce.

If only he had ordered lookouts during the night!

His reverie was interrupted as two overhead hatches were opened, giving the pirates a chance to examine their surroundings. Their prison room was not more than five feet high, but ran the full width of the ship. It was enclosed fore and aft with sets of heavy double doors, and timbers supporting the upper deck structure stood every six or eight feet all through the room, giving it the appearance of a gloomy forest of tree trunks.

In addition to Aruj's group of Greek pirates — who henceforth would be referred to as Turks so consistently that they began to think of themselves as such — there were perhaps twenty other men in the room, and light provided the reason for a quiet welcome. They were quartered in what appeared to be the sick bay, and only one of the occupants was sufficiently alert to carry on a conversation.

Nursing the stump of what had been a hand, he spoke to them in Turkish, "Brothers, I don't wish you evil, but I'm glad the battle was short. Whenever those cannon fire just above us, we are deaf for an hour. I didn't hear any return fire, are you traders?"

Aruj told of their capture.

The one-handed man shook his head in sympathy. "In'shallah." As God wills.

Aruj asked about their new masters, the feared Knights.

"Fierce men," he was told. "The best sword fighters in the Mediterranean. They are expertly led and have not the slightest fear of death. Good engineers. Their fortress on Rhodes is a miracle of walls, parapets, protected firing stations and connecting passages."[1]

The man thought for a moment, then continued, "They are strange, I swear. They come from all over Europe, they even speak different languages. Those of each nation have their own hostels and their own foods, much like the guilds in Istanbul. Once you've been in Rhodes for a time, you can recognize the different groups by the symbols on their hostels, and you will see the same symbols on those knee-length coats they wear."

"How many of them are there?"

"Not many. I imagine on this ship there are not more than fifty, and in the city there are so few that their houses take up only one street. My guess is there are not eight hundred altogether."

"Who does their work — other than slaves?" Aruj inquired.

"The Knights amount to a ruling class of sheiks. Rich men, ashore they hire and train natives as soldiers, workers and servants. At sea, mostly slaves such as yourself. Religion swears them to care for the sick with their own hands, going so far as to nurse enemies taken in battle. Totally devout, they should be respected as sincere— prayer and worship of the Prophet Jesus occupies part of every day. I suppose that's why you Turks refer to them as 'The Religion.'"

He confirmed what Aruj already knew; the chances of gaining his freedom were slim. Muslims offered their captives the opportunity to adopt Islam, which meant freedom from chains, but on Christian rowing benches a man's religion mattered not at all. Many on the Knight's benches were themselves Christian; criminals, debtors, men who had sold them-

---

1.   The Knights had occupied Rhodes for three centuries. Fearsome warriors, they were respected, even admired by the Turks.

Rhodes at the time
of Aruj's visit.

selves or who had been taken by impressment gangs.

If Aruj was to be freed, it could only be through ransom.

Their conversation was interrupted by the entrance of a half dozen guards who set about securing short leg chains that would fasten the prisoners to the rowing benches. The guards spoke some Turkish and gave instructions in that language. With a flash of insight, Aruj tried his Greek and one guard answered him in that language. He resolved to test this man by the oldest known method of making friends.

Earlier he had secreted a gold link bracelet in his loin cloth, taking care to be unobserved. When the chance was right, he slipped it to this guard. His analysis of human nature was correct, for when the leg ironing began, the new friend volunteered to take care of the special fitting Aruj's large size would require. The other guards were more than willing to leave the volunteer to his chore and, once he had set to work, the man opened a conversation quietly, out of the hearing of others.

"You are a wise man, Barbarosa, the others would have seen that trinket when they stripped you, and it would have disappeared like magic. I know a pair of ladies in Rhodes who will provide me lodging and pleasure for the entire winter for this piece."

Although the term "Barbarosa" was a name by which first he, and then his brother Khizr would become famous, the nickname meant nothing to Aruj. They were talking in Greek and his Italian was not good enough to realize that he had been addressed familiarly as "Red-Beard".[1]

"I need Information." He told the guard. "Some now, perhaps more from time to time."

The guard nodded. "I'll take you on as a special interest. If I claim you for my own, the other guards will leave you to me. What do you need to know?"

"How long do we stay at sea?"

"Cruises vary, sometimes until October — God knows what you Mohammedans call the month — but it won't matter a camel fart to you. Slaves remain aboard for the entire season unless there is repair or return to port."

"I have heard that slaves work on fortifications during the winter months."

"Yes, or roads or whatever is needed. Its the best time of year for you. The Knights hire you out to private contractors so they can make a profit on your services. You are permitted to earn a few coins for yourself. Sometimes you can get a woman. The Knights themselves are a queer lot. They have nothing to do with women — boys or men either. They take a vow to have no sex, and they observe it. But you can have all you can pay for."

In spite of his circumstance, Aruj was recovering some of his spirit. "If these men indulge in neither women nor boys, the companionship of the five fingered wife must be common among them."

"I expect so — but then, many of them are too old for such pleasure."

Aruj then asked the question nearest his heart. "What about ransom?"

The guard looked around to see if he was overheard, "It's a good source of gold for the Knights. Don't let them think you're a nobleman. You'll be inspected for marks of wealth; crafted sandals, good teeth — maybe if you wear underclothing. Let me see your hands."

Somewhat puzzled, Aruj turned up his hands, callused from rowing and from sword drill. His informant inspected them. "You are no nobleman. Those are the hands of a working man, but since you were the captain of that pirate galleot we just took, you will have a special price. Nothing like a prince of the kingdom, but heavy enough to strain the purse of any Turkish ladies interested in having your services again."

---

1.   The Turks today spell the word without the "a" — Barbaros

He stepped back and admired the smooth shackles he had placed on Aruj's legs. "Are those comfortable, Barbarosa?"

Aruj shook his head ruefully, "As good as I can expect."

The guard bent to the task of measuring the connecting leg chains.

"Ransom is simple. Your name will be posted and anyone can take the information to Constantinople. Then its up to your friends. They must send an agent to Rhodes to bargain. The exchange itself is simple. Your agent pays and you just get on whatever ship you want and sail away."

His work complete, the guard picked up the small anvil and water bucket. "Remember, Barbarosa, your body and soul are in our keeping. Keep your mouth shut, do as you are told, and from time to time I'll stop around."

The new galley slaves were brought into the sunlight of a large open well midships where they could get a look at their new home. The ship was about one hundred and eighty feet, somewhat longer than a standard war galley, much higher, more than twice as wide, and deeper in the water. Three tall masts afforded sails big enough to move it in even a light wind. Interior timbers as big as a man's body braced a hull sheathed in at least eight inches of seasoned oak, the heaviest ship construction Aruj had ever seen. A ship's gun could hardly pierce such protection. The entire hull was decked over at two levels, with two higher decks — which he learned were called castles — located both fore and aft. The result was an ungainly, double ended craft, so ugly as to offend the senses.

Oars owned the lower deck where they could reach the water easily. Only oar ports gave light. The heavy gun deck flooring served as a solid roof. On each side, sixty chained human engines, each with his own oar, were crowded in a space not more ten feet by eighty. A center catwalk gave the bosun's rawhide whips and dried bull-pizzles easy access.

The ship's guns were its most impressive feature. Aruj's knowledge was limited to estimating their size and range, for no light ship such as his could afford either the expense or the weight, but he counted four large bombards in the bow, four medium on each side, and a half dozen lighter, easily moved guns amidships. Enroute to his rowing station he had passed storage bins of stone balls extending thirty or more feet along the lower deck. There was no ship afloat in the Mediterranean that could stand up to such firepower — if it could be brought to bear.

He soon discovered that with fighting men, slaves, working seamen, and Knights themselves, this ark now serving as his home floated seven hundred souls — an unreasonable number, he thought.

The new galley slaves were stripped, doused in a vile smelling liquid, made to scrub their underarms and crotches, and their heads were shaved. With some amusement, the guards informed them that since most Turks were lousy and carried various diseases due to their strange sexual practices, this treatment was for their own benefit. Stark naked, without the Islamic dignity of turbans — which could never be worn on a Christian ship — they had become sheared sheep, donkeys for caravan, goats for slaughter.

Aruj was the first choice of the bosuns. "Send this big red head with the small dingus to the first starboard oar." A few observers laughed at the slighting reference to Aruj's sexual equipment, a mild foretaste of the chafing and insults he would bear from now on. The speaker continued, "That oar bank can use his muscle on the inboard oar, and there is a debtor on the middle oar who has been circumcised. They can compare codpieces."

Sure enough, Aruj was to find that one of the three men who shared with him his bank of oars was a Frank debtor who had sold himself into slavery for three years. But as a non-slave, the man was entitled to wear brief shorts, so the condition of his foreskin was not immediately evident.

There was, Aruj soon discovered, a great difference in a galleot oar of fifteen to twenty feet and the thirty-five foot brute that was to be his enemy for the foreseeable future. As the inside man on his bank of three oars, his loom had a somewhat longer distance to travel than those outboard of him, and the three feet between his back and the looms behind him left little room for a man of his bulk. Most rowing was done from a seated position to take advantage of leg and back muscles, but under some conditions the men had to stand and fall back, and in such case, he found it nearly impossible to squeeze his bulk into the small space. provided. He was further disconcerted by the loose play in his loom allowed by the leather slings that held the oars to the thole-pins.[1]

But worse than the heavy oar, worse than the cramped space, worse than the leg chains, was the smell. At sea, the slaves were never freed

---

1.   On large ships, wooden looms quickly wore through against iron , so leather sleeves, or slings, lubricated with olive oil or tallow, were used.

from the benches, and the chains gave them just enough room to slide back and relieve themselves directly into the open bilges below. The memorable stench that rose like a fog from the waste and decay more than justified the sailor's tale that you could smell a Christian war galley at sea before you could see it. Nevertheless, in a surprisingly short time, he adjusted to the lack of space, to the primitive toilet facilities, and to the rhythms of oar loom movement. He was to learn that sufficient will could mold a man into any shape and that stress created strength in those who survived.

The new galley slaves were given a wooden bowl as a piece of personal equipment. His Frank bench-mate was an outgoing man who offered advice on the food. "You will be given a small hand of meat three times a week. Unfortunately for you Muslims its bacon from the pig you despise. I'll be pleased to trade you for my salt fish which we also get two or three times a week. The fish encourages a painful looseness in my bowels."

Aruj advised his new friend that his Islamic conscience would not be troubled by unclean food. "When do they feed us?"

"Twice a day. I imagine it will take two men's rations to fill your huge frame, but you can have all you want of biscuit, rice, sugared fruit dried like a rock, and cheap olive oil. If we are on a long pull — no wind, or preparing to fight — they'll soak your biscuit in wine. I imagine the Prophet would approve, wouldn't he?"

The Frenchman proved to be right on quantities and since complaints were answered with a bull's pizzle, Aruj restrained himself from comment. Rancid meat could be digested and the weevils often found in hard biscuit were toothsome.

It was late summer before he set foot on shore. There he broke rocks for the winter months, and when spring came, went back to sea on the oars.

With no word from Istanbul.

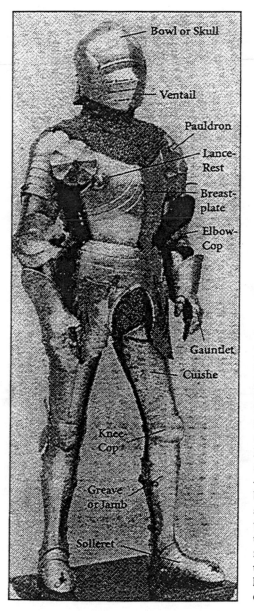

Bowl or Skull

Ventail

Pauldron

Lance-Rest

Breast-plate

Elbow-Cop

Gauntlet

Cuishe

Knee-Cop

Greave or Jamb

Solleret

Typical 16th Century Knight in Full Armor. A suit of armor cost a fortune and required thousands of hours of skilled labor with constant refitting. A good suit was surprisingly effective — its weight was balanced evenly and it allowed good freedom of movement. On foot, a dozen knights with their supporters and skirmishers made up a fearsome force — suitable for defense of a sizable barony. Mounted on a 2200 pound specially bred war-horse (the ancestor of today's Percheron), in battle, they were the tanks of their day. Common in myth and song, they were uncommon in real life. Some peasants lived their lives without ever seeing one.

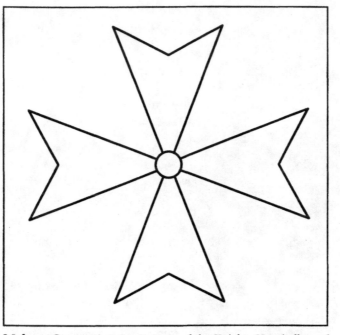

Maltese Cross. Christian insignia of the Knights Hospitallers of Jerusalem, later the Knights of Rhodes, still later the Knights of Malta. The ancient order itself still exists with annual ceremonies. Mostly second or third sons denied inheritance because of primogeniture, these warrior/pirates were all aristocrats of impeccable lineage — each applicant had to have four noble grandfathers. In an age of religious zealotry, these men were perhaps the greatest believers, the most sincere soldiers of Christ. The Knights were extremely wealthy. Many devout nobles throughout Europe (frequently in an attempt to purchase their own entry into heaven) left great bequests of property or money to the Order. Never numbering over several hundred at any one time, they hired or enslaved most of their supporting fighters.

4

RANSOM

1501

Having expected Aruj's return by mid summer, Khizr was concerned after three months, worried after four, and convinced of the worst by autumn. So when the news finally came, even though bad, it was welcome.

Aruj was not dead. There was no information on Isaac, but at least Aruj was alive and apparently in good health.

A Syrian trader brought the news that a giant red haired pirate called Aruj had been taken by the Knights near the coast of Anatolia, south of the village of Vahti, and was now a galley slave. His galleot had been sold as a prize. That was all the trader knew, but it was enough to energize Khizr. His first call was on a Jewish merchant who maintained an unremarkable gold shop in the immense covered bazaar provided by the Sultan for all traders.[1] Would the merchant call together the consortium associates who had financed Aruj's venture, and find out what ransom they would be willing to raise?

The merchant cheered him up somewhat. "Aruj is worth a great deal to us. Not only has our investment with him profited handsomely, our Muslim members have an obligation to him in brotherhood. I can't offer any totals without talking to the others, but I'm sure that help will be forthcoming."

Khizr asked about Prince Kourkhoud, the best known member of the consortium, and was told, "He is the oldest son of Bayazid, and should be in line for the throne, but he is not warlike, and the Janissaries would

---

1. The Istanbul Bazaar was a 16th century architectural marvel and is still one of the world's largest markets and shopping centers

be opposed to him. Also, he inherited his grandfather's taste for young boys, so his sexual pastimes have not produced offspring, and if he were to become Sultan, the question of entitlement to the throne following his eventual death might set off a civil war. He is not expected to succeed to the throne.

"Still, he is faithful to his obligations. As you know, the southern coast of Anatolia is practically within shouting distance of Rhodes, and smuggling from Bodrum on the mainland has been common since Jem lost the war with Bayazid. Rhodes buys food each year, and the Knights could use a few barges of corn. I will see that word is sent to him, but we will have no answer for months — if at all."

The remark about a war between the Sultan and his brother aroused Khizr's curiosity, but for the time being he had more immediate concerns than an Ottoman civil war a generation ago. He thanked the Jew, and continued on his errands.

A week later, the Jew was proven right. The local members of the consortium were willing to put up ransom — although when the Muslim partners settled on their shares, the Jew's personal contribution equaled the total of the three, a generosity not lost on Khizr. Later, when a galley reis known as Sinan the Jew approached him for employment, he took the man on as a ship's officer, even though he was thought cursed because of a stray eye. "Without a man of your religion," Khizr assured the Jew, "my brother might still be pulling an oar in a Christian galley."

The consortium was willing to provide thirty thousand aspers for Aruj, an amount roughly equal to six hundred Venetian gold ducats. In accordance with Islamic strictures, no interest would be charged. Since a year's pay for a Janissary was only sixty aspers (plus spoils if at war) it was a good offer, and Khizr was heartened.[1]

Khizr would have liked to go to Rhodes himself, but his youth would work against him. The Knights were all mature warriors — some elderly — and they held youth in disdain, especially Muslim youth. He needed an older agent who could brave winter weather at sea.

Within hours, he found himself standing outside Osman's villa.

The younger of Osman's two wives met him. The third daughter of a peasant, she was sufficiently attractive that prostitution would have been

---

1.   A Venetian gold ducat contained 3.5 grams of gold — about fifty late 20th century U.S. dollars. Value comparisons mislead, for the purchasing power of gold has varied over the centuries.

a likely future for her. Consequently, Osman's offer of marriage seemed generous. He provided her with escape from the farmyard or bagnio. In return she helped his first wife in both kitchen and bedroom. A small price to pay for lifetime security, she thought, and she was grateful. The young woman and Khizr, being close to an age, had developed a friendship as warm as Muslim strictures permitted between a married woman and her husband's male friend, and she greeted him happily, alone in the front of the house. "Your presence gladdens my heart."

Before any unseemly exchange might occur, she added, "I will call my husband."

Osman came directly from the garden, wiping his hands on a cloth. He had aged little; still erect and quick of movement, his eye was keen, his hand steady, his fierce Turkish mustache still imposing — if a bit gray.

The wiry Turk welcomed his guest with a bone crushing embrace. "Welcome, welcome, my young merchant king! You've not graced my humble home for too long. We've missed you. Tonight, in the square near Mehmed's Mosque, there is a karaghuz shadow play by a famous traveling band — a black-eyed performance. It is both instructive and enjoyable, and makes light of important persons. Now that you are here, I have someone to explain it to me."[1]

Khizr treated the volubility of his friend soberly. "I am truly sorry that time does not permit me to stay the night, Osman Efendi. I come with ill news and with a request of great difficulty."

Instantly grave, Osman dismissed his wife with a nod and motioned his guest to a couch. "Whatever I have is at your disposal. My house, my sword are in your hands. May God protect you."

"Would that your prayer had been heard six months ago. I have just learned that my brothers have been taken and are now pulling oars in a Christian galley."

The older man had been to sea for a lifetime and needed no further explanation. "In'shallah." As God wills. "Were they hurt? Is Aruj sound in body? I can hardly imagine him being taken without bloodshed."

"I don't know any details; I only know that he was taken by The Religion. I know nothing about Isaac, but I assume they're together."

---

1. Karaghuz was satire and humor. Shadow images of puppets projected on a sheet/ wall. The puppets were hidden to comply with Islamic restriction on idolatry.

Osman drew a long breath. "Then they are held by the Knights. Things could be worse. Those men are fierce warriors but, unlike most Christians, they keep their slaves healthy and treat them if they are sick. As a rule, they are also willing to do business." He looked intently at his young friend. "I will go to Rhodes. At once."

"You were in my heart the minute I heard the news."

Osman went on. "When I first went to sea, no True Believer would venture within a day's row of the Stronghold of the Hellhounds, but since Jem lived there, trade is common."

Now it was Khizr's opportunity to follow up the remark the Jewish merchant had made about the war between Jem and Bayazid. He asked for the story — and how it might apply to his problem.

Osman told him. "When Mehmed died, he had only two sons, Bayazid and Jem. Bayazid was the first to reach the city after his father's death, and he bribed the Janissaries to declare him Sultan. Jem, who was governing in the East, raised an army but it was no match for the Janissaries. He fled, first to Persia, then to Egypt, and finally, when no Islamic state could protect him, to the Christian Knights of Rhodes who welcomed him. Bayazid considered himself well rid of Jem, and he paid the knights forty thousand gold pieces annually to keep him out of Turkish territory. Eventually, while visiting Italy with the Pope, Jem succumbed to a bottle of arsenic-laced wine. His poisoner is not known, but his passing saved Bayazid's treasury a tidy sum.[1]

"That bit of history helps us in our trouble. A fortress at Bodrum on the nearby Anatolian mainland is still manned by the Knights, and since the years of Jem, commerce between Rhodes and Turkish territory is common. Traders have no difficulty approaching the Knights, especially under a Frank flag."

Khizr responded. "I have listed a request at the waterfront for a felucca. I should have several offers in a few days and would be grateful if you would make the choice of ship yourself."

"A felucca is exactly what I want. Small, fast, and a good sailer. By working the coast in short stages I can make it in three weeks — barring storms."

Khizr flushed with affection. Tears of gratitude welled not far from

---

1. Before Jem's demise, the Knights "loaned" him to Pope Alexander and to Charles VIII of France. He toured widely throughout Europe in an effort to whip up enthusiasm for a crusade which never developed. As strange as Jem's story seems, it is historical fact.

An early view of Istanbul's Covered Market — known today as the Grand Bazaar.

the surface and he looked down at the floor. After a minute, in control, he said, "A friend has more value than gold and pearls. My gratitude knows no limits."

Osman leaned forward and placed both hands on Khizr's shoulders, his fierce mustache almost touching his young friend's face. "Friend of my heart, one passes out from God's blessing if he keeps not his brother." Then he leaned back. "I'll make arrangements for a cargo to pay for the trip."

Khizr produced an envelope containing several financial documents. "You may draw on my credit, here is a seal for you to use. My family will always be in your debt. If you should meet with misfortune, please know that we will provide for your wives."

One was a trader's certificate with which Osman could buy a boat and hire a crew; the others were eight letters of credit, each with a face value of one hundred gold Venetian ducats. Instruments of this type were common commercial exchange in Christian Europe, and were increasingly in use among banking Jews in Islamic states. They would be readily accepted by the Knights.

"Six of these come from our backers, and are intended for Aruj," Khizr explained. "The other two can pay for Isaac."

Then Khizr proceeded to take a long step into fantasy — an indication of the character that was developing in the young man — the kind of inspiration that was to make him an unmatched leader for tens of thousands of men.

He thought of the crew.

There was no possibility of buying them out. No common family possessed the price of a slave. Once taken, a man was considered dead by his family. Life as a pirate was a high risk occupation; one in which no participant could expect safety or protection if chance went against him. Barring the very rare recapture of the ship on which he was held, chains and an oar loom were a captive's permanent fate.

Khizr appeared slightly embarrassed, but his voice was firm. "Find out what it would cost to bring home the crew. Act as though you might be able to pay market slave prices for the men sold in a group, and if the price is right, go so far as to place a fair amount in pledge. We will probably have to forfeit the pledge, for there were forty men in addition to my brothers, but as long as The Religion have promised to hold them, they will not be sold."

Osman turned away for a moment, then facing his young friend, said calmly, as though he were dealing with a sane proposition, "I'll get the best price, and if the pledge is to be lost, we can worry about that when it happens. One need not swim until one is in the sea."

W inter can be a surprisingly lovely time in the Aegean. For a few days after a cold front passes and its rains have emptied themselves, the north wind has no strength and the air welcomes voyagers with a soft embrace. The temperatures of summer no longer bake the white-washed houses, enraptured lovers do not perspire unseemly, afternoon naps are shorter, and the air seems to acquire a special clarity, making the sea a rich azure. Even winter waves can be gentle.

As a passenger on a small Serbian round ship, Khizr enjoyed just such weather enroute to Lesbos. Any ship headed west this time of made slow progress, and the clumsy coaster was worse than most — it could not sail within six points of the wind. Further, the cautious owner would sail neither at night nor out of sight of land, thus increasing the distance and time. The trip that Khizr last made in less than four days coming east absorbed nearly three weeks going west; plenty of time to review the information Osman had brought.

Osman's trip to Rhodes had been relatively fast and, once there, it had taken him little time to discover that Aruj was alive and in good health — and that Isaac was the impractical fool who had challenged the galleass with an arquebus. He also learned that Pragos and five other men had been sent to paradise through the courtesy of stone cannon balls and that four additional men could not be located — probably already sold.

At that point, his mission languished.

In his meetings with the priest who represented the Christians, Osman had claimed that Aruj was simply an island pirate who spent his profits on wine and women, assuring the priest that his mission was to buy the crew at slave prices. If the ship's reis could be thrown in, so much the better.

But his story made little difference to the price demanded.

In relating the bargaining, Osman complained to Khizr, "For men of religion, the Hellhounds can put an Arab rug merchant to shame! Would you believe that the first figure quoted by them was two thousand gold ducats for Aruj! After days of argument they retreated to fifteen hundred, but from then on the figure remained firm." Osman shook his head in remembering. "I tried everything. I made these old eyes spout water like a spring rain, but it was of little use, that offspring of a she-dog wouldn't budge.

"I could do no better, and I was using my time to secure a cargo to help pay for the trip home when a messenger reached me with a request to accompany him to a central building — sort of a mosque — which I knew to be an official place of some importance. When I arrived, the priest with whom I had been dealing was there along with a dignified, older man who did all the talking. Rather than a jerkin, as the Christians refer to the short leather jacket common on Rhodes, this man wore an armless woolen overshirt, a long vest which reached his knees. On this garment appeared a woven design of family arms, or a guild, as well as the odd Christian cross the Knights use. He wore a sword that must have weighed twenty pounds."

"A Knight?"

"I assume so. Certainly a nobleman. He carried as many years as I — with greater ease, I am forced to add. He asked me if I knew Prince Kourkhoud, and I assured him that my acquaintance with the Prince was limited to seeing him once as a boy many years before, when his

Felucca.

father, Sultan Bayazid, offered entertainment during a celebration of the circumcision of his sons.

"Then he asked me what my very top offer was. I sensed that I was not dealing with any souk merchant, and I told him the truth — that I had been entrusted with eight hundred Venetian gold ducats.

"The official thought for a moment — I could see that he had little opinion of my appearance or intelligence — then he accepted. But he added a special condition. I quote him exactly as I remember, 'Turk, we will let you have this pirate for your eight hundred ducats, but you must pay now, in advance, and we will not deliver him to you until next year. Another season on Christian oars will do his soul some good.'

"I agreed instantly."

The reduction in price made Khizr immediately think of Kourkhoud. He must have contributed in some way. But no one was ever to know. A few years later, when his brother Selim seized the throne, Kourkhoud was garroted with the royal bowstrings and went to his grave without enlightening anyone.[1]

Osman continued his discussion of money, "I realized that you might

1.   Prince Kourkhoud's shares in Aruj's ventures are well known — but Aruj seems
      never to have mentioned repaying any ransom to him.

see neither the eight hundred ducats nor Aruj again, but I had to make an instant decision. The Knight, if that's what he was, impressed me as a man of honor. After I accepted, he instructed the priest in a language I didn't recognize — although I suspect it to have been Latin — and the priest drew the contract papers.

"While the time was right, I also struck for the crew and got them to accept a cash pledge with full payment to be made upon exchange next year. To tell the truth, I'm sure that whiskered priest thought that such a purchase was unlikely to the point of impossible and was happy thinking that the pledge would be forfeited."

"How much did you have to leave in pledge for the crew?"

"Only a tenth."

"What was the price for each man?"

"Fifty ducats."

Khizr did some arithmetic, "Thirty times fifty equals fifteen hundred ducats. A tenth of that had to be one hundred and fifty. You only had the eight hundred I gave you." He left his question unsaid.

"I made the crew pledge out of my own gold. The Knight was pleased to have my money as well as yours."

Khizr was stunned. Well into his sixties, with nothing more than his own savings and his house, Osman had risked his life security for a proposition that any responsible person would judge to be a sentimental day dream. The young man looked at his older friend; a graying, unimportant ex-captain of a small trading ship who, despite his experience and wisdom, was hardly educated beyond calculating sums and signing his name — a man content to live out his days quietly in his flower gardens — and he wondered what internal force ruled this unassuming person. Osman must have obligated everything he owned to raise that much gold.

That afternoon engraved a lesson on Khizr which lasted a lifetime. One did not have to be a king to make a kingly gesture. The qualities of a man are inside; externals mean little.

Aloud he said, "May God find a special place in heaven for you. May I live to repay."

Osman spread his hands and shrugged. "The least I could do was give you more time. If the pledge is forfeited, In'shallah!"

With the facts in hand, Khizr was ready to return to Lesbos with the news. Osman offered to take him, but he declined, "Thank you. A Serbian is leaving this week and will take me to Mytilene. Use the time with your wives."

A s soon as the Serbian tied up in Mytilene, Khizr was first home with the sad news of Isaac; then, well ahead of waterfront news, to the widow of Pragos. Before he set out on the half day's walk to Pragos' olive groves he discovered, to his mild surprise, that Pragos, an ex-Janissary, had entrusted his declaration of inheritance to another ex-Janissary — Yakub.

Khizr arrived late in the afternoon. From the south, silver gray olive trees marched regularly down a gentle hillside adjoining a white stone house. Framed by narrow gardens of winter flowers and a low stone fence, the comfortable structure was protected from the north by an mature stand of pines, some fifty feet high. In Anatolia, the place would have been the pride of a large Timar fiefholder, and he was impressed.

The young wife of Pragos was still more impressive. Khizr was startled. She was the most beautiful woman he had ever seen. Women of her quality were nonexistent in Mytilene, and in Istanbul they were secluded. The closest comparison he could make was with expensive courtesans, but they used facial decoration, kohl-darkened eyes and brightly painted nails. Her eyes needed no outline, her short fingernails and toenails wore no paint, and her skin, as far as he could tell, had never known stain. Her long ebony hair worn in the court style, restrained only by a clasp, reflected the slanting sun with tiny jewels of light and honored a complexion as white as her open linen blouse. With a flowered skirt worn to just below her knees, the sleeves of her cotton blouse rolled up to her elbows, the girdle for her slight waist the same leather worn by farm women, she carried herself with the simple air of Khizr's young sisters.

Despite her beauty, she was unaffected, gentle — even shy. Dressed as she was and speaking directly to a strange man, one could hardly believe she was a Muslim wife, let alone a Sultan's concubine. But simplicity neither obscured her allure, nor kept from him the light musk of her sexuality.

He introduced himself. With the ease of innocence, she told him she knew who he was and invited him inside. The room into which he stepped was typical of a well-to-do landlord farm, a central living area opening on to kitchen and rear courtyard. Other doors apparently led to sleeping rooms. Even in this comfortably large home, there was no one else in evidence. In some surprise, he asked, "Do you live alone?" She was hardly a peasant woman used to running a farm in her husband's absence.[1]

"My water comes by means of troughs Pragos installed from the cistern. I have workers in the groves, and I have two old men who bring me firewood and water for my cistern if the rains fail. I eat little and need to go the market only once a week. I manage very well. But you didn't come up here to inquire after my circumstance. Do you bring news of our pirate venture and of my beloved Pragos?"

For all of his effort to display no emotion, Khizr trembled for this beautiful woman and the devastating loss she faced. Without speaking, he took her arm. His inadequate camouflage alerted her and her hand involuntarily went to her throat. She allowed herself to be led to a low couch. Seated, a small vein in her throat betrayed her anxiety.

Remaining standing, he blurted, "Please remember that to die in the service of the One True God is to live in peace and happiness forever."

She took his hand in a fierce grip. "Is he lost then?"

"Yes, since last year. Along with my brother Isaac."

She continued to look at him for a moment as her eyes filled and fountained over her cheeks. She dropped her head and, as though talking to herself, said, "For the first time in my life I had found a man who showed love for me, the first man to make a woman of me — and now he is taken before I have borne his child. Like a tree without fruit, I am condemned to barrenness!"

Khizr was dumb with pain and sympathy. Clumsily, he reached out to touch her, and she gratefully took his hand to place on her bosom as though to draw strength from its warm masculinity. He could feel her body tremble through the softness of her breast, but she seemed unaware of the intimacy. Only the incredible flood of tears.

After a few moments she calmed, rose, and walked unsteadily to the outside door, opened the top half, and stood framed in the slanted sunlight, gazing at the meadow, bare this time of year. It was a perfect winter afternoon, no breeze, a few insects ratcheting their noisy travel as they reconnoitered the limited fragrance of a small herb garden. He moved to stand behind her, close enough to look over her head at the meadow and its bordering trees.

---

1. In all Islamic countries, women alone were absolutely safe.

Through the thin fabric of her shirt, the slight breeze gently bathed him with her fragrance; the slightest hint of sage, a signal of jasmine sweetness. Without warning, desire flooded him.

She spoke to the meadow, this time in a cultured, sultry voice that dispelled the impression of innocence. "My name, Son of Yakub, is Myrrh, a bitter wood which must be burned to yield its fragrance. In my name is much of my life. With the loss of Pragos, my life returns to the same bitter path it has followed since my birth."

In his desire, he was betraying Pragos. Ashamed, he could only clear his throat, and they stood without speaking for several minutes, until she murmured, "Stay with me. Don't leave me with the devils of loneliness."

The spell was broken.

"As long as you need." He moved away from the furnace of her beauty. Evening was pouring into the room, bringing a chill. "Can I make a fire for you?"

"A small one. And, please pour us each a cup from one of those." She indicated stone jugs on a wall shelf. "It is very strong, a favorite of Pragos — he called it brandy and said it was made by the Franks."

Having something to do with his hands was a relief, a way to divert his outrageous desire.

Myrrh closed the door, accepted her cup and immediately drank it. She studied him as he refilled it, finally saying, "You remind me of Pragos. You are younger, but in many ways I think you are much like him." Seating herself she went on, "Tell me of yourself. How long have you sailed? What did you see in Constantinople — did you see the Sultan? Have you children or wife? For whom do you care? Talk to me of your life."

Nervous and garrulous, he sat beside her and poured out his young life, including, for the first time, his affection for the blonde courtesan in Mytilene. As a confession of sorts, it relieved him. Myrrh listened intently, nodding from time to time, seeming to approve, and her understanding and concern forgave any embarrassment.

She was curious about his love affair, his feelings for a professional woman. On rather treacherous ground, she asked about their lovemaking. Was his desire for her constant — enough to keep him from other women? Did she make him happy as a man? Did she fulfill a need in him?

Then he pressed for her story.

One imaginative version of harem life.

After a long moment she began, "I was taken by an agent for the Sultan's harem when only twelve, shortly after my first menses — no, not taken," she corrected herself, "my father sold me. At the palace I was taught the truths of The Prophet, poetry, music, and I was trained for a man's pleasure.

"When I was sixteen I was pronounced fit and given my own room. Every night when I was not in menses, along with others I appeared in the Sultan's baths. I have a talent for music and played or sang at least once a week while the Master of Two Worlds ate. In my fondest dreams he would drop the handkerchief over my shoulder — a signal which would call me to his chambers — and I would have his son in my belly the next day.

"But no. For three years I followed this pattern, still not called. I learned the satisfaction in giving and receiving pleasure with other women. It was not approved, but was common. If one acted with discretion, nothing was said. But my true wish was to be needed by a man. Without that I was not complete."

He shifted back a bit on the low couch and Myrrh kept her hand on his knee as she continued, "The rejection was destroying me. I felt that I was worthless.

"Then, with no warning, I was told to bathe and perfume myself for the following night. The Sultan had chosen me. I hardly knew what to think; the sky had fallen. When the time came I was led to a low opening and gently shoved into his darkened bedchamber by the eunuch. I had been instructed to enter the foot of the bed by lifting the cover at the bottom and to make my way up along his body. He made no sign he was aware of me until I was level with his face. Then he turned to me and told me to hold his member. Have you ever conceived of holding the essence of God himself in your hands? I did, and as soon as it hardened, he mounted me and rode me for a brief minute or two until his pleasure erupted. Then he pushed himself away and told me to leave."

She trembled, her eyes in pain but no longer in tears. Khizr made as though to stroke her face, she took his hand in both of hers and pressed it firmly. "Do I offend you? Do you want me to stop?"

"Please, no. Your trust honors me."

With a deep breath, she continued. "It happened one more time and the experience was practically the same, except it was not as painful and I didn't bleed. I did not become pregnant. After that he never took me again. What was wrong with me? Everyone told me I was beautiful, I knew enough about the techniques of the sleeping rooms to know that I was skilled — nevertheless he did not use me again. My life was over at twenty-four."[1]

"And then, miracle of miracles, Allah took pity on me.

"Women of the harem who have not attracted the Sultan's approval or borne a child by their twenty-fifth year are frequently married to officers or officials. I was given to Pragos. At the time, all I knew was that I was to marry a Janissary captain, an old man of forty who was about to retire. I presumed that I would still be rejected, but at least I would have a family name."

Her hand trembled where it lay on Khizr's knee.

"With Pragos, I was reborn. I discovered the pleasure a woman can experience with a man, but most important, for the first time in my life, I was needed and appreciated. He cared for me, he wanted me, he used my skills with enjoyment and gratitude. Now he is gone." She couldn't help an involuntary sob. "It will all be a dream and I will be condemned to loneliness and rejection. Why am I wasted? I need to give. How can God do this?"

---

1.   Myrrh's tale is an accurate portrayal of Harem life.

Then, after a moment, "I begged Pragos not to go to sea. These olive groves were his reward for service as a Janissary, and I brought a dowry of jewels from Bayazid, a fortune really, which I carefully hoarded. We had more than enough riches. Pragos never realized that gold was not important to me, that all I wanted was him."

Tears overcame. She dropped her head on her arms in his lap, crying again in ragged hiccups.

A confidant of his sisters and expertly introduced into the physical relationship with a woman by his beloved courtesan, Khizr was sensitive to the emotions and needs of women. Her revelations left him over-whelmed. Above all, his intense sexual hunger for this injured bird burned him with guilt. Torn with conscience, embarrassed by his thoughts, un-certain as to what to do, he awkwardly placed his hand on her back, and, without any intent, reassured her with a gentle stroking. The warmth of his hand through her light cotton shirt seemed to give her comfort. Her sobbing eased and her body relaxed.

Involuntarily, he felt himself becoming erect. Acutely embarrassed, with her arms and head across his lap, he realized she would surely feel him through his thin pantaloons.

For long minutes she remained quietly against him, giving no indica-tion that she was aware of his obvious masculinity. Then she raised her-self and sat for a moment, as though considering a complex problem. Finally, she made her decision and, with a slight nod to acknowledge his engorgement, whispered, "Khizr, your desire compliments me. It makes me feel a whole woman. I feel in you a warmth and understanding. Please don't think me abandoned, but tonight of all nights I want to be needed, or go mad. Will you permit me to love you?"

Khizr was amazed. Bewildered. Excited. He answered by instinct, "It would be a gift of which I can hardly conceive."

A silent triumph, perhaps gratitude, suffused her face. She raised her-self on her knees, brushed back her hair and, with an air of determina-tion, leaned over and cupped him in her hands through his pantaloons. His partial erection was instantly mature, demanding. She frantically unhooked his girdle, tore open his clothing, and held him against her face as though a talisman from which she could draw strength. The frank-ness of her statement and the quickness of her action removed any re-serve. He moved forward to her as she began a ravenous nursing, and almost immediately felt his pleasure coming in a rush, imperative, un-stoppable. The result was a frantic, magical release for both of them — a perfectly balanced combination of firm and supple, yin and yang, male and female.

Each had filled a need in the other.

Relaxed, and grateful for the tyranny of love, he held her face and told her that he would undertake to provide anything she needed. He told her of his hopes of somehow finding ransom for the crew. She inquired in great detail as to the particulars of such a ransom — dwelling for a longish time on the amount needed and on how it might be provided.

Then, impulsively, he stood up and cradled her aloft in his arms as though she were a toy, his confidence and masculinity restored. "Show me the sleeping room." With a convulsive sob she tightened her arms around his neck and nodded toward the far doorway.

The strength of his unceremonious youth, plus the postponements induced by her skills — which she unleashed on him with vengeance — combined to use up most of the night. As he was to realize during moments of reverie in later years, that was the magic time he became a man. What had begun for him as a fortunate adventure became a giving rather than a taking. It taught him more about the obligations of a man to a woman, about the true rewards of a lover, than most men would learn in a lifetime.

He never forgot the night — or her. And with good reason.

The following week she was found dead of self administered poison, and after the authorities, with Yakub's prodding, had confirmed her wishes, her declaration, witnessed by two elderly farmers who worked for her, committed the olive groves and her jewels to the ransom of Aruj's men.

It was enough to bring home the crew.[1]

---

1.   Details of Aruj's ransom are not known, but Myrrh presents an enchanting possi-bility.

A harem musician.

Karaghuz Puppets. Of Persian or Arab origin, and made of either thin wood or metal cutouts, they were puppets whose figures were backlighted on a screen or sheet. Manipulators provided their voices and background comment — which ranged from everyday Turkish life (as these two seem to indicate), to moral and historical humor/satire. Very popular in a population largely illiterate.

5

ARUJ BARBAROSA

1504

Khizr returned to Istanbul and occupied himself with pottery trading and education for another full season while Aruj practiced his rowing skills on a Christian galley. Late the second year, the large red-head was released and arrived in Istanbul on an Alexandria pepper ship, philosophical about his experience and impatient to recover lost ground. By the next sailing season, with the backing of the same consortium, he had another, larger, galleot with sixteen oars on a side and a crew half again the size of the one he had taken to sea two years earlier.

There was one other major change in the operation; Khizr joined the new ship as a full partner. He had finished two years of an education few men of the time possessed and, at twenty, had clearly progressed from youth to man. While not the equal of his older brother in arm wrestling or heavy swordplay, as a seaman he was as good, and in matters of the mind was clearly superior. Full of life, knowledgeable and energetic, he was also an inspired teacher of nautical skills and an enthusiastic participant in sailor's games even when the jokes were on him. He was clearly respected well beyond the degree warranted by his years.

The brothers made a good team: both brave, able, and ambitious — one a man of action, one a man of thought.

They chose the Southern Adriatic and Ionian for their hunting ground. It was a long voyage around the Peloponnesus, but that portion of the Eastern Mediterranean was about to become profitable. Since the days of Mehmed in mid-15th century, Venice and Turkey had been signatories to various treaties which allowed the Venetians to maintain ports in the eastern seas with profitable trade privileges. However, Bayazid had been slowly expanding Turkish control of the the Greek mainland and the Pelopennesus for two decades, taking many of these ports by land, a strategy that culminated in 1499-1500 with an engagement with Venice which the Turks refer to as the first battle of Lepanto.[1] Venetian ineffectiveness and cowardice allowed the Turks to prevail and the Venetians were forced to yield several ports. For the next few years, before Venice recovered its will-power, freebooters such as Aruj and Khizr profited. Attacks on Venetian traders were no longer uncommon, and spoils could be openly sold in Turkish markets with the slightest excuse.

During their first season the brothers encountered a round ship of more than five hundred tons enroute to Venice from Trebizond with a load of Persian silk. Ordinarily a ship of this type would have been travelling in a Venetian convoy or would at least be carrying soldiers. But the prices of convoyed merchandise were fixed by Venetian law, and out-of-convoy soldiers had to be paid. Not only alone, this ship hoisted sail and attempted to flee, a move bound to arouse the hunting instinct.

With no soldiers aboard, it was easily taken.

When the crew was interrogated, the marketing problem was quickly solved. Two of them claimed to be enslaved Turks. Since the enslavement of Turks was forbidden, these crewmen were sufficient excuse for customs officials to permit sale of the cargo in the main trading center at Coron in Turkish Greece. The crewmen's knowledge of Islam and The Sharia was less than scanty and they spoke only a Greek dialect, but Khizr argued that the Ottoman Empire possessed dozens of dialects as well as many misguided souls poorly acquainted with the basic law of Islam. Moral imperatives had never operated with discernible effect on Aruj himself, and he was amused at the moral adaptability of an educated younger brother, at least half-Greek himself, who was well aware that Greeks, particularly those who spoke no Turkish, were as likely as to be True Believers as they were to witness another virgin birth. They immediately set course for Lepanto.

Their profits bought them another galleot and, upon Khizr's insistence, a dozen of the new arquebuses. Since the fiasco with Isaac, Aruj had been cool to the complicated muskets, but Khizr argued that a ball, which relied on weight and shock value, could punch through wooden

---

1.   The Bay of Lepanto is the present day Gulf of Corinth.

A late 16th Century Battle Cruiser under short sail. The oars are raised.

rower shields more effectively than an arrow, which obtained its distance through shape and lack of resistance.

He also revealed his own youthful vanity. "We should not be backward. People will hold us in higher regard if we use the latest arms."

By the end of the second year they had repaid Aruj's ransom and had bought the consortium's interest, freeing them of obligation. With freedom from debt came impatience. Wider fields beckoned. In the third year, the gray robe of winter had not lifted when Aruj, after enduring a long day on the Mytilene dockside, first raised the subject of new fields of endeavour.

Arriving at the waterfront compound the brothers used for the winter, he dropped to the comfort of a pile of silk rugs taken from a protesting Syrian, leaned back, and reflected, "We are rich men, but money is not our religion. We should yearn for greater things. Time is passing us by. I am now in the thirtieth year of my birth and you have seen twenty-three summers. It is seven hundred and eighty years since the Hegira."[1]

Khizr quoted a poet: "It is written that if you thirst when your well is full, you shall never know peace. Though fed, hunger shall curse you all of your days."

Aruj had a jaundiced opinion of his younger brother's habit of quot-

---

1. Hegira. The flight of Mohammed from Mecca, the beginning of the Islamic calendar.

ing poets and sages. A man could never tell whether those green eyes were serious or not. He ignored the homily. "Our father is dead, mother is content with her own household. We have endowed our sisters with bride prices. I've argued with my last Arab merchant. I'm tired of Mytilene. The time has come to move to wider fields."

Khizr approved, again in poetry. "You have flung open the gates of my heart, O respected elder brother. I have waited these many months for the Bird of the West to spring from your heart. I, too, yearn for a wider world."

Aruj looked at him with some surprise. "You agree quickly. What's happened? Now that your blonde courtesan has moved to Sigri, are you lonely, or is some irate husband planning to extend your circumcision?"

While Aruj's nose for information was good, it had failed to smell out that his brother had made the move to Sigri possible for the lady in question by investing in a small shop where she and her lame brother could provide comfortably for their parents. The young man maintained his penchant for reticence about personal intimacies.

Khizr crossed the room to a wall cabinet, took out a folder, spread maps on the table and answered without poetry. "To deal with your questions and speculations in the order offered: Yes, I miss her comfort. No, there is no husband whose knife threatens my happy friend." Tapping the papers, he went on — this time in Arabic. "I've been thinking about the West and our Muslim brothers in Africa, and I see no reason we couldn't join them."

Aruj was startled, speechless for a moment. "That was Arabic you were just spouting, wasn't it?"

"When thinking about Africa, I realized we had no Arabs on our crews. So I have drilled myself in the language. I will only ask one or two extra shares for teaching and interpreting."

Aruj recovered from his pleased surprise quickly. Never one to waste time in reflection — or praise for that matter — he nodded as though such an accomplishment was to be expected and he returned directly to the subject in hand. "About half the crew are islanders and some won't want to leave. You should poll them. The waterfront is quiet this time of year, and there's no shortage of men." With something approaching pleading in his voice, he added, "I suppose I can't take my women."

"Can they row?"

"Ah, but the young Circassian . . . to leave a dainty flower just as the petals are ripe...." But Khizr didn't rise to the bait and, after a moment, Aruj added grimly, "I suppose you'll carry trunkloads of those costumes you decorate yourself with, and I've yet to see one of them row!" Ever since Istanbul and the Galata Saray school, Khizr had managed to make himself notable by his dress — an affectation which, in Aruj's view, was not suitable for a fighting man.

Ignoring his brother's sarcasm, Khizr slid the maps across the table and addressed the question of destination. "All I've heard from you has been wishful thinking about soft winters and the cool flesh and pink tongues of dark beauties. I knew you would wake up some morning with that tiny thing that does most of your thinking pointing toward Tunis. So I prepared. Here are Venetian maps of Sicily and the Cape Bon area of Africa, and a chart of the port of Tunis. The people are True Believers. The King will offer security and a winter layup for a percentage of our take. The climate is good.

"There is no better harbor for us while we learn the Western Sea and Spanish ships."

ight weeks later, carrying a son of Yakub on each quarterdeck, two unique galleots rowed abreast into Tunis harbor and saluted the Goletta, the fort at the throat of the lagoon where the dock and harbor facilities of the city reposed. Christians mixed colored pigments into the tar or pitch which protected their hulls, and these ships were an artist's delight. Peering through nine hundred miles of salt crust were cream-colored hulls set off by dark green railings and fretwork, white booms and masts, red oars, and bright red iron ramming beaks. For all the world these were small, prosperous Genoan merchants.

Another of Khizr's ideas; one that was to pay great dividends.

The city of Tunis was impressive in its collection of manure, tolerant of its flies, and accustomed to its own filth. Its public water supply, common to all Islamic cities, once used, transported sewage down open gutters to the salt flats of the warm, essentially tideless sea and created a stench offensive even to noses accustomed the bilges of galleys long at sea. The "Flowery Bride of the West", as some referred to the city, was more like an aged Cairo prostitute.

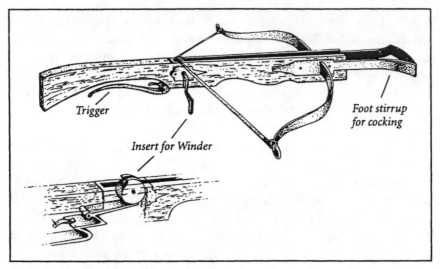

Trigger

Insert for Winder

Foot stirrup for cocking

Crossbow.

Khizr and Aruj, happy to stretch their legs, went on foot to the castle. In a city accustomed to such exotic visitors as jungle animals, giant black slaves, and a fair skinned she-slave riding a white mule, two large red-bearded seamen inspired little attention.

At the castle, they easily sealed their bargain with Muley Mohammed, long the prisoner of his rich table. The girth of the elderly Berber, who termed himself "Sultan", restricted him to raising a limp hand in approval. He agreed that the new arrivals could reside in or near Tunis, use the harbor as they pleased, buy such supplies as they wanted, repair and build ships, and recruit new men if they wished. The lagoon was protected from weather and there were adequate facilities for human replenishment during the winter layup period. The rotund Muley demanded a tithe of prizes in return for these harbor and market privileges, and the sons of Yakub considered it a bargain.

They wasted no time. Within the week they had gathered their crews from city pleasures, taken on hard biscuit, salt meat, olive oil, water, barley grains — and hired three local seamen acquainted with Italy's coasts. Once prepared, both ships rowed north, intent on the shipping lanes above Citavecchia, Rome's seaport. It was, they were told, virgin territory for pirates.

Three weeks later and hundreds of miles from Tunis, during a hot,

hazy, windless day near the cliffs of Piombino where the channel between Elba and Italy makes a narrow passage, Aruj and Khizr were prepared to give birth to a dramatic new era in the Mediterranean.

Two majestic cargo galleys, separated in trail by perhaps two hours,
stroked slowly over the glassy sea within hailing distance of the rocky
coast. From the promontory on which the pirates crouched, only the
first great galley could be studied in detail, but there was little doubt that
the sister, less distinct in the sea haze, was a close, if not exact, copy.

The galley was oversized. About one hundred and fifty feet long, it
was exceptionally wide, perhaps thirty five feet. With rowing benches
taking up sixteen feet on the sides of the ship, there was plenty of space
for boxes and tarpaulined bales in the middle. Extra large covered decks
on the bow and stern made the craft appear awkward, but provided more
space for fragile cargo and gave comfort to passengers and soldiers.

Just below the Christian flag was the pennant of the Pope. Recognition was instant; even Lesbian pirates knew of Alexander.[1]

Certain that it had nothing to fear, the great galley loafed along com-
placent and unaware. The flags it flew were sufficient protection from
any state in the Mediterranean which owned expensive war galleys and,
with a full complement of soldiers, it considered itself safe from anything less than a warship.

Nevertheless, with the audacity that was to make the Mediterranean a
Turkish lake, Aruj and Khizr had other plans.

Within minutes, the first large galley would see a galleot rowing around
the nearby rocky promontory with a dhow in tow, a small local fisher-
man taken earlier. The galleot crew would be wearing knee length cut-
offs such as those worn by paid seamen, and the men on its steering
platform would boast doublets typical of merchant dress. Genoa was
just a few days north of Piombo; there would be little doubt that it was
an Italian trader.

Khizr's camouflage was about to return its investment.

Two hours earlier, when Aruj had proposed an attack, the pirate crews
considered the idea impossible. If through any miracle, the pirates survived the heavy guns to reach boarding range, they would be dealing
with three times their own number of armed men. Simply to be seen

---

1. Alexander Borgia was not only a world class lecher, but a greedy trader-speculator
   well known throughout the Levant.

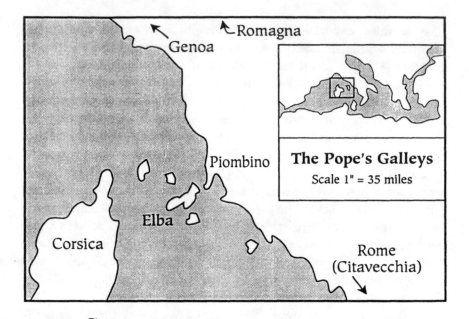

might be fatal. On a pursuit, their thirty-six single-rower oars were a poor match for sixty multi-rower oars. Close to shore, the galleots might reach land before being overtaken, but the Italian countryside was hardly hospitable for fugitive pirates.

With absolute disregard for the odds, Aruj was a tiger thirsting to attack, and Khizr quietly agreed with him. One brother wanted to fight for adventure and joy; one was willing because he saw an opening. But even the strongest pirate captain was to some extent hostage to his crew. While a leader might inspire, men could not be driven where they would not go. Out of sight on the back side of the small peninsula, the crews on both ships had joined in an open meeting.

Although Aruj talked himself hoarse, the men were clearly not willing. Standing on his afterdeck, a battle cloth tied around his head, he argued, "In the name of God, are we women that we don't dare wring the necks of these infidels?" He slammed an oak pike down on the taffrail with force enough to break the hardwood shaft. "If I have to do it alone, I intend to cut the balls off those pork-eaters."

Still there was no acceptance, and finally, frustrated beyond reason, he played his trump card. "Masters at arms," he roared to the shipmasters, "throw half your oars overboard!"

Without a full complement of oars, the pirate galleots would be all but immobile. Even though they might hide until immediate danger was past, there would be little chance to get safely back to Tunis.

No one moved to obey.

Aruj addressed the hesitation in his inimitable style. "You miserable sheep, if I have to throw oars myself, I'll do it!" He drew his sword, leaped to the first rowing bench and, balancing himself with one hand on a mast stay, promised, "The first man who gets in my way will have to hunt for his head!"

Before anyone moved, Khizr seized an oar, held it aloft and shouted, "I have an idea!"

If these men were cowards, they would hardly be six hundred miles into hostile waters in two frail shells. They were willing to listen.

"Our ships will fly Genoan colors. We'll take off turbans and dress in Christian clothing. They won't be alarmed at a small Genoan trader, and we can row right to them — ram and board. Once we engage, in twenty strokes Aruj can be around the point with his ship to hit from the other side. The Crosskissers aren't armed or expecting battle, and with a hundred of us on her in minutes, we can have that ship under control before they can wind a crossbow."

"How about the second Christian?" A still-dubious crewman asked.

"We can take the first one and escape before the other knows what happened. Many of the rowers on that first galley will be slaves wanting to pull their hearts out for freedom. The other galley is two hours astern, and can't overtake us. We can be out of sight by nightfall."

Another fifteen minutes of deliberation, questions, ideas, explanation, and an agreement was struck. Now, two hours later, Khizr's ship stood ready. He had forbidden gun-fire for fear of noise reaching the second ship, but rowing benches were cleared, swords were handy, cross bows wound and placed at hand, and half-pikes made razor-sharp. An aggressive spirit — the excitement of blood — sparkled across the crew like a lightning strike in the hot, still air.

Above, on the promontory, lookouts watched the first commodious galley, sails hanging slack, continue to slide along the placid water, the steady slow beat of the coxswain's tambour thrusting against their hearts. On the galley's covered afterdeck, thirty or forty lethargic officials and women could be seen reclining under canvas rigged as a shade, doing their best to breathe through the stench that rose from the ship's bilges. Half naked soldiers, none wearing armor, were spread out on the foredeck, languid, nearly comatose under the burden of fire pouring from the sun.

For waiting pirates in hidden galleots, unable to see their prize, the tension was tangible. Stroke by stroke, fortune was bringing them the chance of a lifetime. If their disguise failed, death or slavery waited. Fear knotted muscles and stimulated blood. Although they had been assured that death against infidels would entitle one to an Islamic eternity of pleasure, as far as was known, no traveller had ever returned with verification.

A shiver of anxiety from one of the lookouts, "Look there, do I see wind?" The man focused on a slight irregularity on the glassy sea. A wind would surely foil their plan, for the prey would move offshore and put sails to use.

But the disturbance on the water smoothed out.

Onward came the grand galley, a symphony of indolent coordination: raise oars, hesitate, stroke. Slack for a moment, then raise oars, hesitate, stroke — a picture of relaxed confidence.

Finally, lookouts on the bluff dropped their flags and the play opened. Khizr put his ship into motion around the bluff. Seeing the first large galley he was apparently surprised, for he immediately altered course to intercept and ran up a Christian flag to join his Genoan colors. Interested, the large galley ceased rowing. Grateful for a break in the monotony of the day, its passengers made their way to the rail for a closer look at the visitor.

The Genoan clothing of the pirates on the galleot could be seen, and several pieces of Italian body armor were easily visible. One of the deck officers on the Pope's galley showed his knowledge of the laws of Genoa, "Some of them must be soldiers. The Genoans require paid soldiers on all traders, you know."

The ships were closing at an angle, and when they were not more than three ship lengths apart, confusion appeared on the deck of the galleot. Oars were suspended at the top of their beat while several men ran toward the bow. The tow line to the dhow parted and the galleot's oars suddenly dipped and commenced a strong pull, heading directly for the waist of the large cargo galley. Four strokes, and the galleot drove its ram home full-length in a thudding crash that locked the ships together.

The sharp impact of the ramming knocked down most of the unsuspecting Christians, and before they could gain their feet, a solid rain of steel arrows pinned them down — closely followed by a nightmare of swords, axes and half pikes. Screaming, "Allah al'allah a'ukbar Aaallah!",[1] the pirates poured over the larger ship in a torrent of swordplay.

The ramming was Aruj's signal. Less than a crossbow shot away, his galleot rounded the point and joined the fray. (Aruj's crew was to claim afterwards that they covered two hundred yards in ten strokes — if true, a record approaching a miracle — but even if their speed was overstated, their enthusiasm was not).

Once engaged, the pirates were in a state of excitement that made each of them ten feet tall. Inspired, they would not be stopped. They paralyzed the Christians with their frenzy and in only minutes were in command of the larger vessel.

The relative position of the attackers was fortunate; the second Christian galley couldn't make out anything unusual. Khizr's ramming was hidden and, while Aruj's attack was visible, his approach was facilitated by slave rowers who cast their oars loose, permitting him to secure alongside and board over the outrigger and gunwale. At a distance, Aruj's small ship laying alongside the large galley appeared to be normal for exchanging visits. The galleots might have brought news. Fortune had also smiled on the pirates in the matter of sound. The victim had not been able to fire either cannon or muskets, and eight miles of sea filtered out hand-to-hand clatter.

The sister galley appeared to have taken no alarm, its slow beat and course unchanged.

All was quiet and orderly on the pirates' new possession. Oars cast off to facilitate Aruj's boarding had been recovered, the Christian soldiers were secured in the bilges and below cargo decks, bench slaves waited in breathless silence. The Christian flag remained aloft. Commanding the quarter-deck of the new prize, Khizr ordered the quartermaster, a tall recruit from the Tunis waterfront, to back the galleot off and disengage its ram. The new man, Aydin, a Muslim who had escaped slavery from a Spanish galley, by virtue of his strength and natural talents was a valued man in his chosen trade. On the basis of his knowledge of the Italian coast, Khizr had hired him as a guide. Today he would show a talent for

---

1.   War cry praising God. "God is great."

leadership and the quality of a quick mind.

"I have already ordered disengagement."

The protesting sound of wood being forced confirmed him. The yard-wide hole in the large galley's hull could be easily covered with sail cloth. They were ready to make good their escape.

Alone on the quarterdeck, Khizr gave no order.

No wind slatted the sails. The galley slaves were as quiet as a burial-ground. The oppressive heat seemed to blanket noise. Languid and glassy, the slowly undulating sea, its surface hammered flat by the sun, softly raised and lowered the hulls of the giant galley and its two small escorts in gentle, synchronized swings. Like a dog being driven from the house, the abandoned dhow seemed reluctant to leave. The second Christian still showed no alarm, his pace unchanged.

Aruj came aft to join Khizr. They looked at the distant galley, then at one another. The thought was spontaneous and simultaneous.

Attack!

In a voice that could be heard the length of the ship, Aruj screamed, "Rowers remain in chains for now. Soldiers and passengers out of sight, kill the first one that makes any noise!" His battle excitement at full pitch, he took a few seconds to raise his arms in a wrestlers victory arch. "We'll wait for the other cross-kisser to row into our arms like a rat to cheese."

Khizr shouted instructions to Sinan on the deck of Aruj's galleot. "That ship is yours. Keep your Christian appearance. Hold off as he approaches, and be ready to strike from the opposite side."

As Sinan began to swing away in Aruj's galleot, the tall Aydin made a running jump over ten feet of water to the deck of the smaller ship, re-gained his footing, and shouted up, "I'll make a good Christian for you!" Khizr felt a rush of kinship for the warrior and, as he prepared to board his own galleot, he offered a silent and exaggerated salaam across the water between them.

Within minutes the galleots had separated from the stationary Christian and were resting on their oars a few cable lengths away. As the second fat hen, now less than a mile away, clucked her way incuriously to the waiting foxes, the adventurers were ready to begin their second long odds gamble.

The adventure and its recitation eventually became the mainstay of hundreds of long evenings, but even imaginative embellishment could not exaggerate the long odds. Or the exhilaration from steel-strung nerves. These minutes were life at its purest, its most clear.

Moving toward them in maddening deliberation, the second galley managed to construct a half hour of suspense, but when it finally pulled alongside, the second act of the drama proved anticlimactic. The attack was different in that there was no ramming. The two galleots nudged their bows at an angle against the second large galley in what appeared to be poor seamanship and, before the Christians suspected an enemy, Aruj was tied to the starboard side of the victim with his new galley. Boarders struck from both sides and the victim was easily taken.

There was one surprise — delivered by a large gun on the first Christian. Galleots were too light for cannons, nevertheless, most pirates had experience with Turkish "man killers" — light, half pound muzzle loaders. With commendable initiative, three of Aruj's more imaginative men decided to fire a heavy bow pedrero[1] on their new ship. During the wait for the second victim to join them, they discovered how to pack the detachable powder chamber and insert it, to hammer down the wedges that forced the chamber forward into the breech, to ram a stone ball into the barrel, and to unsling the gun from its restraining ropes in order to turn it for aiming. As the attack commenced, they lit the slow fuse and watched it burn with pride.

In a way the firing was a success, for the explosion made a great noise and produced an impressive cloud of black smoke. But the fact that the varying sizes and shapes of the hand-made stone balls required adjustment in the amount of powder was information the volunteer gunners didn't possess. They had packed too much powder for a close-fitting ball and the gun had not withstood the over-pressure. A huge and deadly crimson flower blew the gun open at the breech and awarded the gunners instant passage to heaven. The battle over, they got to receive their reward in heaven as shahid — outstanding warriors killed in battle, honored by burial in their battle clothing to testify as to their bravery upon arrival in heaven.

Once the second galley was secured, no time was wasted. The Muslim slaves on the Pope's ships were freed from chains but remained as rowers for the voyage south. The new shahid gunners received brief prayers, were weighted and dropped overside, and the small fleet set full sail and all oars for Tunis.

---

1.   Type of cannon. Cast iron successor to the bombard.

Pedrero – Successor to bombard. Stone-firing. Cast in one piece. Range and accuracy improved over the bombard.

The large galleys themselves were too cumbersome and too expensive for pirates to operate. Nor was there a market in which they could be sold — a buyer would have to forfeit them upon arrival in any European port — but the hulls could be broken into usable materials. The new pedreros were too heavy for galleots, but were valuable, necessary, for anyone who might someday be a king.

Aruj retained them for himself.

In the next days, as the small flotilla strained southward, a count of the treasure was taken, and no sane man would have anticipated the total. The cargo represented a King's ransom. Pope Alexander had died a few months earlier and his personal holdings were being shipped to Romagna where his son Cesare Borgia was Duke. Since the large galleys were considered secure, they also carried the dowry for the daughter of King of Navarre, about to be married to Cesare.

Within the cargo spaces of these galleys were over four hundred pounds of gold and silver specie,[1] four chests of jewels, ten huge shipping chests of silk, and twenty tarred and waxed barrels of spices in the lower hold of the second ship — each worth its own weight in silver. Objects of art, hundreds of porcelains and tapestries were boxed. Alexander prided himself on his patronage of the arts, and there were a large number of crated portraits by Italian and Flemish painters, but the pirates had no idea of

---

1.   In 1504, when this capture occurred, silver was worth approximately half as much as gold. Later, after the discovery of the great silver mines of the New World, silver began a steady decline in value.

their value, and since Islamic law prohibited representation of the human form, they were considered heretic works of the devil, and summarily thrown overboard. Finally, there were nearly three hundred Christians suitable for the slave market or ransom.

Custom provided a ratio of shares between captains and crews, and the King of Tunis was also to be considered, but Khizr and Aruj agreed that small items, not to be charged against the accounting for the prize totals, should be given to the crew for barter. During the days it took to reach Tunis, these goods set off nonstop trading, a contest won by the only Egyptian among the pirates. Any self respecting fighting man knew that steel daggers, short swords or breast-plates were worth far more than several hand-weights of such foolishness as scented oil, perfume, powders and pastes. The Egyptian who didn't realize this wisdom was made a rich man, in time to become a respected merchant prince in Tunis.

Two weeks later, flying the green banners of Islam and firing everything that could hold powder, the two largest galleys ever seen in Tunis stroked slowly past the Goletta into the Tunis lagoon. They might well have been a kef hallucination — except that even non-eaters saw the same apparition.[1]

By sundown, every soul within a day's travel was in Tunis.

Notice had been sent to Muley Mohammed that his tithe would be delivered the next day, and an hour after early morning prayers, a procession led by horns and drums invaded the peace of the city. At the head of the column were Aruj, Khizr, Sinan, and Aydin. Immediately behind them came a parade of Muslims freed from the rowing benches of the Pope's galleys — their recent nakedness covered by new cotton trousers and turbans. Next were women and bareheaded Christian noblemen under guard. Behind them were chained Christian soldiers still wearing Vatican tunics.

Last, secured only by light ankle chains, was a group of Christian galley slaves, mostly debtors or criminals. With these men, in a dramatic move that would catch the attention of all of North Africa, Aruj was to lay the cornerstone of a kingdom.

The treasure and captives represented the wealth of a Spanish Dukedom. When the tales spread to the hinterland, the effect on the Berber natives, who conceived of wealth as a single camel or donkey, was explo-

---

1.   Kef, marijuana, was eaten more than smoked.

sive. Before their first raiding season was over, the sons of Yakub had become the most famous pirates in North Africa.

The procession nearly filled the palace square.

Standing before the spherical Berber King, Aruj spoke in a voice loud enough to be heard by everyone. "God has given us a great treasure taken from the cross-kissers. There are camel-loads of gold and silver, silks, jewels, and rare spices. These are divided by weight and your tithe is set aside."

Aruj paused and indicated the women. "For your special honor, we present thirty-nine she-slaves. You may choose your tithe from among them." Muley made a deprecatory gesture — and licked his lips. Aruj went on, "Also here before you are nearly three hundred new slaves. Once sold in the markets, your great House will receive your tithe. Further, there are fifty nobles for ransom to be divided in the future."[1]

He allowed a moment for onlooker appraisal before indicating the freed Muslim rowers. "To your right are our brothers in God who were enslaved on the ships we captured. They asked to come before you today to give thanks to your great kingdom for their freedom." His speech was interrupted with shouts of praise from the newly freed Muslims — and applause from the bystanders.

His bones warm in his fat, the Berber king inclined his head graciously to his fellow religionists.

Then Aruj indicated the galley slaves, last in the parade. "That leaves this final group of prisoners standing directly before you. Here are ninety seven victims of their own religion. Most were condemned to rowing benches for such crimes as stealing bread for their children or failure to pay the rates of usury charged by money-lenders. A few are here because they sold themselves into slavery."

Inasmuch as Aruj seemed ready to continue, the King nodded, but didn't speak.

"With your indulgence, sire, my brother will give our message to these men in their language, repeating as I speak to you."

Aruj continued speaking to the King in his new, slow Arabic, while Khizr translated for the Christian slaves.

"Bagnio traders priced these men last night, and I now place a tithe of

---

1. Aruj was not being entirely honest. A half dozen of the more beautiful women had been quietly reserved and secluded.

this value on your table." Suiting action to words, he placed a bag of gold before the King, then turned to the slaves. "You therefore now belong entirely to my brother and me."

There was a small stir. Turks were rumored to behead prisoners on very slight pretext.

"Your misfortune is to have been born into a religion where no man has a brother. We True Believers do not chain our brothers to galley benches. To show the greatness of God and, following the instructions of the Prophet, we now give each of you a chance for the good fortune of Islam where all are brothers.

"Your freedom is hereby granted.

"For those who accept the True Faith, we will give employment either ashore or at sea, and each will receive four loaves of bread daily in the measure soldiers are paid. Those who do not accept the True Faith must make their own way by selling their work wherever they can, and when chance offers, they will be exchanged for any True Believers taken prisoner by the Christians."

The offer was more than magnanimous. It overwhelmed prisoners and audience alike. Explanations were offered among the spectators for those who had not heard Aruj or understood Khizr. The prisoners, accustomed to brutality at home and whips at sea, could not at first understand what had occurred, but as comprehension spread, those willing to believe the unbelievable began dropping to their knees, some in tears.

"Papers will be waiting for you to carry. See the officials at the entrance to the square. They are prepared for you."

In a preplanned move, a dozen smiths with small anvils and hammers set to work to break off the light leg chains, one or two blows for each man. The square was transformed into live theater. Overjoyed slaves freed of chains, hardly able to believe their good fortune as the red bearded adventurer regally disbursed a small fortune in human flesh.

A more effective or dramatic flourish would be difficult to conceive. Such a theatrical gesture appealed to the emotional nature of a religion purposely made dramatic for an illiterate people. It represented charity, Islam at its finest. The Prophet had specifically said that the freeing of slaves gave merit. As Khizr had pointed out when suggesting the scheme, Berber tribes of the interior, poor men who didn't share in "Sultan" Muley's wealth, would be impressed with such profligacy. The age old distrust of country folk for city folk, jealousy of the poor for the rich, made those tribesmen a fertile ground in which a generous, flamboyant gardener might plant seeds for a future kingdom.

Before the week was out, every one of the slaves had accepted Islam. It took only a simple declaration, and for men whose main goal in life had been to avoid starvation or the whip, one God or another was very much the same.

Ornate pedrero in museum storage.

6

GROWTH — AND DEATH

1505-1517

Now that the brothers had true wealth, Khizr handled most of the money decisions — including one to build a powder-mill. With nearby oak forests to make charcoal, saltpeter on the adjacent African coast, and the greatest brimstone mines in the Mediterranean only three days away in Sicily, it was a good investment. They also bought two more galleots outright and accepted the pledge of four independent reis and their ships.

Aruj paid little attention to anything but the ship's guns they had taken from the Pope's galleys. A kingdom could not be acquired without cannon.[1]

With eight ships operating, it didn't take long for the brothers to discover that the ex-slaver who, years earlier, had told Aruj the western Mediterranean was alive with fat merchant ships, had been correct. From their base in Tunis the coast of Sicily was only two days away, the Kingdom of Naples five or six, the rich Balearic islands perhaps six or seven, and Corsica and Sardinia just beyond the Balearics.

By 1509 they owned ten galleots and had nine independent reis pledged. They had become a recognized maritime force, so large, in fact, that Tunis was cramping their operations — as well as their egos. Aruj's ambition was developing an appetite of its own. Like the grave, it was never satisfied.

As tenants operating by permission, they were subject to the King's authority, a circumstance that became increasingly unacceptable, espe-

---

1. Cannons were worth more than the ships that carried them. Spain issued them to her ships for each voyage and removed them upon return.

cially to Aruj. He would have preferred to take over Tunis, but Muley Mohammed was a Hafsid who traced his lineage to the Almohavids, a Berber dynasty which at one time had ruled North Africa, and as an heir of the tattered remnants of that glory, and a decent ruler by Arab standards, he could claim the loyalty of the local population. Without an army, Tunis was out of reach, as was the entire North African coast. Either the Spanish or their lackeys were established at every acceptable port.

However, the island of Djerba, well down the eastern coast, offered possibilities. Said to be the legendary home of the Lotus Eaters who welcomed Ulysses, there was a large harbor-lagoon with natural sand barriers stretching in some cases for twenty miles, creating a near perfect anchorage for shallow rowing vessels familiar with storm movement of the sandbars. A slight rise of land just inside the lagoon could be armed, making the island easy to defend.[1] It fed itself handsomely. The only claim of ownership was a tenuous history of having been part of ancient Roman Tunisia, and thus inherited by Muley Mohammed. That corpulent gentleman had no interest in the place, in fact he urged his increasingly powerful guests to take advantage of its sunny climate.

Djerba had drawbacks. It was remote, demanding four days to reach the passage between Cape Bon and Sicily, the true beginning of the Western Mediterranean. It had no suitable timber for ship construction and there were only a few small native settlements of fishermen and farmers. Plunder and slaves would have to be sold elsewhere. For men with long-range ambitions however, the island's pluses outweighed its minuses.

In 1510, the brothers moved their operation there.

Djerba was a paradise for those who wanted sunshine and relaxation; but for men of action, life took a bit of adjustment. The gentle natives were physically much like Hamite Egyptians whom they resembled in their aversion to hard work. Khizr credited diet for their passive nature. Quoting from Homer's poem of the travels of Ulysses, he informed Aruj, "Odysseus said that the natives were simple people who didn't eat meat or wear many clothes. They spent most of their time eating lotus, a fruit that made one forget all cares."

"Where can I find some of this lotus?"

"No one knows for sure, but it was probably the fruit of the sidr tree. The Arabs dry it, make a paste and a kind of cake out of it."

---

1.   Early defense-works already existed there.

Djerba fortifications as they are today.

"I respect your learning, but sidr fruit is nothing but a red date — flea shit. The Arabs feed it to their camels to keep them pacified. I haven't found anything on this island that will turn a man's head, and the women aren't fit for anything but milking goats. Although I admit I favor the local date wine."[1]

---

1. Modern historians doubt that Ulysses ever got that far south and west. His "lotus land" was probably somewhere in the Aegean.

While life on the island was quiet, there was a good deal of activity at sea. The brothers had not yet developed the galley tactics that Khizr was to use with such success in later years, but their ships cruised regularly and widely out of their new base. During their years on Djerba they were the first pirates to mount guns larger than brass half pound "man killers." The fact that these brothers, on a remote island, could obtain and use such expensive and sophisticated weapons indicated a potential well beyond that of common pirates.

Each brother pursued a different interest. Khizr never failed to make at least one long cruise each season, but a dockyard became his special project. He brought skilled workers from Tunis and, with them, trained a cadre of shipbuilders. The island grew no worthwhile timber, so he made a learning circumstance out of materials disassembled from captured ships. In later years he was to credit much of his success in creating whole fleets of galleys to the experience he gained on that sunny island.

At the height of his adult powers during his thirties, Djerba taught Khizr the limits and possibilities of administration and governing. Aruj left the management of the island up to him, and he became an owner of slaves, an employer of paid workers, a ruling official — even a judge to settle quarrels. With all these tasks waiting, he threw himself into work with noticeable abandon. There were days when he never wore silk, and his beard was apt to go a month without trimming.

Aruj was impressed. He couldn't resist asking, "You're keeping two Cypriot maidens — why don't you dress up for them?"

"We stay undressed most of the time."

In fact, Khizr had little time for the pleasurable activities associated with undressing.

Aruj had little interest in the shipyards. He lived at sea in the summer and spent winters traveling in the interior among native Berber tribes. His brilliant costumes were the envy of primitive men such as the Tuareg, "Blue Men", who colored themselves and their robes with indigo, men to whom display was a pleasure of life. He was lavish with his gifts, he was taller and stronger than even the fierce Zoaves; none had never seen a swordsman of his power.

In the course of his visits, Aruj passed a single, constant, message to these desert dwellers. If they wished to share in coastal riches they needed Turkish guns and Turkish ships. The Berbers increasingly came to hear him and, in the fourth year, his long winter months of eating sour goat curds and rancid mutton bore fruit.

A Berber sheik who had been dispossessed of the city of Bougie by the Spanish asked Aruj to help reclaim it.

On the central coast of North Africa, west of Tunis, Bougie was surrounded by fertile countryside and richly timbered mountains. Ample food and easy defense complimented a harbor suitable for shallow draft ships, and the population was large enough to provide workers. It was an excellent base for galley operations.

Aruj and the Berber Sheik planned a joint invasion — Aruj's ship's guns to reduce the Spanish fort overlooking the harbor; the Berber's army to take the city from the rear. Once taken, the Sheik was to have his old throne and Aruj a free port.

That was the agreement; Aruj's personal plan differed.

On his return from the interior he stopped first at Khizr's home. Overlooking the shipyard and lagoon, the comfortable residence, like most of Djerba, somehow seemed temporary. The whitewashed village, a more or less haphazard collection of mud and brick structures, slept under a sky ungentled by cloud. Ships in the lagoon cowered in the unrelenting sun. On the beach the surf used the least possible effort to sporadically rinse a few feet of sand. Even the ubiquitous flies were indolent.

It was not a bustling scene.

"Young brother," Aruj observed, "We become too satisfied with our easy life. The married man considers the single man a wastrel, the ox looks down on the ass and the hare. If we stay here longer, we will despise the adventurer. Its time we moved to where the sun shines on power and fame."

Khizr did not disagree.

Aruj described the Sheik's plan, and then his own. "By the Beard of the Prophet, here is my chance! Once my guns have opened the fort and I've put it to the sword, I'll move into the city and have that Berber donkey by the balls before the first day is out."

Again, Khizr had no objection.

Bougie lay about five hundred miles from Djerba, and heavily loaded ships could barely make fifty miles a day. Tunis delayed them for food and gunpowder, and by the time they finally arrived off Bougie, Aruj was itching with frustration — an ailment that was shortly to be inflamed by the discovery that even though well placed, their light ship's guns worked slowly on the fort.[1]

After weeks of steady bombardment, less than ten feet of the wall had been broken open. Food supplies for the ships offshore were growing short. Spain might send warships at any time that would make quick work of their galleots. Summer had been deceased for some weeks, bringing a daily possibility of storm at sea. Worse yet, autumn rains and the late planting season, on which their families depended for food, were seducing the Berber tribesmen. Their numbers were quietly diminishing every day.

When Aruj announced, "I'm going after those Christians tomorrow!" Khizr was again agreeable.

The attack opened impressively. However, after the first twenty or thirty men, the flow slowed. Only a few at a time could enter through the narrow breach, and the Spaniards were ready for them with sword and pike. At first, success had seemed only moments away, but the Turkish battle charge faltered — first to disorganized screams, then to an occasional cry barely heard over the clash of battle. In a few more moments the collective heart of the group would be lost, and with it would go victory.

Aruj beckoned for a "legup" propelling him to the top of the wall where, visible from all points, swinging his huge sword, he cut through one Spaniard after another. His "Allah al'allah howah a'ukbah!" permeated the entire struggle. A pulse of renewed determination pounded through the attackers, and for the first time they were able to establish a small perimeter inside the wall. The Spaniards were tiring and the battle hung in the balance.

But the balance tilted sharply.

Surprised, unbelieving, his sword fallen, Aruj stared at the spray of blood erupting from his right arm. A Spanish lead musket ball had swung him half around as it tore his arm off from just below the elbow, making it a useless appendage held only by the cloth of his heavy shirt. He picked up his sword with his left hand, but with the shock and the loss of blood, he staggered, slumped, and sat down. His men managed to reach him, take his sword, hand him down, and carry him away.

---

1.   Siege distances of the day were hardly more than a hundred yards, closer than a Galley could afford to be. Guns had to be off-loaded and fired from shore barricades.

With the loss of Aruj's fighting presence went the siege of Bougie. A tourniquet, a fast galleot, and a skilled Arab surgeon in Tunis saved him, but he would be a long time healing.[1]

With Aruj out of action, Khizr took the fleet back to Djerba. Alone there, Khizr expanded his interests from the building of ships to their employment. He spent the entire season at sea, coming ashore only to off-load spoils and resupply. Without anyone to share his decisions, he experimented to his heart's content with new techniques of attack, finally settling on a "team" of one larger galleot escorted by two or three lighter ones — mimicking an armored Knight protected by nimble men-at-arms. On each of the larger ships he managed to put at least one twenty-four pound pedrero, and one of his small flotillas could present a victim with a boarding nightmare of two hundred armed visitors.

A long year passed before Aruj saw Djerba again, but when he did, the giant was his old ebullient self, wearing his new silver arm and ready for battle. The arm was a marvel; in many ways stronger than the original. "I can use the whole power of my chest and shoulders to control the thing. Watch." He selected a small post, closed the pincers on it, and the wood crumpled as in an iron vise.

Then he added, "There is sometimes a cursed itching I get in fingers that no longer exist, and an ache in the wrist I no longer have. But I have recently discovered a cure. I place the stump in the warm nest of a she-slave."

Thanks to Khizr's work, the brothers now had twenty eight fighting galleots, eight of which carried fifty oars. More importantly, the crews were trained in the new tactics he had been developing — tactics that were to make him famous and eventually to make Turkey queen of the Mediterranean. With this fleet, regardless of Bougie,[2] they were ready to make a firm bid for their destiny, and when news reached them that

---

1.   Islamic surgeons and medicine were probably the best in the world at the time.

2.   The brothers made another attempt at Bougie before moving on. It too failed.

Ferdinand of Spain had departed on life's last voyage, they realized that for the rest of the season Spain would be occupied with crowning Charles as his successor. There would be no Spanish war galleys sailing near North Africa.

Only a short season remained, but they had no intention of letting it waste. Djidjelli, a small, well-located seaport east of Algiers, had a harbor protected by reefs and shoals. Small, it had been abandoned by Spain. The city's inhabitants were blood relatives of the desert Berbers whom Aruj wanted to enlist in his campaign for a kingdom, and they were willing to host Muslim brothers.

The move came in two sections. Aruj took the first group of fighting galleots and, after tying up loose ends, Khizr followed with the remainder of the fleet, carrying supplies and men. By the time he arrived it was well into autumn, and Aruj welcomed him with bad news. Djidjelli was still eating in October, but with two thousand hungry pirates as guests, arithmetic argued that stomachs would be growling by mid-winter.

Aruj was involved in, even hostage to, the problem. How he performed in Djidjelli would be important to his reputation with the desert Berbers. Explaining the urgency, he told Khizr, "These people tell me that they need two thousand salma[1] of dry corn and we'll need a thousand for our own men. Take eight ships back to Tunis. Buy enough corn for the winter."

To "buy enough corn for the winter" was easier said than done. Khizr had spent several days in ports along the coast during his trip to Djidjelli and had discovered that food shortages existed nearly everywhere. Corn would not be available in the quantity needed. Nor would distant Djerba be helpful. Food on Djerba was mostly mutton, fruit, fish and green vegetables — which neither traveled nor stored well. He decided not to burden Aruj with this information, accepting the problem as one to solve himself.

Sicily was the granary for eastern Spain. It was late in the year, but if the last of the annual corn ships had not already sailed, a couple of those might solve Djidjelli's problem.

As soon as fresh water and biscuit were aboard, he departed with eight galleots on a course for Sicily, and four days later was loitering in the

---

1. Spanish weight used for grains — about 400 pounds. Prior to the discovery of maize in the New World, all grains were known as "corn."

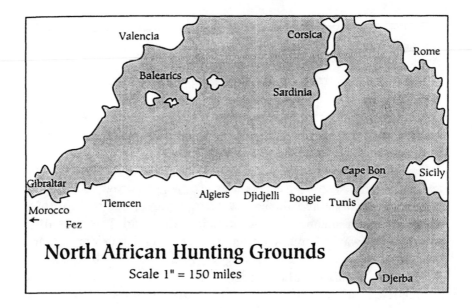

Valencia

Corsica

Rome

Balearics

Sardinia

Cape Bon   Sicily

Gibraltar

Algiers Djidjelli Bougie Tunis

Morocco

Tlemcen

Fez

North African Hunting Grounds

Scale 1" = 150 miles

Djerba

shipping lanes commonly used by ships bound for Valencia or Barcelona.

Arab scholars developed the concept of zero, thus making advances in mathematical abstractions possible — but in the case of Khizr's anxious pirates, "zero" was no abstraction — it was a very real circumstance. As the days passed, the sea set a lonely and bare table. Days turned into nervous weeks until finally, Khizr's seasonal weather fears were realized. The sky and sea informed him that he had to make a decision which might mean the success or failure of his mission.

The day dawned gray and mousy, exploring its world in short advances, uncertain and ready to retreat if challenged. The sea reflected the sky's gray character and mood. Gone was the lively sapphire blue; absent was the jaunty wavelet. Instead, with monotonous regularity, a dull, oily undulation slid sullenly under their hulls and rolled deliberately, angrily, eastward. Beyond the horizon, there could be no doubt; wind was urging the sea to attack.

If he fled two or three days south to a safe beach — the course any sane galleot reis would choose — his small fleet would be well out of the only area in which corn ships might be found. By the time they could reposition themselves they would have missed the last possible ship for the season.

On the other hand, if he remained at sea, his men might never need corn again.

The feeding of Djidjelli dictated his decision.

Canvas was rigged to shed rain and sea. Masts were shipped and, along with deck guns, secured in the bottom of the hulls. Extra bailing buckets were broken out. The bilges were pumped dry and all disposable weight was jettisoned. Saying, "We'll have little thirst if we founder," Khizr ordered most of their drinking water overboard.

Contrary to conventional galley wisdom, he decided to face the storm head on. Ballast was moved aft to raise the bows, and drogues consisting of spars and canvas lashed into bundles were prepared, ready to be thrown overboard as sea anchors to hold bows into the wind. Late that afternoon the crew was fed double rations. Extra bailing details were set, and it was none too soon, for a fast-moving cold front struck just before nightfall, its thunder, like cannon fire, driving storm clouds ahead of it. Throughout most of the night, like dogs before the whip, the small ships flinched from squalls and lightning, cowering before nature's anger.

But the storm was short-lived and dawn brought good news. The "bows on" technique had kept the hulls dry enough to be bailed successfully, and the drogues had maintained seven of the eight ships in sight of one another. By daylight, even though danger remained their companion for some hours, the issue was no longer seriously in doubt. By the second night the worst was over, and before nightfall on the third day, they found the eighth galleot, damaged but floating.

The entire fleet had ridden out the storm, a feat of unprecedented seamanship.

As if to congratulate the seafarers, the weather apologized. A sunny autumn calm settled on the water, allowing them to dry, to recover equipment, and to reship their ballast.

And fortune joined in wishing them well.

Four Spanish corn ships — nearly three thousand salmas worth — had ridden out the storm behind a Sicilian bluff. On sight of the pirates, the crews fled inland.

No effort was wasted to chase them.

The grateful citizens of Djidjelli went so far as to formally declare Aruj "Sultan" and by spring he had recruited more than two thousand fighting men from among their desert cousins.

The Brothers now controlled two seaports, nearly forty galleots and, together with their seamen, could put four thousand fighting men in the field. It didn't take Aruj long to develop his strategy. "This isn't the time to wear out our asses on rowing benches! Now we take territory!"

Shershell, a bit less than a hundred miles west of Algiers, was claimed by one Kara Hassan, another Turkish pirate who had gathered nearly a dozen independent galleots into a motley fleet and declared himself King. Aruj selected it as his first objective — partly to eliminate competition. "As Bayazid said to Jem when he seized the throne, 'An empire is a bride that cannot be shared'. I'll send Sinan with a handful of gold to propose an alliance. Sinan's wandering eye and the gold he carries will convince the Turk I'm genuine, and once I'm inside his walls I'll deal with him quickly and directly."

"Elder brother, you think more like a Christian prince every day."

A week later the brave but simple-minded Kara Hassan welcomed Aruj as a fellow Turkish king. The festivities were hardly underway before Aruj unlimbered his scimitar.

Next was Algiers. Governed by a Sheik named Selim, the city had a split personality. Its harbor was dominated by a Spanish fort on an island known as the Penon, but the city itself was walled and independent of the harbor. The Sheik wanted to extend his reach and he turned to Aruj for help. An invitation to visit was extended.

And was quickly accepted.

The direct approach used at Shershell couldn't be repeated in Algiers; the sheik had too many armed men. But for a man of Aruj's imagination, it was only a matter of weeks before opportunity presented itself. On a casual social visit he found the sheik unarmed and alone in his bath. Using his powerful silver arm skillfully, it took but a moment for him to strangle the unfortunate man with a towel — leaving no marks — and to quietly depart.

The public crier declared that the sheik had been felled by some type of seizure; a failed heart or heat stroke.

Aruj seized control of the city.

He and his brother were not welcomed by all. In a matter of weeks a plot to assassinate the new rulers emerged. It cost Khizr a small bag of well-spent gold to learn of the details and , with knowledge of the plot and plotters, Aruj seized the opportunity to make a dramatic statement.

He selected a Friday when most of the people were gathered for prayers in the main mosque and, while the faithful were prostrated toward Mecca, the heavy doors were suddenly barred by Turkish guards — imprisoning guilty and innocent alike. Aruj, whose Arabic was by now good, left his prayer mat and delivered a sermon, the gist of which was that good citizens should show better civic manners than to rise against their rulers.

His lecture was punctuated by guards who made their way picking and choosing. Twenty unfortunate plotters were bound with their own turbans, taken out and made to kneel on the ground, and the congregation was herded outside to watch the festivities. In a burst of instant, carefully planned violence, the twenty kneeling men were simultaneously beheaded, each with a single scimitar stroke. To the pleasure of Algiers' flies and as a lesson in citizenship, the plotters were left as they lay and the audience instructed to quietly return home and pray for their new leader.

The Arab proverb, "God has an army called Turks, and when he is angry with us, he turns his army on us," now had meaning for the citizens of Algiers.

Only one major native challenge on the coast remained. The Arab "Sultan" of Tenez announced his intention to avenge his cousin, the Sheik, and he marched toward Algiers with a force of nine thousand. Aruj hurdled out of the city with only a thousand crossbowmen and two hundred arquebusiers, met the numerically superior force two days from Algiers, and cut it to pieces. Giving parole to the survivors, he mounted the "Sultan's" head on a long pike and carried it on to Tenez.

The city was pleased to swear loyalty.

Handling ground forces with skill proved that Aruj had become a capable general of land warfare, a development clearly understood by Berber and Arab chieftains. One by one they swore loyalty.

In one year the dreams of twenty and the plans of ten had borne fruit.

S pain was concerned. Established in Algiers, the brothers' captures at sea were sufficiently rich to pain the treasury. The Spanish lackeys in North Africa who depended on Spain for protection were crying alarms and fears, and a new Pope was vigorously complaining that a strong Islamic kingdom in nearby North Africa threatened European Christianity.

Something, it seemed, must be done.

Charles, who was to be the main opponent of Islam for the next thirty years, was the grandson of not only Ferdinand and Isabella of Spain, but also of Emperor Maximilian of Germany. He had been raised in Flanders, a part of the Netherlands owned by his maternal grandmother. Inasmuch as he was new to Spain and he spoke no Spanish when he arrived in Madrid, he depended largely on Flemish and Papal advisors.

Barely nineteen and unprepossessing — five feet eight and one hundred forty pounds — his Hapsburg inbreeding was betrayed by a protruding jaw and lower lip. Ugly, shy, and retiring, he was nevertheless intelligent, courageous, conscientious. Lacking the pride and vanity of most monarchs, he disliked flattery and he chose his officials for ability rather than obsequiousness. He was to become one of the great rulers of the century.

He was also rigidly, fanatically committed to Christ's Kingdom on Earth; seriously viewing himself as Christ's personal defender and agent.

Characteristically, his decision to wipe out the "vile Mohammedans in Algiers" was quickly made, and with a similar urgency, his military acted with unusual speed, sending thirty war galleys and five thousand soldiers at the first sign of spring.

Once arrived on Algiers' beach, Admiral Diego de Vera's lack of skill in amphibious warfare was evident. The expeditionary force spent several days making a poor affair of putting soldiers and horses on the beach out of reach of Algerian cannons. Aruj waited patiently behind city walls until the Spanish forces were in their greatest confusion, then, with every fighting man who could carry a sword, burst out of the city gates, charged down the long beach and struck the Spaniards in camp. It was totally unexpected and stunningly successful.

The ships avoided harm by moving a bit to sea, but the beach was soaked with Spanish blood. Over two thousand Spanish soldiers were slaughtered and five hundred were captured for the Algiers slave market. Admiral Diego de Vega returned to Spain with half of his force carried on casualty lists.

Algiers was no longer a simple "pirate nest".

Throughout the winter, perceptive men in Europe, including the Pope, urged Charles to try again, and he was willing. This time he would fight the European kind of war with which he was familiar — cavalry supported by men in armor. An army of ten thousand was dispatched to Oran, a Spanish stronghold on the African coast west of Algiers, and placed under the command of the governor of the city, the Marquis de Comares.

When word of this force reached North Africa, Aruj was visiting the King of Fez, a Moroccan city crowded with Muslim and Jewish refugees from Spain. The King promised support and Aruj decided on an aggressive strategy. He moved the fifteen hundred mounted Berbers he had with him into the city of Tlemcen, a historic Almohavid stronghold and a major terminal for inland caravan traffic to Morocco. He knew he could not hold the city indefinitely, but he was to be the bait while the King of Fez struck the Spaniards from the rear.

Aruj's small force denied the city to the attackers for three weeks, but when the promised forces from Fez failed to materialize he was forced to abandon the defense. He broke out of the city at night and disappeared in the direction of Algiers.

De Comares realized that Aruj would have to pass over an open valley to reach the safety of a river crossing, and he detached a fresh cavalry group to cut off the retreat. Twelve hours later, as the leading column of Spanish horsemen erupted on to the valley floor, they found Aruj's force further than expected, cresting a low rise a few dusty miles ahead, and a race to the river crossing commenced — the Algerians whipping the last strength from exhausted animals, the Spanish cavalry pounding into gallop. Each group could now see the other plainly, the spent Turks praying for the river, the fresh Spaniards smelling blood. The approaching clank of Spanish armor and drumming of hoofs was a rhythm of death played in hovering dust — pursuers and pursued choking in a fog of sweat and fear.

With less than a half-mile remaining before the river, Aruj called out a detail and ordered, "Slaughter the four mules that are carrying gold and rip open the sacks. It will delay them enough to let us get to that stream. We'll get a guide rope across and hold it for you!"

The soldiers assigned to the decoy complied, and the Spaniards, now not more than three hundred yards away, could see the gold as it spilled out.

ARUJ
Two Views

As seen by Christians

As seen by Muslims

For perhaps the first time in history, the cupidity of Spanish soldiers had been overestimated. The thundering cavalry didn't hesitate.

A small detachment of Aruj's horsemen reached the river, emplaced guide ropes and succeeded in crossing the river. But his main body, with the Spaniards close enough for pikes and cutlasses, was forced to halt and form a defensive perimeter just before reaching the river. With the backs to the river, they were immediately engaged, and for a time managed to hold their own.

A short distance away, waiting to cross, the way was open for Aruj to escape, but he would not abandon his men.

Ignoring the shouts of those near him, he raced in wild spray along the river edge to the small hillock where his men were making their stand. He was an apparition. On a white Arabian, a maroon cloak billowing behind him, his bright turban decorated with peacock plumes, a glittering scimitar raised above him, his "Allah a ukbah, aallaaah!" was an inspiration. In a day of individual combat, this kind of courage could be the turning point in a battle.

But not today.

Unhorsed, with a half dozen wounds, he fought on his feet, his silver arm broken loose from body straps, a scream on his lips, his scimitar cutting a swath through his attackers.

Until he was run through by a Spanish pike.

On his knees, braced against the pike, head thrown back, sword aloft, cursing his enemies, he died.

7

BARBAROSA HAYREDDIN

1518

The King of Fez arrived outside Tlemcen shortly after Aruj had fled. After a long look at the shining armor protecting several thousand muscular Spanish torsos, he concluded that Aruj no longer needed help, and he alternated between a canter and a gallop back to Morocco.

When the pitiful remnant of Aruj's force staggered into Algiers with the tale of his demise, they brought two other bits of news — one good, one bad. The bad news was that after Aruj's death, his men on the west side of the river had surrendered under a flag and laid down their arms, only to be murdered by the Spaniards. The slaughter was observed by survivors from the hills across the river. Not a man, they said, was spared.

The good news was that the Spaniards apparently were not following up their victory. Although scouts had watched for two days, the Christians made no move to cross the river. After searching in the sand a half mile or so from the battle scene — probably looking for the abandoned gold — they had departed toward Oran.

This intelligence was confirmed two weeks later by Berber tribesmen — to whom nothing in the desert was secret — when they reported the Spanish army in Oran re-embarking for Spain. De Comares apparently felt that by killing Aruj he had accomplished his assigned task. The African summer was torching the hundreds of sandy miles he would have had to traverse, in armor, dragging a siege train, in order to reach Algiers — a walled city whose harbor was already controlled by a Spanish fort. He had cut the head from the serpent and saw neither glory nor profit in the headless remnant. Instead, he contented himself with installing a tame

Arab ruler in Tlemcen who agreed to pay an annual tribute of two thousand Spanish crowns, twelve Arabian horses, and six falcons.

Garcia de Tineo, the Spanish lieutenant who wielded the fatal pike, was authorized to incorporate the profile of Aruj into his family coat of arms, and the sword and cape of Aruj became a famous trophy in Malaga, known as "La Capa de Barbarossa."[1]

In Algiers, the pirates showed their approval of Khizr as a new king by awarding him Aruj's nickname. Khizr's beard was not as red as his brother's but it had an auburn cast, and his abilities were a full order higher — entitling him to what had become a term of respect among the ship captains.

The general population was a somewhat different proposition. The new Barbarosa needed to win their approval. For this reason, the Spanish withdrawal was more than welcome. Rather than organizing a panic defense of the City, he could take the time to court the native Arabs and Berbers. By nature he preferred to abstain from the methods of Aruj; by intellect he reasoned that their loyalty could be obtained with less pain and long term expense than through the sword.

A man who believed wholly in his own strengths and abilities, Khizr was more concerned with carving out a kingdom from the rough framework left by Aruj than with an eventual claim to heaven. The reassurance of religion as well as its forms occupied a marginal place in his life. But, not wanting to use force, and not having a "legal" claim through an established royal family, he would have to be legitimatised by God.

The Renaissance, now warming Europe, was totally unconceived in Africa. In Algiers, religion provided authoritative answers to a world virginal of reason. If God blessed a new King in Algiers, the new King would certainly be accepted.

Khizr put it to Sinan, "Since God rarely takes the trouble to show His thoughts directly, it is up to me to see that He is apparently satisfied with my rule."

For weeks Khizr publicly wore the coat of a devout believer. He buried his brother in the style that might be expected of a devout Muslim prince concerned with the soul of a deceased predecessor. Devastated at his loss, he ordered an impressive funeral with a regiment of paid mourners, gave

---

1.   Ironically, Aruj's cape eventually became a popular Christian religious attraction under the name, "The Cloak of St Bartholomew."

munificent gifts to the poor, and built a small mosque dedicated to Aruj's memory. For weeks, Khizr was seen only as a mourning Prince, inquiring of Imams, distributing alms, and highly visible at daily prayers. Properly respectful of the status and authority of the local Ulema,[1] he insured that their decisions were enforced and that their cash operating needs were fully met.

There was no opposition to the new King from the people of Algiers.

Once the passing of Aruj had been properly observed, Khizr was human enough to enjoy the prestige his status awarded. His penchant for dress was given full reign. "Bird of Africa," "Sunset in motion," "Walking mosaic," "Bridegroom", were only a few of the comments he inspired. No-one who had fought alongside him, however, was misled by his sartorial indulgences. They knew that he would not long be satisfied with the trinkets of prestige, and their faith was rewarded, both in the city and at sea.

In the city, the new Barbarosa now had taxing power, and he set about using it imaginatively and firmly. With the revenue, he provided public water, street cleanliness and security of the market area, established the first schools where children could learn to read the Koran, and spent months improving city defenses, using paid laborers. By the beginning of the next season, instead of an impoverished Arab town, he owned a healthy, walled city that could defend itself against several times its number.

Then he returned to his first love — the sea.

During the winter of his reorganization and improvement in Algiers, the news of Aruj had spread widely and, with the pirate king no longer at sea, many traders would be sailing without escort. The iron was hot for striking. The new Barbarosa believed himself to be the greatest galley commander in the Mediterranean, and it was time to prove himself, free of his brother's shadow.

Before the season was out, Barbarosa's ships were instructing one another with a simple flag code, and an effective search net sixty miles wide could be cast with three "flotillas" of four or five ships each. He could support an effective patrol of the strait between Cape Bon and Sicily or, if he wished, scour a wide swath for shore-hugging ships along the Italian coast. Results were beyond the wildest expectations, and by the end

---

1.   Islamic judges. Special class of religious and juridical scholar/officials.

of a single season he could mus-
ter more than thirty ships.

During this same season he
also took the best single prize of
his career — one which was to
indirectly lead to his first victory
over the great Genoan Admiral,
Andrea Doria.

On the first day of good
weather following a late summer
storm which he had endured on
a protected Ligurian beach,
Barbarosa's flotilla picked up a
large Christian cargo galley that
had been caught at sea and
blown two hundred miles east-

Andrea Doria is a national hero in Italy, for
whom, perhaps prophetically, the ill fated passenger liner that sunk off New York was
named.

ward. It had suffered extensive damage and succumbed quickly to the
chamade[1] of five galleots striking from all sides.

Through pure chance, he had struck another El Dorado — the flagship of the Lomellini family of Genoa carrying the entire year's profits
from their enterprises in Southern Spain. To put honey on his cake, there
were a half-dozen wealthy merchants as passengers, all exceedingly anxious to arrange for their own ransoms.

There was also a Spanish noblewoman — a treasure who would change
his life.

With the great Lomellini ship in hand, he headed for the closest port,
his old home of Tunis. There, he could sell the plunder to Tunisian traders and, as a new King, could pay his respects to Muley Mohammed who
had welcomed him to Tunis fifteen years earlier — now elderly and wasting away of a debilitating disease that had melted his generous rotundity
to a mere two hundred pounds.

In Tunis, Barbarosa managed to find a lot of time to spend with the
new female captive. One of his captains, Ochiali — a convert to Islam
and a devout student of Arab culture — urged the custom of azl on him,
saying, "The Prophet has ruled that congress with female captives is per-

1.   Chamade — Great noise at time of attack. Gongs, horns, guns, screams combined
     in outrageous volume to disconcert enemy. A Turkish specialty.

mitted as long as you leave no seed. Withdraw your weapon in time to fire it on the ground. Her value at ransom is not reduced and she suffers no shame."

Barbarosa's response was, "You are more in love with desert Arabs than any Turk. How do you think a Christian noblewoman would react to such treatment?"

"When I practice azl, there are never any complaints. No she-slave would want to return to Spain after tasting my delights!"

Azl or no, Barbarosa's personal standards would not permit him to force such a woman, nor did he send ransom notification to Genoa.

Named for her queen, Isabella, she was twenty years old and had been married for two years to the Spanish Ambassador to Genoa, a man in his sixties. When captured, she was returning from a visit to her terminally ill father in Spain and would ordinarily have returned to Genoa by coach but, without notifying her husband, at the last moment she had seized the opportunity to make a relatively fast sea voyage. She ignored her fellow passengers, merchants typical of the commercial culture of Genoa, and her disdain had been resented. These gentlemen, concerned solely with their own fate, made no mention of her in their own messages for ransom, consequently, she was not missed with the Lomellini ship.

It would be months before she was known to be in Africa.

Her dignity and bearing interested the new Barbarosa; her beauty bewitched him. She possessed a quick sense of humor, spoke both Italian and Spanish and, unlike the women to whom he was accustomed, could read and write. He had never known a woman such as this, and he resolved to win her heart — in effect, to court her.

Close to forty years old, he was a man falling in love for the first time.

Preoccupied with the sale of the Lomellini treasure and bemused by his Spanish Countess, he dallied in Tunis, failing to anticipate the reaction of Genoa. When the Pope's galleys were taken, the Vatican had attempted no retaliation. With that in mind, he did not foresee the strong reaction that occurred in Genoa over the this capture.[1]

One of the more powerful families in Genoa, the outraged Lomellinis launched a strong campaign in the Genoan Senate, demanding punishment. They used not only family influence but went to some lengths to

---

1.   In the case of the Pope's Galleys, Julius II, in office only short months when they were taken, hardly would have launched an expensive effort to salvage the wealth of Alexander.

persuade individual Senators with time-honored Italian handshakes.

The Senate was convinced.

Traders and bankers, Genoa had allowed its fleet to decline. The City/
State maintained only a few galleys for ceremonial purposes, but had a
tool immediately at hand — a well known condottiere who owned war
galleys and would sail for anyone with his price. Fifty years old and famous for handling armies as well as ships, Andrea Doria was the best in
his business.

His instructions were to destroy the pirate ships in Tunis.

There, Barbarosa received barely one day's notice of eight war galleys
west of Cape Bon. He was in trouble. Galleots could not fight war galleys. Nor would he be protected in the lagoon, for the fort had been allowed to lapse and was neither manned nor armed. The logical course
would be to abandon his ships and flee inland, but by now he was a
seasoned commander, a veteran of nearly twenty years of galley warfare,
a brilliant tactician, and an excellent judge of human nature. Like a river
stronger at the mouth than at the source, from youth he had become
very much a man.

He would find a way to fight.

Within the hour he had the merchants from the Lomellini galley delivered to him. When he offered them their freedom for information,
they were pleased to tell him whatever he asked — especially after their
attention was called to a stack of prominently displayed bastinados.[1]

According to them, Andrea Doria had been a journeyman in his allegiances, working first for France, then the Ducal States, then the Pope
and, in recent years, the Genoans. He was descended from an old Genoan
family and for some time had been maintaining a residence in Genoa.
He was known to be close to prominent members of the Senate and,
having political ambitions of his own, would welcome such a mission. In
a military sense he was a professional and unlikely to be swayed by hate
or revenge. Greed however, operated on him with keen effect. To the
knowledge of the merchants, he had little acquaintance with North Africa or Muslim pirates, had probably never visited Tunis and would have
to rely on others for its appearance and geography.

Their information meant several things to Barbarosa: Doria would

---

1.   Long slender rods, most commonly used on the soles of the feet. A Turkish spe-
     cialty.

not know exactly what to expect in Tunis and would probably have a low opinion of pirate ships and appearances. Political ambitions would make him impatient for recognition and reward. He would avoid unnecessary damage to his expensive galleys and, this late in the season, would be concerned about weather.

Barbarosa summarized, "My guess is that Doria would be satisfied to destroy a pirate fleet and not inclined to mount an attack on the city itself. If I am right, and he is a man who will accept the shadow for the body, we can give him a fleet to sink."

The plan he developed became folklore; a charade which pulled victory from disaster.[1]

Besides Barbarosa's own flotilla, there were six coastal traders and two pirate galleots enjoying Tunis hospitality. He passed the news of Doria's impending visit to the owners, explained his plan, and offered each of them a sacrifice price for their ships. All but one accepted and were paid. The one reis, whose refusal demonstrated a clear lack of respect for a Turkish King, was promptly chained to one of his own oars.

The first Barbarosa would have tied him to a cannon mouth.

The next morning presented a typically hot day. The unctuous sea in the outer harbor was spread before the sun, inert and inattentive to the eight formidable red and gold visitors lazing on its face. As the sun began its skyward journey high enough to draw oil from flesh burdened with armor, Doria's soldiers could see a pirate fleet inside the lagoon prepared for action. The cream-colored Lomellini galley, with a banner of Islam at foremast, was in the center of a line of galleots, feluccas, roundboats, barges with oars, — apparently everything in Tunis that floated. To a stranger, not knowing what to expect, the "pirate fleet" would be impressive.

In reality however it was a hollow shell. Four of the galleots were hulks that only hours before had been fitted with new masts, sails, and oars. The eight others were the locals Barbarosa had acquired the previous evening. Everything else was a ragtag collection of miscellaneous junk.

His own ships had disappeared. Overnight, he had unshipped the masts and sunk them in twenty feet of water

From the outer harbor, Doria's seamen could see the pirates prostrat-

---

1.   This was Barbarosa's first meeting with Doria, and it actually occurred while Aruj was still alive and convalescent. Otherwise, it is reported accurately.

ing themselves in prayer before battle. Once prayer was finished, a cannon was fired, oars were manned and, led by the Lomellini galley, the
pirate "fleet" got underway through the lagoon throat. Two and three
ships at a time passed through the channel fronting the fort, flying flags
and streamers, blowing trumpets, and beating drums and gongs. They
were making their challenge.

Doria blessed his good fortune. The fools were going to attack! It would
simplify his task. Once he had dealt with them, he could be enroute to
reward in Genoa.

Within minutes the forces were engaged, and as any reasonable person would have predicted, Doria's heavy galleys made short work of the
pirates. The captured Lomellini galley was the first to turn tail. It avoided
a ramming, fled for the beach, and its fighters — apparently few in number — abandoned ship. Following its lead, the whole pirate fleet dis-
persed, each ship rowing for its life. In moments, the sandy shore was
decorated with fleeing men, making themselves scarce in the general direction of the city walls.

On his flagship Andrea Doria assembled his staff and ordered, "We
have performed the task we were assigned. We can't waste time chasing
those greasy heathen; by now they're within the walls of the city, and
we're not equipped for a siege. Send a detail to the city walls to demand
any hostages and treasure the heathen are holding. Put a crew aboard the
Lomellini galley, and burn everything else that floats. Put men ashore to
level the fort. When that's done, we'll clear for departure. I don't want to
be storm-caught in this shit pocket!"

In response to the detail of soldiers sent by Doria, the merchant hostages, who had been held all night in close confinement and knew nothing of Barbarosa's strategy, were, as promised, freed. They were quickly
passed out the city gate with "all the treasure that could be found" — a
few chests of silk. Once aboard Doria's ship, anxious to be enroute home,
the merchants "knew for a fact" that the pirate Barbarosa had fled inland
with a train of mules the night before.

They also forgot, or failed to mention, their missing female companion.

It took five days to level the fort, and Doria was gone as quickly as he
had come. That winter he was to be voted Admiral of the Galleys by a

grateful Genoan Senate.

In a way, he had won the engagement. Barbarosa had given up the Lomellini ship and lost some usable galleots. Most of the small craft in the harbor had been destroyed, and the fort damaged. But he had suffered very few casualties, he still had the bulk of the Lomellini treasure, he had saved the city of Tunis, the fort could be rebuilt, and like a phoenix from the ashes, his fleet rose from the harbor floor as soon as Doria's sails were below the horizon.

In less than a day Barbarosa was enroute to Algiers with dry ships and his blonde treasure.

Once there, he set her up in her own villa with Spanish speaking servants. She was given escorts and the privilege of city exploration — and purchases in the souk.[1] The active and varied life of the Muslim city fascinated her and, since many of the people were fugitives from Spain, Spanish was commonly spoken and familiar foods were everywhere.

Life in Algiers also had comforts not normally enjoyed in Italy. Her residence provided a fully tiled bathing-room with flowing water, a sunken tub and a separate bathing enclosure with an overhead spray — as well as a facility that disposed of waste with running water. Naturally fastidious, and used to European bathing by water in buckets and passing waste by the same primitive transport, she realized that life with an African King had certain advantages. He was an excellent companion, pleasant to be with. She thought him a handsome figure, was attracted by his masculinity, and was particularly impressed by his personal cleanliness — discovering it common among upper class Muslims — in his case unusually so.

Shortly afterward, he went to sea for a month and his absence had a beneficial effect. She was a young woman in the beginning bloom of her sexuality, and her husband's interest in that area had been exhausted before their marriage. Marital fidelity in Genoan society was observed largely in the breach, and in another season or two she would surely have experimented herself. Why not try life now, so far from home, with this bronzed story-book figure?

By the time Barbarosa returned from sea, she had made her resolve.

He visited her villa on his first evening. Some distance from Tunis itself, nestled on a low hillside near the ruins of ancient Carthage, the

---

1.   Term for the local market in all Arab towns.

cool, shrub-enclosed structure was a sanctuary where he could dismiss such frustrations as a cannon dropped overboard in thirty feet of water by a clumsy crew, or the insolence of greedy Arab traders. Impregnated with hundreds of miles of sea, a feathery evening breeze caressed the garden and enveloped the flowered hillside in its soft embrace. Ship lanterns in the distant harbor accented the darkness, and small glass lanterns on low tables highlighted Isabella's golden hair.

Taking a glass of wine and assessing her radiance, his spirits were lifted. "Countess, your beauty takes my breath." He seated himself beside her. "Do you grow accustomed to our evenings?"

"Yes. It's much better than Genoa this time of year."

"Would you like to stay?"

"More than I thought when I was first brought ashore, but I wonder what my future is. I still can't think of my mother without pain."

"Your husband, too?"

"In honesty, no. As I told you, I was betrothed to him while still in convent. He was older than my father and we have little in common." She smiled and tapped his hand lightly. A detectable current pulsed between her finger tips and his wrist. "European women frequently do not have freedom to choose a husband, any more than in Algiers."

"Then you'll choose to remain in my city?"

She looked at him intently and didn't answer directly. "You are interesting in many ways."

He picked up on her flirtation. "I carry you in my mind as a desert warrior dreams of cool water. You could not be cruel enough to remain in Africa without granting me your favors."

"I'm your slave. Would you take them anyway?"

"I have promised myself to leave the decision to you."

She was a woman intent enough on seduction to abandon coyness. "Then you may ask."

Inspired by her invitation, he reached the wine, poured for both, and raised a silent toast. When they had both drunk, he set aside her glass and took her face in both hands — the first time he had touched her in a familiar way. Looking closely into her eyes, he said, "The Arabs have a saying that a day without love is like a day without sunshine. I have waited too many days for you."

She cast her eyes down and, in Arabic, shyly asked, "Then, master, would you like to visit my little sister tonight?" She leaned back and, catlike, stretched herself on the couch.

He was caught by surprise. The expression was one commonly used by Arab prostitutes as a solicitation, and he had no idea she was aware of the phrase — let alone in Arabic. Swallowing, he managed, "Your servants have been taking you to the wrong places." (He was later to learn that erotic words and phrases — or outright obscenities — were a secret stimulation of hers during their lovemaking.)

She wanted to see him naked. Untanned except on his hands and face, with only a light dusting of reddish hair on his chest, his fair body was as smooth and clean as rainwashed marble. Towering before her, his massive torso and clearly defined muscular structure made her weak. For the first time in her limited experience, thighs tingling, she felt herself involuntarily flooding. She leaned her face against him and found his flesh as fragrant as it was smooth.

His touch was gentle, his caresses skilled, his patience and concern for her pleasure an entirely new experience. At the beginning, there was the quiet hiss of her silken robe as it whispered down her breasts, then her own sharp intake of breath as he tasted the intimacies of her body. Seemingly endless caresses set the stage for a joining that seemed to last for hours — with her pleasure reaching new heights every few minutes — a plateau of excitement so intense she cried aloud, nearly fainting.

When finished, he held her for a moment, but she was too undone to raise from the couch, so he went to the bath first. By his return, she had recovered enough to offer her evaluation. "My dearest lord — I had heard that sex could be enjoyable, but had grown to doubt that I'd ever experience it. It was so wonderful, so exquisite!"

She had found the attention, the affection, the physical and romantic gratification she needed and, as time passed, her earlier life slipped more and more into dim memory. When his son Hassan was born — the only acknowledged son Barbarosa was ever to have — he took the somewhat unusual step of a formal marriage.

Barbarosa was never to restrict himself to the pleasures of only one woman — his appetite was huge and catholic — but she was to occupy a unique position. As long as she lived, he never called her anything but "Bella" — a short version of Isabella, as well as a compliment in Italian.[1]

---

1.   Little is known of the mother of his son Hassan. Barbarosa did have a taste for blondes, and such liaisons were not uncommon.

B
y the end of the year, with a season and a half passed since Aruj had gone to meet the Houris, much of the North African coast was the fief of the new Barbarosa. His wealth would ransom a king, and his fleet was larger and better trained than that of some small European states. Even so, Algiers was a long way from being a world power. Without support, Barbarosa could not long survive a Spain willing to pay the price of his removal. He needed to ally himself with a great power.

The obvious place for him to turn was Turkey, the Ottoman Empire.

Barbarosa called together his advisors, men deserving of the name by which they were becoming known: "Corsairs" — swift warriors of the sea. They were a diverse assemblage, representative of the heterogeneous Mediterranean world. All but two were "renegados".[1]

One of the two was Tourghut, known in Europe as Dragut. Younger than Barbarosa, and eventually to become a great Admiral in his own right, he was from a poor family in the Turkish coastal town of Charabulac. Adopted and raised by the Turkish provincial governor, he had learned gunnery with the Turks who were overhauling Mameluke armies in Egypt. When his mentor died of a fever, he chose the sea. A technically educated man, he had become the chief specialist in the new science of ship's cannon. Among the captains, he had become Barbarosa's closest personal friend.

Aydin, known as Cacha-Diablo (Punishing Devil) by the Spanish — a nickname that was proof of the fear he inspired among them — had been a Muslim slave in Christian Corsica, where he had escaped from a Spanish rowing bench by worrying the fastening rings of his chain loose with a sawing motion (that left lifetime scars on his lower arms), then torching a small felucca and setting it adrift among Spanish shipping in the harbor. In the excitement, he stole a ten foot dhow, and with neither food nor water, rowed and sailed the cockleshell three hundred miles to North Africa. All while still wearing his leg chains.

He had been with Barbarosa since the capture of the Pope's galleys. Unusually large, he was as tall as Aruj and weighed nearly as much. Like many large men, when not in battle he was gentle and good humored — especially with women and children.

Sinan, the "Jew from Smyrna"— the man Khizr had hired from the Istanbul waterfront after Aruj's ransom — was a notable reis not sworn

---

1.   Christians who converted to Islam, a common practice.

to Islam. A thinker with a mathematical bent, he was to become a famous maritime scholar and inventor of navigation formulae — despite the disfigurement of a "stray" eye with which he was born. Jokes were made about which eye he used on his telescope — the one that looked straight ahead, or the one that looked sharply to starboard — but not in his presence.[1]

Sinan the Jew.

Salah (Antonio renamed) was the humorist of the assembly, an affectionate, cheerful man, and probably the only one of the group whose sexual preferences were unbiased — anything and anyone suited him. Oddly, he was the only reis in the group who observed the Islamic injunction against alcohol. Originally from the Genoan island of Khios, he had learned his trade in the Aegean, and had brought three galleots west while the brothers were still headquartered on Djerba. His ships were the cleanest and best kept in the fleet.

Ahmed was a bit younger. He had risen from rower to bosun to reis in two years at Djerba and one at Djidjelli. Like Aydin, his size was enough to cow most men. He was known as an exceptionally hard taskmaster. His courage and rough edges made him feared; his prowess in battle was epic. The other captain in Barbarosa's inner circle who was Muslim by birth, he was the most irreverent. In battle, his exultant blasphemy matched his raging confidence.

Ochiali, a Calabrian, also destined for eventual fame as a Turkish Admiral, was the youngest reis. He had offered his services while Aruj was getting his new arm in Tunis. Exceptionally unattractive, he was short, bandy-legged, coarse-featured with a voice so hoarse he could barely be understood across a deck. Known as "Scaly Head" from an early bout with ringworm, he had been a youthful Dominican Novice studying for

1.   Sinan's home of Smyrna is present day Izmir. Jews held many influential offices in the Ottoman Empire, some close to the Sultan himself.

Ochiali – Also spelled Uchi-ali. Two views. The ages of Barbarosa's renegados and lieutenants, such as Ochiali, have been manipulated. Their subsequent careers and ages at death reveal that most of them could not have been ship captains until later. Detailed information on their early years is hard to come by, so most of them are arbitrarily introduced in 1518.

the priesthood when captured in a raid on his Calabrian village and chained to a galley bench. He was grievously mistreated by a sadistic Muslim bosun, but an attack on a ship's crewman by a galley slave was cause for instant death. His choice was to accept Islam and, once he had done that, he became a volunteer and entitled to protect his honor — which he did by calling out his tormentor and killing him with his hands. Like many converts, his acceptance of Islam was more intense than those born in the faith.

His one weakness, if it could be called that, was women. He kept a harem of at least a dozen, and his performance with them, as well as with the female captives his ships always seemed to take, was admired as heroic.

Included in the meeting were local experts in such unwarlike subjects as taxation and juridical procedure, men who had never been to sea but who were part of Barbarosa's rule for varying reasons. One of them was a Moorish scholar newly escaped from Spain, a walking encyclopedia of the Spanish court and personalities. Another was a young Berber, a re-

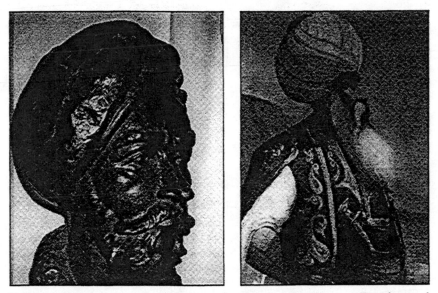

Dragut – A bust and a painting — young & old. Known in Europe as Tourghut, and nicknamed by them "The Drawn Sword of Islam" he was a warrior of courage and abilities second only to Barbarosa.

cent graduate of the Islamic University in Alexandria whose father, a judge belonging to the Ulema, had been imprisoned and executed by the ex-Sheik — the same gentleman who expired in his bath after a visit from Aruj.

In all, there were six local advisors, a dozen captains, and a visiting Turkish official who was a stranger to all but Barbarosa. Rumor averred he was an agent for someone high in power in Adrianople, the old capital where Selim's son Suleiman was governor, but since his arrival a week or so earlier he had been Barbarosa's guest and rarely seen.

It was early morning. The braying donkeys and clanging hammers of masons, now in their second year of strengthening defense parapets, sounded faintly in the room. Tea in samovars was available for those with eastern tastes. The new vice, coffee, was hot in silver urns, and sweet cakes and fruits were scattered in serving platters. Once the seats were filled, Barbarosa stood at the head of the table and, among friends, adjusted to the warmth of the day by removing his brocade vest.

He spoke in Arabic. "According to information from our brothers in Spain, the offspring of a dog, Charles, now realizes that when his men —

Selim I (the Grim). 1512-1520 (two views). Son of the peaceful and scholarly Bayazid, he was a throwback to Osmanli Sultans. In eight years on the throne he conquered more territory than his father did in thirty — mostly in civilized Africa and Asia. Concerned with purifying and consolidating Islam, in one campaign he gifted more than fifty thousand Persian shiites with early passage to whatever paradise their apostate beliefs entitled them.

may their souls be tied to an Egyptian crocodile in hell — failed to pursue their attack after killing Aruj, they made a mistake which he plans to rectify. If he chooses to send enough force, it is doubtful that we can stand against him — no matter our skills and good resolution. It would be very much to our long-range interest to have support from outside Africa.

"Today I'm going to talk about Turkey."

There were nods of approval.

He introduced the Turkish visitor by describing him. "Our visiting brother comes from Adrianople where he is a member of Prince Suleiman's court. He is well acquainted with the policies of Suleiman's father, Sultan Selim." Giving him an entry into the discussion, Barbarosa turned to him and wanted to know if Algiers were to be offered as a gift, would Selim accept, and might some kind of support be expected? "Your knowledge would benefit us. Take all the time you wish. What you have to say will remain in our hearts."

The visitor's description of Selim was graphic. "He has become known as 'The Grim' for good reason. He is as mean as a spear-stuck boar and cruel enough to serve as a public executioner. It is widely believed that after he forced his father, Bayazid, to retire to the Crimea, he had the old man poisoned. One of his first acts upon seizing the throne was to have his three brothers garroted by the royal mutes.

"But his cruelty is tempered by a strange sensitivity. He is a poet of great feeling and expression, and he writes frequently for his own enjoyment. His oldest brother, Prince Kourkhoud, was a patron of men's backsides, but brave nevertheless. Once Selim seized the throne, Kourkhoud realized that the mutes would be visiting with their bowstrings and he asked to have his life spared, insisting that he had no interest in the throne. When the request was refused, he accepted his fate with grace and he prepared a poem of loyalty, love, and farewell to be delivered to Selim after his execution.

"Kourkhoud's poem triggered Selim's emotional side. He wept openly for a day after the poem was delivered, then, to make himself feel better, had Kourkhoud's executioners executed."[1]

The visitor believed that Selim wanted to establish an all-encompassing Islamic Empire. The Sultan, he said, not only wrote and spoke in Arabic himself, but encouraged use of the language. Arabic language, customs, and arts were very much in style in Istanbul.

To a man, the listening group was fascinated, each one totally absorbed in the recitation. Even the outside noise seemed to subside. The guest paused and Barbarosa offered a comment. "For those of you who don't speak Turkish well, it helps to realize that the language is not at all rich. It does not lend itself to art or poetry and cannot be written except by ear and then only very roughly. Arabic is far more useful. For this reason alone, Selim is wise to encourage the use of Persian or Arabic."

Aware of Barbarosa's interest in languages, the guest nodded agreement, and continued, "When Selim captured Egypt, he also solved a lasting problem. Upon his return to Istanbul he brought the Prophet's cloak and sword, which will convince many of the Faithful that he enjoys The Prophet's mandate. He also brought the Caliph of Egypt with him, and the old man has not been heard from since. From now on the Sultan will be the Caliph. Only one man will speak for Islam."[2]

---

1. Selim's reaction to Kourkhoud's poem was widely approved.

2. The Caliph might roughly be compared to the Pope. Originally the office-holder had to be a descendant of Mohammed's daughter (there were no sons), but later on, non-descendants laid claim to the office and the question divided Islam for centuries. Selim settled the arguments with his sword.

He assured the men there was no doubt that Selim would accept Algiers. He added that concrete evidence of such approval — soldiers and guns — was certain to be forthcoming. "Selim is a warrior, a practical man. He will understand your danger and he acts instantly on his decisions."

When his speech was finished, support from the group was unanimous.

The decision made, Barbarosa turned to the visiting official, "Dragut reis will carry you to Istanbul. May I charge you with passing of my offer and some gifts to Selim?"

"It would be an honor."

During the following weeks before departure, Barbarosa charged Dragut with delivering letters to his mother in Mytilene, and an oiled packet to a "widow" who owned a small market in the village of Sigri.

When finally prepared, the gifts for the Sultan were impressive, filling most of two galleots. There were precious stones and pearls, crafted gold jewelry, a collection of esoteric African birds, two Arabian stallions and four mares, as well as aromatics and other curious objects not seen in Istanbul. There were also forty beautiful maidens and forty pretty boys, each carrying a purse of one hundred gold sultanins.[1]

In four months Dragut returned.

On Lesbos, Barbarosa's sisters both were well. His mother was happy to hear of Barbarosa's new son. The golden-haired "widow" who lived with her lame brother in Sigri had dictated a letter for Dragut to write and carry, the gist of which was that she was "nearly fifty and lived mostly in her memories." She was "Touched and exceedingly grateful for the lovely jewels I found in the packet" and added that some of the village fishermen still remembered the miraculous escape from the storm by Aruj nearly twenty years ago.

From Istanbul, the news was equally welcome. Selim was pleased with Barbarosa's gifts. He was not only willing to accept Algiers into the Empire, he appointed Barbarosa Beylerbey of North Africa.[2] Along with a note saying, "The gifts do me honor", he sent the official trappings of an Ottoman Viceroy: a coal black Arabian stallion, a jewel encrusted scimitar with Selim's tugra engraved on the hilt, and a silken banner with two

---

1.   A Turkish gold sultanin was worth almost two Venetian ducats.

2.   A Beylerbey (bey of beys), was normally a ruler of a major division of the Empire. In the case of Algiers, it was meant to honor Barbarosa.

horse tails. He also promised a thousand Janissaries as soon as weather permitted.

Such quick acceptance of Algiers was to be expected from Selim. His view of a pan-Islamic world with Turkey at its head fit hand in glove with several hundred miles of new territory in North Africa.

He also awarded Khizr an Islamic name: Hayreddin[1] — Defender of The Faith — an indication that the new Beylerbey was expected to further Islam with his sword. Like the Spanish who burned and raped their way across the New World in the cause of their God, Selim's religion was a single-minded obsession.

Unofficially, the nickname Barbarosa had already crept into wide use, so a compromise of "Barbarosa Hayreddin" was generally used.

The Mediterranean had its greatest galley Captain. Turkey had a new Viceroy. Islam had a new Defender of the Faith.

---

1.   Hayreddin is a Turkish spelling, but most writers use the Arabic phonetics — "Kheir ed din" or similar.

16th century Christian war galleys. These narrow, shallow craft carried approximately two hundred rowers and as many more fighting men. Note the bow cannons on these models.

8

ALGIERS COMES OF AGE

The 1520s

In the spring of 1520, Selim died an early and painful death from cancer, eased only by generous opium dosage in the final months. On receiving the news of his passing, Ochiali observed, "Selim the Grim has ridden forward on that great adventure we all face — to meet the many he has sent on before him."

Aside from his cruelty, Selim was a man of great ability, one who, in his nine short years on the throne, made Turkey a world power and the absolute leader of Islam. He not only used his fearsome armies to conquer, he adopted much of the culture of his conquests by insuring that Arabic arts (which reflected Persian influence) were adopted wholesale. Turks, warrior nomads with no written language of their own who traditionally borrowed cultures from their conquests, were receptive, and Istanbul became not only the center of orthodox (Sunni) Islam, but a champion of Arabic arts and literature.

Upon Selim's death in 1520, his twenty-five year old son Suleiman returned to Istanbul from Adrianople, where he had been serving as Sanjakbey, bringing with him his inseparable friend, Ibrahim. Born Greek, Ibrahim was taken slave by a wealthy widow who educated and gave him to the young prince Suleiman as a companion. Arriving in Istanbul as Suleiman's advisor, he was to become a great military leader, wearing the hat of Commanding General of the army whenever Suleiman himself was not in the field, and he was later to be appointed Grand Vizier, an office he held with distinction for fifteen years — a fruitful and strong period of Ottoman greatness.

The promise of Suleiman's reign was auspicious. He was the 10th ruler in the Ottoman line and he took office during the 10th month of the 10th century of Islam — favorable numerals for Muslims to whom the figure 10 bore a mystical significance. As well, the names Solomon and Abraham were names of men approved by God as great leaders.

Another good omen for the future — somewhat more practical — was Suleiman's lack of brothers, a circumstance which spared Turkey the royal fratricide that by law accompanied assumption of the throne. When a new Sultan was selected, royal brothers were strangled with the silken cords of the royal mutes and pregnant women from the old Sultan's bed were drowned. Male children of the Sultan's daughters were always strangled at birth. While the custom generally accomplished its desired end of avoiding civil war, it caused pain and resentment well beyond the royal siblings and their supporters. Both Suleiman and Turkey were fortunate to avoid the abhorrent exercise.

A product of three centuries of absolute family power, trained from earliest childhood to believe in his own omnipotence, and now personally the richest man in the world, Suleiman was recognized by his subjects essentially as God on Earth. His power was absolute. A wave of his hand could make corpses of thousands, his slightest whim could set into action the most powerful government and military force in the world, a scribbled signature could grant a kingdom.[1]

Suleiman nurtured an insatiable curiosity about the people and cities of his Empire. One of his first questions concerned North Africa: What was this remote land? Who were the people? Why had his father appointed a pirate as Viceroy?

Ibrahim produced beautifully drawn maps and his answer took the form of a medress history lesson. "Physically, the area is a narrow coastal strip that stretches eight hundred miles along the northern and northeastern coast of Africa. There is little or no intercourse with lower Africa, for a great desert divides the land. There are good ports which support trade and which have timber nearby; larch especially is plentiful. The climate is healthy and allows crops twice a year in much of the country."

The Sultan interrupted to ask about religion.

"Sunni Islam is universal. There are a very few Jews who have been

---

1.   Touched by the pleas of a widowed Christian Queen, he promised her babe in arms the throne of Hungary, and when the child reached maturity, kept the promise.

Suleiman – In middle age and as a youth. He wed much of his time and authority in the codification of kanuns — secular laws first introduced by his great grandfather, Mehmed. He was to eventually place the twenty three kingdoms and millions of people of his Empire, whose only justice had previously been the sometimes vague and occasionally conflicting interpretations of the Sharia (Koranic Law), under a detailed and universal code. Throughout the Islamic world, he became known as "The Lawgiver", a worthy successor to Hammurabi and Justinian.

driven out of Spain in the same movement that brought many here to Istanbul. There are no Christians. There are small pockets of Shia believers in the far west — Morocco."

"Language?"

"Arabic. One reason your father liked the area, I'm sure."

"People?"

"Three intermixed and sometimes hard to distinguish types: Arabs, Berbers, and Moors. The Arabs are remnants of the early armies of Islam. The Berbers are natives, a fierce tribal desert people who eventually came to dominate the Arabs. Moor is a name originally applied to Berber natives of the ancient kingdom of Morocco in the far west, many of whom have Negro blood.[1]

"The first conquerors, the Carthaginians, were merchants. Then the Romans came on the scene and destroyed Carthage. In its place, Tunisia,

---

1.   "Moor" comes from the Greek "mauros" — dark skin.

as most of North Africa was then known, grew to be a strong and cultured state and a major division of Rome itself — a source of food and wealth for the Empire. However, as the Roman Empire slid into decay the armies of The Prophet swept across on their way to Spain. The word of Mohammed was gratefully accepted."

"Who rules today?"

"Until recently, the area was a mare's nest of petty princes and corruption — a fruit tree ripe to be picked. The only nearby Islamic state, Egypt, has shown no interest. The Mamelukes your father left in Cairo have been content to occupy themselves in their cool gardens with their male playmates; they think of North Africa as the 'Mahgreb' — unknown west. Spain maintains a few coastal forts — one of which is just offshore from Algiers — and controls a few Spanish tribute cities ruled by Berber and Arab jackals.

"Your Viceroy, Hayreddin Pasha, has made himself master of most of North Africa from his city of Algiers."

"From where comes this Hayreddin?"

"His father was a Janissary captain honored with a gift of land on Mytilene by your great grandfather, Mehmed. Hayreddin and his older brother Aruj — a notable fighter who was killed by the Spanish — operated as pirates from Mytilene against Venetian shipping. Your uncle, Prince Kourkhoud, was one of Aruj's backers. Fifteen years ago, they moved to North Africa and established the Kingdom of Algiers. Barbarosa leads his ships personally every year and he has never suffered a defeat. Enemies as well as supporters know him as the unequaled galley master. No one on earth can match his knowledge of sea warfare."

He added a prophetic remark, "The Empire cannot afford to be without this man."

From Suleiman's first days, Algiers was allowed to operate freely within the Empire, and during the decade of the 1520s, operate it did. By the middle of that period Christians were losing over five million ducats of insured shipping annually — wealth that made Algiers a flower of the African coast, a marvel of comfortable, even ostentatious, homes and gardens. Life there was as safe and enjoyable as in any European city; better than in most.[1]

---

1.   A Spanish historian, Diego de Haedo, wrote, "(Corsairs were) ready to sink with wealth and captives... gold, silver, pearls, amber, spices, drugs, silks, cloths, velvets etc., rendered (Algiers) the most opulent city in the world."

E arly in the decade Barbarosa acquired a lifetime friend — a man he was eventually to choose to be his successor as the Pasha of Algiers.

Arriving at a Sardinian rendezvous with Dragut during an early season voyage, he received an unusual gift. As Dragut boarded Barbarosa's galley, he was bursting with pleasure. "I have brought you a treasure, o great sailor of Mytilene."

Mistakenly, Barbarosa assumed that the "treasure" would be a blue eyed maiden.

Instead, Dragut gave Barbarosa a young man, a eunuch, and he sang youth's praises at length. "He is the brightest, most entertaining youth I have known. I freed him from an al-fail[1] who owns most of this part of Sardinia just south of here, and I have had him with me every day since. He was altered just last year and the operation hasn't affected either his good nature or his strength. Under your guidance he should become a trustworthy servant and useful to you in appraising those men you select to govern your city."

Barbarosa's voyage that spring lasted over a month, giving him ample opportunity to get acquainted with the youth. Day after lazy day, when not raiding, he summoned his new slave, and their friendship grew rapidly. Back in Algiers, Barbarosa introduced him to Isabella and his son Hassan with instant success. The eunuch was honest in his accountings and absolutely loyal. His outstanding characteristic, as Dragut had predicted, was his excellent judgment of men; he seemed to possess an intuition of the type ordinarily the exclusive property of gifted women. All eunuchs were called Aga as a term of address; he chose for himself the same name as Barbarosa's son and thus became known as Hassan Aga.

During the early part of this period, Barbarosa's personal life also reached its richest apex. Drawing on his childhood and the status enjoyed by women in his family, he welcomed Isabella as a valued confidant and conversationalist. An intelligent woman, she became his intellectual counterweight, a friend with whom he could joust on wide ranging topics. Even the subject of religion was fair game.

Barbarosa's native distrust of superstition made him willing to debate the inconsistencies of his own religion. When Isabella challenged the "narrow" outlook of Muslims, Barbarosa explained, "Muslims, Chris-

---

1.   Al fail. An Arabic term for a dominant homosexual.

HASSAN AGA

Exactly how Hassan Aga came into Barbarosa's possession is not known. One Christian historian claims that Barbarosa himself ordered the castration of an intelligent youth, but it is unlikely.

tians, and Jews all descend from Abraham, but Muslims are closer to Jews. Both have strict food laws, circumcise males, forbid a priesthood, worship only one God. They both consider women less than men.

"That's not a bad idea, you know," he added as he looked into space.

She ignored his thrust. "Why do you hate the poor Christians?"

"The Christians, who are far from poor, follow practices distasteful to us. They worship icons and idols. They eat unclean food, obey priests, don't circumcise men and have three gods: the father, the son, and the holy ghost — four, if you include the mother of Jesus." Then he gravely intoned a prayer as though in Mosque, "There is no God but God, and Mohammed is his prophet!"

She raised her eyebrows.

"They also pay too much respect to women," he added, gazing at the same spot in space.

She made a face and he continued, "But, to tell the truth, we respect Jesus. Its the Cross-kissers of the Roman Church we hate. The Prophet ruled that Jesus was himself a prophet, and thus to be respected. A great Islamic scholar once answered a critic who asked how Mohammed got to heaven by replying that He climbed the ladder left for Him by your prophet Jesus. Can you imagine the Pope making such a remark?"

She answered his question with a question. "Judges here are all religious scholars. Are all Islamic laws in the Koran?"

"Yes and no. Mohammed was a Bedouin and his laws were those necessary to survive in the desert. For example, men are encouraged to take extra wives — how else can a widow care for herself ? But His Words do not always exactly answer all questions, so his pronouncements have been expanded to rules called Sunna, The Tradition."

"How long is the Koran?"

"It has 77,934 words in 114 surahs."[1]

"That's a miraculous count. I didn't know you were an imam."

"I cannot claim 'Hafiz' — I don't know the book by heart. To memorize the numbers I just gave you was work enough."

"Why are Muslims always at war?"

"Mohammed says war is the sword of God. And we seek vengeance for Christian killings. When the Christians captured Jerusalem they butchered every Muslim man, woman, and child, and then turned on the Jews, herded them all into one synagogue and burned them alive."

"Explain the Shiites."

"They are mostly cruel people who consider women to be creatures without souls, like animals. Some Shiites circumcise women by cutting off the sex button, the little man in your boat that gives you so much pleasure." He gently squeezed her venus mound.

"Circumcision of men has been a health measure since Abraham, but when Shiites do it to women, the real reason is to remove pleasure from sex and therefore to insure faithfulness. Some shiites even sew up all but a tiny opening on the sex flower."[2]

Trying a bit of raillery herself, she said, "Four of the five major duties of a Muslim are concerned with oneself — daily prayers, pilgrimage to Mecca, Ramadan fast, and recital of the Creed. Only the giving of alms has concern for others."

He refused to rise to the bait. "Mohammed was a good and kind man and His words made life better for many people. He was very human. In violation of custom and law, He had congress with the beautiful young wife of his adopted son, but a later revelation from God permitted it. When His youngest wife Aisha, with whom He was very much in love, fell behind the caravan and spent the night in the desert with a handsome young tribesman, He alone believed her protestations of innocence, and again, God supported Him with a revelation."

---

1. Chapters.
2. See glossary for detail (infibulation).

She couldn't resist. "Those revelations were certainly fortunate."

He looked at her. "Now, Bella, what was the result of His human weakness and His kindness? It was this: from that time The Law requires four witnesses to convict a woman of adultery — and only in Europe, where adultery takes place in city squares — can that many witnesses ever be found. His love and trust have benefited Muslim women for almost a thousand years."

He concluded, "Well, whatever you think, we have El Buraq, the horse of Mohammed. It has the face of a woman, the tail of a peacock, and can leap across whole deserts in one bound!"

She patted his intimate hand.

M uslims, collectively (and inaccurately) known as Moors, had ruled Spain in a fair manner for centuries. Moorish art set world standards. Architecture flourished — the Alhambra, a palace in Granada, was the equal of any building in the world for beauty and function. While Christians were burning books in an attempt to destroy all traces of such "heathens" as Socrates and Plato, Islamic scholars in Spain were translating (and saving for the world) Hellenic culture and knowledge. The Moors laid only light taxes against non-Muslims, commercial and land-owning privileges were available to all, and Christians and Jews were free to practice their own beliefs. Sephardic Jewish cities such as Toledo, Cordoba, and Grenada became world famous centers of learning and intellectual freedom.

The Moors were an industrious, inventive people whose energies built roads, created seaports, and founded cities. Water, an integral part of Islamic religious practice, brought not only cleanliness to cities which became the healthiest in the world, but made a garden out of thousands of hectares of arid land. A common saying of the time was "Only an Arab can fully understand the importance of water."[1]

With time, however, came decline. Islamic theocracy would not adapt to change and ruling dynasties began to self-destruct in a welter of internal jealousy, intrigue, and family feuds. In the late 11th century, a Christian Knight, Rodrigo Diaz de Vivar (El Cid), conquered part of Valencia

---

1.   Muslims were required to wash before prayers (five times daily) and after sexual congress (fewer than five times on most days).

in a picture book campaign that exposed Moorish weaknesses. Seeing opportunity, freebooting Christian princes and their trains of noble adventurers who coveted Muslim riches were soon ready to emulate El Cid, and as a fig leaf the Pope blessed a Crusade known la Reconquista (The Reconquest). El Cid's treatment of the Moors had been humane, but as la Reconquista inched down Spain over the centuries, greed and narrow religious zealotry gave license to brutality and despoliation.

Isabella of Spain. As unpleasant as she looked.

When the last Moorish kingdom, Granada, surrendered in 1492 to the Spanish armies of Castile and Aragon — Ferdinand and Isabella — the Spainards, following a practice that had become tradition, lied. In return for a promise of religious freedom, the city capitulated, but before the dust settled, Ferdinand issued an order of expulsion or death for all non-Christians.

Most of the Jews managed to escape, but there were simply too many Moors for all to flee, and those who remained became in effect slaves — forced to accept Christ en masse — baptized by buckets of water thrown at a crowd. Those who had property coveted by the Church stood an excellent chance of being burned alive in the unique ceremony of faith in Jesus known as an auto da fe — a procedure that served the dual purpose of ensuring the salvation of the sufferer's soul and of passing title of his property to the Church.[1]

Known as Moriscos, these Moors remained secretly loyal to Islam. They conducted prayer at home, gave each child a secret Muslim name and delayed circumcision until adulthood — a ceremony certain to test personal commitment. Many appealed to their Muslim cousins in North Africa, and large numbers were brought over.[2]

---

1.   Not only were property owners burned alive, but if they had died of other causes, their corpses were dug up and burned in order that the Church might have "legal" title.

2.   In the twenty five years following 1492, a half million Moriscos were brought to Africa. Algiers was a prime mover in this traffic.

A group of eight hundred Moriscos, vassals on the Valencia estate of Count de Oliva, asked Algiers for transportation and suggested a date on which the Count and most of his men would be away — a good opportunity, they thought, to appropriate the Count's treasure. The magic word "Treasure" caught the eye of Barbarosa himself, and when his sixteen galleot flotilla surreptitiously arrived at Oliva's beach, the cloudy, moonless, night proved perfect.

In three hours of torchlight a flood of humanity carrying life's treasures poured into the narrow galleots like water in an irrigation ditch, pooling in low spots, eddying into unused spaces, and filling some of the ships to the gunwales. Meanwhile, Morisco guides led a party of Corsairs to the Count's estate where his two guards gratefully allowed themselves to be immobilized while his vault was emptied.

Around midnight, to report on the evening, Aydin seated himself under a lantern hung by the forward mast of Barbarosa's flagship. "We have loaded two hundred families and they are satisfied that no one is missing. Some ships have more than others and we should redistribute as soon as we can. We will also need more water."

"The treasure?"

In the dim light, Aydin's flash of teeth could be seen through his villainous beard. "I led the party myself, and I promise you the strong-room is as bare as a bride's bottom on her wedding night!"

Looking at the swarthy giant, so hugely enjoying the robbery, Barbarosa observed, "I can see why the Spanish call you 'Cacha Diablo.'" He added, "We can take care of reloading and fresh water on Formantera. Float the ships. When clear, run up a lantern. I'll follow."

In minutes Aydin's ship lantern instructed Barbarosa to launch, and within an hour the faint shore lights had dissolved in the velvet darkness. By noon the next day sixteen galleots stroked their way around the easterly cape of Formentera, a small island in the southern Balearics, and settled themselves stern first, anchors out, on to the soft sand.

Fresh water and passenger reloading took time, and since the following day was to be the first of the month immediately following Ramadan and thus a propitious time for beginning a voyage, they decided to remain over-night.[1]

---

1. Ramadan, a basic requirement of Islam, consisted of a month long daylight fast, (somewhat like Lent). While not required of travelers or soldiers on campaign, few ignored it completely.

The next morning, he was in good humor — exchanging jocular obscenities with the crew as he boarded his ship. Taking position on the steering deck, he turned to review his small fleet.

Something was awry.

There were no lookouts on the island hill!

In a tone that made everyone within earshot jump, Barbarosa barked his anger at the nearest officers. "I'll be a donkey's prick if I see a lookout on that hill! Get a signal team up there, and if they move at less than a run, I'll open their backs to their lungs!"

As the officer ran to obey, Barbarosa added to Hassan Aga, "Find out who was responsible for setting the watch this morning, and tell him to say his prayers. Before I'm done with him, he'll need them!"

Within minutes, as Salah walked down the line of ships reporting readiness, two men carrying a signal kit could be seen running up the hill. Barbarosa ordered, "Sound the launching calls sounded. Leave a gig to pick them up."

With boarding planks taken up, holding ropes released, capstans turning as they pulled against bow anchors, and a dozen men on pry timbers levering sterns, the ships slid easily into the water. With every ship floating, as the first oars lifted, a sound as chilling as a north wind froze the fleet.

A horn from the lookouts.

All movement stopped, oars were suspended in air and collective breath was held while two messages unfolded from the flags: (1) There were eight Spanish war galleys on a direct heading for their hideout. (2) They were separated by an hour into two sections of four, and the first section should be off the cape in less than two hours.

The situation could hardly be worse. The galleys were arriving from the northeast and the Algerians were enclosed in a curving bay that faced south. The open sea could be reached, but a war galley could row down a galleot like an eagle overtaking a seagull. While eight galleys could not chase sixteen galleots very well and, in a widely spread formation, some galleots would escape, flight would mean the likely loss of half of the small fleet.

On the horns of a dilemma, Barbarosa held his decision for the time being. Passengers were his first problem. He didn't hesitate. He was a fighting seaman. If it would help his fleet, he would abandon every

Morisco in Spain. Flags fluttered and in a frantic fifteen minutes they were tumbled ashore in waist deep water.

He signaled for a crescent formation and a course to the east which gave an option, for a short time at least, of either running or fighting. Obedience was immediate, but as the pirate galleots passed the sandy hook of land, losing sight of the beach and exposing the two contestants to one another, opinions about Barbarosa's intentions were mixed. The arc of Corsair galleots swung out at an almost leisurely pace, and as the distance between the two groups shrunk, fighting seemed more and more unlikely, for the Spanish cannons could be identified as culverins — modern cannons that could punch an iron ball through a light hull from three hundred yards or more.

Nevertheless, a calm Aydin observed to his deck master, "I'll bet you my ship against your sword that crazy Greek intends to fight! We'll see some blood today."

The pirates reached the critical point beyond which there would be little chance for successful flight and, as they did, there was a flurry on

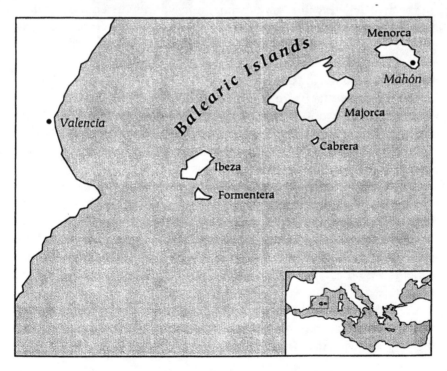

Barbarosa's aft deck. The green banner of Islam was struck. In its place rose a white flag!

Every reis had to reassure himself he was seeing correctly. No Corsair alive believed that the word "surrender" was in Barbarosa's vocabulary. Their eyes denied their minds.

With their target now in range, the first four Spaniards did two strange things — or more correctly, failed to do two expected things. They ceased rowing and they didn't fire their cannons. As far as they were concerned, surrender was logical. By asking for terms, the pirates would avoid damage and might gain a bit of Christian charity. It did not occur to them that their own ships would shortly be broadside to Corsair rams — with their own forward-pointing cannons useless.

The tableau continued to shrink for another tense twenty minutes, each minute slowly moving the opposing forces closer in a strange ballet of oars — four resting eagles within a slowly closing crescent of small hawks while four more eagles flew in on oar-wings to join. Only the sound of the looms, the splash of the waves against hulls, the twitter of rowing signals and occasional voiced commands could be heard.

By the time the second group of Spanish galleys pulled alongside their brothers and a thousand oars rested in the air, not more than a few dozen yards separated any of the ships.

But only for a moment.

Suddenly, the banner of Islam rocketed past the white flag as it returned to its place of courage and pride, and a quartet of screaming horns from Barbarosa's deck stabbed and goaded the corsairs into attack.

Sixteen galleots, as though puppets on a single string, lashed the sea across the few remaining yards, and the graceful ballet turned into a medley of violence as they impaled the larger ships with their razor iron beaks. Once the rams tied the ships together, pirate bowmen presented the Spaniards with a hail-storm of steel arrows and musket balls, clearing the way for boarders. Barbarosa, naked to the waist, a head cloth keeping sweat from his eyes — for once ignoring appearances — was the first to make the leap from his own rambade.

In a cacophony of death, the Turkish chamade was joined by steel striking steel, muskets popping, chains rattling, slaves screaming as oar looms were driven into them, and the cry of wood being torn.

The initial shock favored the attackers, but as the Corsairs mixed with the Spaniards, the onslaught of arrows and musket balls faded, and Spanish armor enjoyed its advantage.

After an hour, the outcome was still in doubt.

Until a single arquebus provided a turning point.

The Spanish commander, General Portundo, prominent in shining armor and helmet plumes, was instantly killed by a musket ball that pierced both his armor and his heart. Without their leader the fight went out of the Spaniards and, one by one, seven of the eight Spanish ships surrendered. The eighth, wiser and more disciplined than the others, had spun around at the first onslaught of the Corsairs, and by presenting only its stern had been able to prevent boarding. When the flag came down on Portundo's ship, it cleared out of the action. This was the kind of rowing the fighting ship did best and in a few minutes its getaway was complete.

Barbarosa had thrown the dice against long odds — and won.

As the first corsair galleots returned from the battle and rounded the cape unharmed, Morisco tumult erupted on the Formantera beach. In an extravagant turn of fate, disaster had turned into victory. A dark specter of whips and chains dissolved in a glorious sunrise of freedom.

The corsair attack had been courageous, skilled, vigorous, and a complete surprise, but it only succeeded because the galleots were allowed to close. Had the Spanish used their cannons, the corsairs would certainly have been prevented from attack and boarding.

Barbarosa had displayed two aspects of his genius: his analysis of the enemy's intention, and his willingness to gamble on unorthodox strategy.

As he later explained to Isabella, "When we visited Valencia, King Charles was in Genoa being crowned as Emperor of the Holy Roman Empire, and most of the Spanish fleet, including Portundo's squadron, was with him. The festivities finished, Portundo, with Oliva as a passenger, returned to Valencia only one day behind us, and when Oliva learned of his losses he offered Portundo a personal reward of ten thousand crowns for the return of the treasure and the Moriscos.

"That's when greed began to make Portundo's decisions. We had only our lives to worry about; he worried about losing the Moriscos and the treasure if we were sunk."

"How did you know that?"

"I knew that Oliva must have come on the scene, for Portundo's fleet broken in two sections indicated a search pattern. He would be after gold and Moriscos. Portundo would not have known that we had seen him an hour earlier, so I moved east past the cape to keep the Moriscos out of sight, and let him think they were still aboard. If he believed the gold and Moriscos were still aboard, he would be reluctant to destroy valuable property. When we dropped our flag at the critical distance to run or fight and the first four Spaniards failed to test us with a few cannon shots I was sure he wanted us afloat.

"Spanish reis and generals have a low opinion of us. I doubt they ever conceived we would dare attack, or that we would be effective if we did. Such pride is a weakness."

Barbarosa was generous in praise of his commanders and he was lenient with the captain who had failed to put lookouts on the hill; sentencing him to only twenty bastinado strokes and a season on an oar.

A triumph for Barbarosa, the adventure with General Portundo also marked a turning point in his development as a galley tactician. During the rest of the 1520s, he addressed the limits and possibilities of guns and of the ships they required.

With cannons came his need for larger ships, but how much larger? Experience had shown the maximum effective size of a galley to be about one hundred fifty feet moved by a bit fewer than two hundred men. Beyond that length, the slightest increase in speed required an astronomical increase in rowers.[1]

Oar looms for thirty foot oars required three feet of fore and aft "swing" space for the rowers. Leaving space for foredeck and quarter-deck, only about thirty benches could be placed on each side of a one hundred and fifty foot hull. Since the days of the early Greeks, the solution had been to group oars in "banks" — rowers seated above and beside one another. In this way, with three oars in each of sixty "banks", one hundred and eighty oars could find their way to water.

This system was referred to as alla sensile — "in the simple way" —

---

1. The ratio of power to speed is a factor of hull length and is controlled by something known to modern ship designers as "standing wave resistance". 16th century galley builders couldn't name it, but they were well aware of its effects.

but it was far from simple. Such crowding required carefully engineered placement of men and benches, and thole pins could not be more than a few inches apart in each outrigger group, tolerances that in turn led to complicated design and construction.

War galleys, like all large ships, grew on the shipways as products of the knowledge and experience of designer-foremen. These master builders were a valuable resource; actively recruited, cherished, and rewarded. But there were none in Africa and with no national tradition of large ship building, few in Turkey. However, on Djerba, Barbarosa had successfully copied smaller galleots, and he thought to duplicate the technique with a full galley if a model could be found.

A war a thousand miles distant provided his solution.

When Suleiman decided to remove the last Christian stronghold in the Levant, he invested the Island of Rhodes with a massive siege. Greatly outnumbered, the Knights sent requests to Europe for reinforcements, and the Venetians, with centuries of experience carrying pilgrims and crusaders to the holy lands for pay, offered the same service to Rhodes. Volunteers were crowded on a new galley and dispatched to Rhodes.

Dragut, returning from Istanbul with a small flotilla, had been forced to wait out a storm in a Greek coastal city where the wine was good and the maidens needed firewood for their hearths. Once out of bad weather and firewood, he had struck out for home, crossing a route commonly traveled by Venetian ships. His lookouts sighted a lone war galley whose rigging appeared to be a shambles and whose rowing was ragged and weak. The ship had made an ill advised attempt to weather the storm, and the fighting men were deathly seasick.

Once Dragut had a chance to look over his prize, he found himself in possession of a two-hundred-fifty ton alla sensile war galley created by Vettor Fausto, a master builder famous wherever galleys were fabricated.[1]

It had one hundred and fifty-four feet of true hull, plus bow and stern overhang, and employed 180 oars in banks of three, ranging in length from twenty-eight feet for the outside (lower) to thirty-two feet for the inside (upper) oar. The tholes for each bank were grouped on a telero frame eight feet outboard, leaving one-third of the oar inboard of its fulcrum — the best ratio for oar thrust. There were three fixed forward

---

1.   Venice had bribed Fausto from his native Crete by the comparatively unique offer of life insurance, a family allowance, and paid education for his children.

firing guns in the bow: one thirty-two pounder and two fifteen-pounders, and there were two lighter guns aft.

Barbarosa set about making a copy.

His enthusiasm for the alla sensile ship was not generally shared. Inspecting it, Ochiali observed, "I don't want to sound too critical, but anyone would be able to breed a camel to a donkey about as easy as train a crew of slaves to operate this creature. It looks like a Lebanese marriage agreement — very complicated."

Barbarosa resisted such plebeian criticism. " You old camel farts have no soul. I am told that this artist, Fausto, plans to build a still more advanced quinquireme — five oars in a bank to you of little education — that may well be the fastest ship since the great Greeks. I would give a purse of gold and a virgin she-slave to examine that craft."[1]

Ochiali remained loudly unconvinced.

Years later Fausto did build such a ship, but once at sea the rowing positions were so crowded that the men could not function in bad weather and a siege of intestinal flux carried off most of the crew on a single voyage. The high fatality count was blamed on crowding and the ship was put up by the Venetian authorities to be maintained as a museum curiosity.

By that time however, Barbarosa had become resigned to a simpler design. His "Fausto Felucca," as Ochiali and a few irreverent wits referred to the one he built, was not a success.

Barbarosa eventually abandoned the idea, and after only a few years Ochiali seldom mentioned it.

Failure of his Fausto Felucca or not, Barbarosa continued to search for a way to project sufficient man-propulsion power without the complications of construction and training required by the "alla sensile" system. Once he settled on the problem without prejudice or precedent, the answer was right under his nose. Like body armor that lasted centuries beyond gunpowder, the alla sensile system of galley propulsion had become obsolete and was not recognized.

Why not more men per oar?

---

1.   War galleys could reach seven or eight knots for twenty minutes or so. Ancient Greek galleys, which had no decking or ribs (their extremely light hulls were made rigid with a network of taut internal ropes) could reach as much as ten. A knot is a measure of speed equal to 1.15 mph.

Large commercial galleys often used anywhere from three to seven men on each loom — to move a heavy ship steadily. Why wouldn't that thrust produce speed in a lighter ship?

Oar looms had to be longer and thicker. Oar blades had to be larger. Tholes needed to be strengthened.

Taking these needs into account, he built a half dozen galleys of relatively light construction using three men on each oar, and the system soon proved to be superior. In fact, it was being simultaneously "discovered" all around the Mediterranean. The "scalaccio" system of multi-rowers per oar, as it became known in Europe, soon became the standard in war fleets. In a single generation, alla sensile large ships were to become mere curiosities.

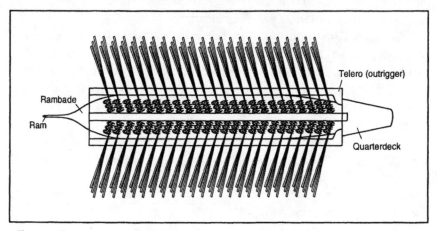

Alla Sensile oar arrangement on war galley.

9

A SEA CHANGE

The 1520s *(cont.)*

The period that saw the enrichment of Algiers also witnessed the continuing decline of a corrupt Roman Church. The split between Luther and Rome widened. Henry VIII created the Church of England. Spain won the first of four wars with France, wars which reduced the power of the Papacy and eventually resulted in a devastating sack of Rome. The printing press gave food to a world of hungry minds with such offerings as Machiavelli's wildly popular *The Prince*, a manual of politics which encouraged Christian Kings to rely less on God and more on human nature.

And syphilis appeared.

A gift from the New World to the Old, this disease first emerged about the time of Columbus' return from America. Within three decades it had ravaged an Europe in which sexual indulgence had become unrestrained. Even the sworn celibates of the Roman Church "lived in orgies and licentiousness". Highly contagious and untreatable, it condemned poor and rich alike to insanity and death. Francis is thought to have been a victim, and the madness of Henry VIII in his final years was possibly a form of paresis. Since celibacy or a rigidly protected marriage bed were the only prevention, fear of the disease encouraged the growth of rigid moral sectarianism such as Calvinism (and eventually Puritanism) — thus furthering the Protestant split within Christianity.

On land, Turkey's armies stormed westward into Europe with a thousand mile advance into Hungary and sister states. At sea, the black-hulled galleys of the Corsairs appeared like dark nightmares to strip away people and treasure from the Christian Mediterranean and its littorals.

With Rome declining, Islam advancing, and Algiers becoming the Ottoman jewel of the West — with all that feast on life's table — Barbarosa had to kneel and accept God's decision in personal tragedy.

No one connected pestilence with the flea-ridden rats that escaped visiting ships. Slaves in the bagnio fell victim first, but within days the whole city was infected. No treatment proved effective. Smudge fires were built, vinegar was poured on face cloths. Ochiali believed in a frequent washing of hands. Dragut relied on frequent changes of clothing. The religious depended on prayer. The only sure way to be safe was to get out of the contaminated area, but this option was forbidden for fear of spreading the disease. With the city sealed off, the lack of fresh food and workers from outside brought everyday activities to a standstill. Death carts, as they collected corpses for burning were the only signs of life.

Within twenty-four hours of the first symptoms, dehydrated from loss of body fluids caused by vomiting, violent diarrhea and high fever, the victim became incapacitated. Ugly swellings, known as buboes, appeared in either the neck or the groin, causing extreme pain and, unless they ruptured, which few did, death followed within hours.

Arab medicine was as good as any in the world, but its physicians stood as helpless with the wife of the Beylerbey as they did with the lowest slave woman. All they could do was try to keep her comfortable. Barbarosa, a man possessed, the problems of his city forgotten, remained continuously at her side, neither eating nor sleeping. He alternately, paced, sat, cursed, wept, and finally — acting out of character — prayed for Divine intervention.[1]

To no avail.

On the fourth day, she died.

Arriving unbidden, remaining unwanted, the pestilence lasted through the rest of the hot summer, yet the only person in the palace to be stricken was the woman Barbarosa loved. No one could explain why some were chosen; some were not. The one treasure for which there was no price, no substitute, had been taken from him, while people of incomparably lesser worth were left untouched. God alone made the decisions.

Isabella's death imposed on Barbarosa a personal turning point. Whether this sea-change in his personality meant he was a greater or lesser man cannot be said with certainty, but for the rest of his life he

---

1.   Muslims normally praise God and swear obedience rather than ask for help.

submitted to God's inscrutable will. From this time he accepted an un-knowable fate, a resignation typical of Islam. His response to Hassan Aga's sympathy was, "The Prophet tells us that even the mightiest will be humbled — 'Death will level their mountains, make nothing their pride, and scatter their days.'"

In'shallah. It was written.

While Barbarosa willed himself to accept, acceptance did not bring him peace. As irresistible as the tide, his anguish engulfed him. Out-wardly, he showed only a slight aging, but inwardly his grief released a peculiar whimsy. For a period he indulged himself in whatever pleasures his mood demanded, and at the end of an evening he often found him-self in the dark bottom of a jeroboam of heavy wine. Finally, a door be-gan to open for him when during a game of high-stakes barbudi, he won a tall, panther-like Abyssinian she-slave. Ochiali, whose luck had grown progressively worse all evening, offered her against the total of his earlier losses. The bet was not one that would ordinarily appeal to a winner — even exceptional she-slaves were hardly worth their weight in gold —

but Barbarosa was playing with his friend's money and he accepted the bet.

Ochiali cried real tears when he lost and, after Barbarosa became acquainted with her skills, he could sympathize. She was that extremely rare prize which the Arabs called "kabbahzah" — a "holder" — a woman with vaginal muscle control that enabled her to grasp him as though in a strong, warm hand — a pulsing movement "like a wolf's tongue". She told him that some of her African sisters were strong enough to injure a man if they wished.

She became the catalyst that brought him out of his personal swamp.

She rarely spoke and then only in poor Arabic, but she awarded herself to him with an unmistakable affection, and her love brought him comfort. Exceptionally

Physician during plague. Fully clothed to prevent contact. Nose beak contained filters for breathing.

slender, she was inches taller than he and her sable flesh had the unique quality of her race; cool to the touch even in the hottest weather. The acrobatic embrace of her long, satin body took him beyond fatigue; her sexual skills made him an empty shell, sated with pleasure, empty of pain and regret.[1]

Unfortunately — or fortunately — within months she was dead from a frailty of the lungs; a weakness of her race, according to Sinan. "The women are frequently affected; many don't live past thirty."

Her loss was another, milder, sea squall, and one after which Barbarosa was ready to resume his life and growth. While he would day-dream for years about an expedition to central Africa to find one of her sisters, his destiny lay beyond wine and slave girls. Her passing marked the end of a period, and his mind dulling excesses faded rapidly — to disappear entirely when he turned his attention to the Spanish fort in the harbor, just offshore from his city-center.

For all the years he had been in Algiers, that walled and hostile presence of Spain was not only an annoyance but a daily insult, a constant reminder of Spanish power. Here was something on which he could revenge himself; a fate he could take into his own hands.

He convened his advisors. "We can no longer allow those swine to dictate our movements. Our guns are too light to open those walls, and I don't want to ask Istanbul for siege guns. We should be able to solve our own problems. I welcome ideas."

A Moorish advisor had a question. "At times the entrance to that fort is unguarded. If the gates can be opened at the right time, could you have a force out there in fifteen minutes?"

"Easily. How would you get the gates open?"

"I know two young Moriscos who have a taste for intrigue and adventure. Send them into the fort as fugitives who wish to convert to Christianity. Where religion is concerned, the Spanish can convince themselves of the most outrageous propositions. Once the boys are trusted they may be able to open the gates."

The idea captured Barbarosa's imagination; sparked his re-grasp of life.

Ruiz and Alphonso could read and write, and Spanish was their na-

---

1.   Sir Richard Burton dramatically described his own experiences with these unusual women more than two centuries later.

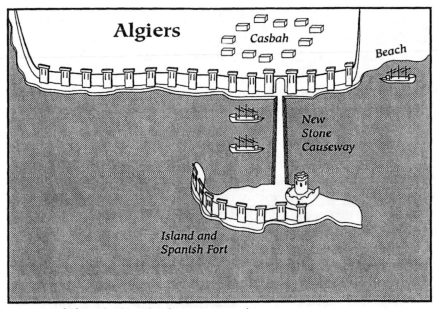

Diagram of Algiers harbor after fort was captured.

tive language. They were enthusiastic volunteers and Barbarosa took a personal hand in their training. The boys admired him with an intensity that was embarrassing and, emerging from his own self-pity with a worthwhile goal to occupy him, he came to reciprocate their affection. When the time came to insert them into the fort, he was reluctant to see them go.

The plan worked perfectly — for a time. The boys "escaped" to the fort and within a week had been accepted as family members into the house of the commander himself, Don Martin de Vargas. These young men, the Captain believed, were the first of many who would see their way to Christ.

Ruiz and Alphonso learned that there would be a special worship celebrating the return to life of the Prophet Jesus, and the gates would be left unguarded while the soldiers attended church for prayer. On that Sunday morning the youths asked for and received a special thirty-minute catechism from the priest before departing for prayer and reflection. Once at the gates, they skillfully performed their dangerous mission, but a mistake, made earlier when Ruiz had rudely rejected the amorous invitation of one of de Varga's maid servants, proved fatal. She, having more interest in the activities of the young man who had wounded her sensibilities than she did in church services, had quietly followed them.

The unbarring of the gates produced suspicion of treachery; the hanging of white cloths on the city-side of the fort walls confirmed it. Running, she interrupted church prayers to advise Captain de Vargas that evil was afoot, and within the hour the spectacle of the two Morisco boys, bound hand and foot and hanging from the walls of the fort, made clear the fate of the scheme.

The corpses were easily visible — a challenge as well as an insult. Barbarosa's captains watched him closely. Since Isabella's death, his personality, which had been that of steel shining with purpose and clarity, had become that of the sea, brutal and impersonal. He said nothing, but he asked Istanbul for siege guns.

They arrived early the next spring.

The heavy murlaccios breached the sandstone wall and, despite a brave defense, the fort was taken. Pleased with his victory and impressed by the Spaniard's courage, Barbarosa called for the Spanish Captain to offer him a place in Algerian forces. Don de Vargas' refusal, capped by grievous insults of Barbarosa's mother and of Islam, triggered the new Barbarosa. He borrowed Dragut's heavy war sword and split the Spaniard a third of the way in two.

With the fort finally in hand, the entire population of Algiers was put to work filling a causeway joining the Penon with the city, creating a stone breakwater and enclosing the harbor. The construction so changed the appearance of the city that a pair of Spanish round ships sent to supply and relieve the fort failed to recognize Algiers and sailed on down the coast — where they were trapped by an onshore wind and easily taken.

Barbarosa now used humor for the first time in months, an encouraging sign of his emotional recovery. He promised to build a Mosque on the Penon with an exceptionally tall minaret in order that future Spanish navigators could find Algiers.

The loss of the fort and its supply ships was a painful insult to the majesty of Spain — a discomfort not helped by Barbarosa's widely publicized offer of a navigational aid — and it capped the growing concern in Spain about an aggressive Islamic state next door.

Charles provided the majority of men and ships for an invasion fleet and solicited help to "Exterminate the vermin and level the city of Algiers to the ground." Genoa hired Andrea Doria with a squadron, the Germanic states of the Holy Roman Empire sent soldiers, the Knights of Rhodes gave two heavy ships and a detachment of armored fighting men, and the Pope paid for seven ships from the Papal states under the command of Fernando de Gonzaga.

Through a network of Morisco spies, Barbarosa received regular news of the assembly of this force but, while the size of the project worried him, the spies also reported a ray of light in the dark clouds of activity. The allies were argumentative, indecisive and were wasting valuable weeks. When late summer came, the fleet that should have been at sea months earlier was still in various stages of undress, quietly rising and falling each day on the slight Barcelona tides.

Fleet Admiral de Moncada, as delays brought the season dangerously close to autumn storms, was well aware of the peril, and he pleaded with Charles to wait another year, "The coast of Africa has at least one storm every year," he argued. "and when a large amount of warm, wet air passes that part of the world, no sea is more vicious than the shallow water off Algiers."

But Charles believed that another six months might see Suleiman dispatch reinforcements from Istanbul. The strike was to be made this very season.

In Algiers, talking to Dragut over a beaker of Djerban date wine brought from Tunis — along with five hundred barrels of gun powder from the powder mill he still owned — Barbarosa discarded any idea that they might challenge the Christian fleet at sea. "They'll have forty or fifty war galleys, plus two or three of those floating forts they call carracks.[1] We have three thousand Moors, Berbers and Arabs in our pay. Istanbul is sending us another thousand Janissaries and has offered rewards to any men in Egypt or the Levant who will join us. We'll disperse our ships among four or five harbors along the coast with skeleton crews and borrow a thousand fighting men from them. Our force will total better than five thousand. That's half the Christians' ten thousand — plenty for a defensive battle."

He spun a dagger on the scarred table. "The city walls are reinforced.

---

1. A sailing ship that carried many large cannons. The predecessor to the galleon.

We have water, and enough food, powder, shot, steel bolts and arrows, to last for months. Our cannon may not be very heavy, but can throw trash iron and chains faster than Spain can breed Christians and ship them here."

Dragut agreed. "We can hold out until Istanbul responds."

So they continued training and stockpiling.

In the vespers of summer, Christian ships finally began to assemble at Trapani on the south coast of Sicily. Although tardy, the Christians had outdone themselves: Forty war galleys and three carracks escorted thirty transports with ten thousand soldiers and a thousand cavalry horses — the flower of mounted Spain.

Then, in early November, like a slow camel train, the armada sluggishly paced itself south to Cape Bon and west to Algiers.

The well-drilled, colorful war galleys moved in concert offshore, flaunting their colors and testing the nerves of the castle cannoneers by parading insolently just out of range. The ponderous carracks simply floated at anchor like Turkish wrestlers, basking in their own fearsome presence. As the Algerians studied their guests, the transports appeared to be in good shape, which meant that their soldier and animal passengers were likely to be in fighting condition. Spread over the sea, the threat dried the mouth of the bravest defender. The faint at heart could feel the lash of Christian galley whips on their backs.

Had Barbarosa not ordered the city gates closed, many would have fled.

Well down the beach, the first transports were warped ashore stern first to off-load soldiers and guns — and by nightfall three thousand fighting men had sand under their boots. The horses were apparently scheduled for the following day.

The city took fear to bed.

Every man who had ever been to sea with Barbarosa was aware of his uncanny ability to forecast weather. A popular description of his reputation among sailors was expressed by Cacha-Diablo. "When no other man has the least idea the next day will bring anything but sun and fair winds, that Greek can sense a bora in his bones, rain in his beard, and rough seas in his balls." In twenty years of seasonal raiding — when seafarers did their forecasting with soothsayers, superstition and guess work — Barbarosa had never lost a ship to weather, including the storm he had ridden out in search of grain ships for Djidjelli.

And now, in this critical time, he had some encouraging news.

"Since yesterday, there has been a steady ground swell from the north and, while I can't measure it from here, the wave level near the shore has increased. Tonight there will be clouds and rain. We can send out a force during the dark that should be able to move to within striking distance of their encampment. By morning there will be too much wind for them to reinforce the beach, and with surprise and spirit we can kill those offspring of Satan like lambs at slaughter. Tell the men that I'll give a she-slave of his choice to anyone who kills twenty Christians!"

To risk a large force several miles from the fortress walls was a significant gamble, but to hear him was to have faith in his luck.

That night, as predicted, rain began. At midnight the Moorish cavalry and Janissaries quietly filed out the city gates. Using every bit of cover, five hours of quiet movement placed them in the brush within a stone's throw of the enemy, horses heads held down, fatigue and wet forgotten, tense with the desire to kill. Then Barbarosa's white Arabian took form in first light, and the strident scream of Turkish war trumpets released them into action.

Burdened by suprise and confusion, the Christians on the beach were no match for the rabid Muslims. Moorish horsemen chewed a great hole in the Christian perimeter for the savage Janissaries to exploit. On the water where Christian reinforcements floated in overwhelming numbers, the ocean turned gray, the sky charcoal, and the clouds emptied themselves of massive floods of water driven almost horizontally. All thoughts of their comrades on the beach were abandoned as the fleet fought to save itself.

Sails ripped, ships were tossed broadside as the wind lifted whole wavetops to join the rain in a devil's spray of salt water. The transports with the animals suffered first. To the dismay and trauma of men who had trained and loved them, a thousand finely bred horses were thrown overboard to drown. On the galleys, bench slaves frantically tore at leg chains as the water rose — bringing death within swimming distance of shore. Huge waves roared onto the beach, smashing everything — boxes and bales of cargo, weapons, masts, rigging, oars — whole ship carcasses.

The storm lasted most of the day. The next morning's sun illuminated nineteen hundred Spanish corpses on the beach, eleven hundred washed ashore drowned, and a thousand men taken alive for the slave market. Twenty war galleys and forty support ships were sunk or driven ashore, some over twenty-five miles away, destroying any Spanish hope of installing Barbarosa's head on a pike.[1]

The Algerians rounded up the survivors on the beach and forced them to bury their dead where they fell. At the same time salvage parties searched debris, the centerpiece of which was a little damaged carrack high and dry on the beach. The heavy anchor had held its bow into the wind, allowing it to ground stern first and, owing to a peculiarity of the sand windrows, it was propped oddly upright with no more than a few degrees of list.

Since the ship contained several hundred fighting men and guns that could be fired, it was a tied, but dangerous dog.

Seeing it, Barbarosa realized there must be nobles or ranking officers aboard and, with the flag of Castile at the masthead, knew they would be Spaniards. Calling for an aide, he ordered, "Notify Salah Reis that I intend to offer safe passage to the men on that ship and I want him to select four companies of Janissaries to protect their surrender."

The aide wanted to know who would carry the flag of truce to the vessel. Barbarosa assigned him the honor. "You will. Get a horse and a white flag for your lance; I'll have your message by the time you are back here. But clean up a bit. After you've seen Salah, bathe and change to your best dress. I'll not have those cross-kissers belittle our dignity."

Pleased with the honor, the young officer drew himself up, touched his turban and started for the door.

Barbarosa held him a moment. "Tell Salah Reis he should expect trouble from our horsemen. They may get out of hand. Many are Moriscos and have great reason to hate the Spanish. He must be prepared to defend the prisoners and he should form the Janissaries accordingly."

"He'll need to move them right up to the shipside."

Barbarosa drily rebuked him, "I should expect so, unless Spaniards have grown wings and can fly."

Embarrassed, the officer clamped his mouth shut and offering no more unsolicited advice, turned to leave.

---

1. Spain attacked Algiers unsuccessfully with large invasion fleets twice in twenty years. This description employs elements of both, although the hurricane — one of the great shipwrecks of all time — actually occurred during the second attack.

Barbarosa added, "First find the four Cavalry commanders and send them to me."

When the officers arrived a few minutes later, Barbarosa told them he was going to offer safe passage to the Spaniards and that as captives they could not be harmed.

"But Hayreddin," the youngest captain protested, "many of my men have lost their homes, wives, children, to those slits of whores, and they live for revenge." Another joined in, "Our men have tasted Spanish blood. We may not be able to control them."

Barbarosa reminded them that enemies could not be injured under a flag of truce, and he grimly continued, "If these prisoners are harmed, I will shut off the pay of your men and will sell their horses to the Arabs. Before I'm done, they will wish, as the thirsty in the desert wish for water, that they were back in Spain." He looked closely at each captain, "Make no mistake. I mean what I say."

A third captain who had not spoken, sighed, "I know what you want, Pasha, and I will try, but it will take more than orders to control them."

Barbarosa had heard what he knew to be true. "I know your problems and I will have Turkish infantry on the beach. But that doesn't lessen my promise of punishment if there's anything less than your full support."

The four took a glum departure. From the balcony Barbarosa saw them, light rain forgotten, gesticulating and arguing among themselves as they walked to their horses. He could also see four companies of Janissaries slogging in their metal shod black shoes across the beach toward the ship. He noted that Salah had chosen a senior Janissary officer for each company — for he could spot the distinctive red boots of their rank — and he was pleased by such foresight.

When the young officer returned in his best dress, Barbarosa gave him a missive and explained its terms. Muslim galley slaves were to be unchained and disembarked immediately. When that was completed, the Spaniards were guaranteed safe conduct and would be held for ransom, terms to be arranged. Surprise at what appeared to be an unusually generous offer was evident on the young man's part, but he had learned to keep his opinions to himself.

For himself, Barbarosa ordered fifty mounted men in ceremonial dress. He took time for a bath and clean clothes, time enough to find the Spanish acceptance waiting. Calling for a white horse, he mounted, and at a

Bagnio women on sale.

canter led the splendidly dressed troop of horsemen to a slight rise less
than a hundred yards from the ship where he could be easily seen. The
breeze still fluttered the Janissary standards, but the rain had stopped
and his escort rested comfortably in their saddles, overlooking the ship.

It took only an hour for the Muslim galley slaves to be freed from their
chains and taken to city baths, but by the time they had cleared the ship
and the Spaniards had commenced to disembark, word had spread among
the Moriscos. A sizable, and hostile, group of horsemen had gathered on
the beach. Catcalls and shouted insults encouraged a half dozen of the
more unruly to put their horses into a gallop, pulling up short in a shower
of sand.

As their numbers increased, their intentions collectively seemed to
jell. Led by one or two of the more rabid, the whole mass of cavalry began to move forward at a slowly increasing pace. In another moment
there would be bloodshed.

On the beach, a Turkish horn sounded. The four companies of
Janissaries formed into ranks by making a quarter turn facing the cavalry. Men in the front rank spread apart two arm's lengths, dropped to a
knee and embedded their eight foot pikes on an outward defensive slant
in the sand. Another horn, and the second rank stepped one pace side-

ways and duplicated the move. The horsemen now faced two hundred impassive, razor sharp pikes braced on the ground, any one of which would disembowel a horse. Two more horns sounded, and the third and fourth ranks of Janissaries unlimbered their short bows — weapons with steel arrows that could pierce three inches of oak at a hundred feet and be strung and loosed six times a minute.

With that fearsome collection of death options blocking their route, one thing was clear to the Moriscos: lives and horses would be lost before that disciplined line could be breached. Enthusiasm began to subside. The group dropped to a walk, then to a reluctant standstill.

For those still wavering, an arquebus spoke from the knoll where the King and his escort sat their horses — a blank shot to call attention to the royal presence. There sat an impassive Barbarosa, surrounded by glitter and pomp. Even if the Moriscos succeeded in satisfying their hatred on the Spaniards, they would eventually have to face the legendary discipline of that marble figure, less than a stone's throw distant.

Their officers managed to turn them and move them away.

The Spaniards were segregated into leaders and led — four hundred and thirteen common soldiers, seventy seven nobles — and taken to the large hall of the palace to await, they were told, for the royal figure they had seen on horseback.

Their curiosity was soon satisfied. With a trumpet salute, the large double doors at the front of the hall swung open and forty black giants wearing green turbans and scarlet pantaloons, holding gleaming scimitars upright against naked, oiled upper bodies, moved quickly and silently to form a line at the back of the room. Immediately after them came red-turbaned Berbers in blue and white capes, each carrying a steel crossbow and a short sword. Finally, surrounded by a personal escort of forty brilliantly costumed Janissaries with pikes and coiled shoulder whips, came the Beylerbey of North Africa in full Turkish ceremonial dress.

With a quick, vigorous stride, he mounted the dais. One hundred and twenty escorts, in a clashing, stamping drill, ranged themselves behind him and froze at attention. The room fell to silence.

In spite of themselves, the Spaniards were impressed. Most of them had been under the impression that the pirates in Algiers were waterfront scum, renegade Christians and skunky Arabs.

Barbarosa spoke in court language — precise, lisping Castilian.

"As fighting men, we True Believers appreciate the courage with which honorable men wage war and I shall obey the code which civilized men observe. I would speak with the ranking officer of your group."

A stocky man, erect in the uniform of a Spanish General, stepped forward. Barbarosa acknowledged him with a slight bow. "A few years ago, beside a small river several days west of here, my brother Aruj fought his last battle against soldiers of your King. Your state has made treasures of his clothing and sword, and songs of his Italian name — Barbarosa.

"When he was killed, his men laid down their arms and gave themselves over to the Marquis de Comares, Governor of Oran, a man feted and praised in your royal court." He paused, and raised his voice: "But, like wild dogs, those carrion-eating bastards of Spain slaughtered every one of those brave men."

In the strained silence, he asked, " What think you of the word of a Spanish grandee?"

Even though he spoke in some volume, his tone was one of query, of genuine curiosity as to the meaning of such an atrocity. It gave a strange sense to the drama; was he intent on revenge or not?

The Spanish General cleared his throat and protested, "But that killing was the work of a few men. They could not be stopped."

Barbarosa looked down his considerable nose. "Had my Janissaries been men of Spanish quality today, those Morisco horsemen would have repaid you for my brother. You have the word of men you call infidels to thank for your lives."

The Spaniard had no response.

Barbarosa continued to the finale for which he had been waiting since he first realized the ship was Spanish. "I promised my brother's memory I would take one hundred Spanish lives for each of his murdered men, and one thousand for him personally." He paused and looked over the room as though counting, then continued, "There seem too few here to satisfy that total today. Also, I have promised you safe passage and The Prophet has instructed us to honor our contracts. Therefore, I will fulfill my promise to my brother another day."

He cleared his throat. "You may all return to Spain as soon as you are ransomed."

Breaths of relief escaped.

"Spain will be notified. All must be paid before any one may leave. When you hear my figures, remember that all the gold in Spain will not bring back one of my brother's soldiers."

He paused and appeared to smile. "Five hundred Spanish crowns for each soldier, and five thousand for each officer."

Even Barbarosa's men were startled.

At that rate the room full of Spaniards would bring enough to build and outfit a small fleet.

He had given the Spaniards a choice: impoverish their families and rape the Spanish treasury — or be slaves.

The story of this lesson in honor did not reach Istanbul for some months. There it was praised as, "Short of striking off their heads, the best lesson the cross-kissers could receive; it hurt them where their hearts are."[1]

---

1.   The actual amount of the ransom is not known — but the incident became famous.

Seige Cannon in Instanbul Museum. This is a smaller, relatively mobile version of the "Basilisk", a Turk siege cannon. The greatest of this type was probably the famous "Cannon of Orban's" (A Hungarian who defected to Turks because his salary wasn't paid). It had a ninety six inch bore, required sixty oxen and two hundred men to move in pieces, used up to three hundred pounds of powder to throw a stone weighing 1450 pounds over a mile, and needed three hours to cool after firing.

10

SULEIMAN CHOOSES AN ADMIRAL

1532

The decade of the 1520s that saw the development of Algiers also witnessed Suleiman at the other end of the Mediterranean following in his father's expansionist footsteps, but looking to Europe rather than to Asia. In his first year on the throne, angered by a Hungarian king who executed two Turkish ambassadors and cut off the ears and noses of others — a sure way to catch the eye of a Turkish Sultan — Suleiman stormed and captured Belgrade, the first major Islamic incursion into Europe for three quarters of a century.

With that success in hand, he assembled an army of two hundred thousand and laid one of the great sieges[1] of the century on the Island of Rhodes, the last Christian outpost in Asia. Heavily fortified and previously considered impregnable, the fortress resisted for six months before the Knights — who had already abandoned their satellite fort of Bodrum on the nearby Anatolian mainland — with their native army near mutiny and fewer than a hundred of their own number remaining, sued for terms, promising never again to take arms against Turkey.

The victorious young Sultan, in his twenties and still somewhat of a romantic, admired the Knight's bravery, particularly that of their seventy two year old Grand Master, Villiers de Isle-Adam. Allowing them a brokered surrender, he permitted them their arms, saluted them as they marched out of the castle to the docks with flags flying, and confided, "It is not without regret that I force this brave man from his home in his old age."

He also provided a Turkish galley to deliver them wherever they wished.

---

1.   During this siege, mining on a large scale was introduced by the Turks.

In distant Algiers, remembering Aruj's two seasons on the oar of a Christian galley, Barbarosa was pleased by the victory. He was also cynical about the good intentions of the Knights. "Suleiman," he said, "is a man to admire. His courage is unquestioned. He personally leads his forces in war. He may be the best horseman in a nation of horsemen. He is said to be fair and just to all. But he has a lot to learn about The Religion. By honoring their bravery with freedom, he may have done a high minded thing, but Turkey will one day suffer."

Dragut agreed. "Had I been in charge at Rhodes, a few years on the oars would have done those old men a great deal of good."[1]

Noble gestures aside, the victory proved expensive; more than twenty thousand Turkish fighting men died, and Suleiman drew breath, sending his Sipahis and Ghazis back to their land holdings. He did however, keep his engineers busy constructing bridges across the Sava and the Drava, tributaries of the Danube — the gateway to central Europe.

At the end of two seasons, rested, with his Janissaries clamoring for battle and its reward, Suleiman called in the levies of horsemen, listened to his soothsayers, mounted his black Arabian, and led his superb infantry, cavalry, and artillery up the Danube valley. There, in five years of seasonal campaigns, three hundred thousand Christians were either to fall before Turkish arms or take up residence in Turkish bagnios, as this young Sultan added most of Eastern Europe's rich lands and agricultural peoples to his Empire. These campaigns proved Suleiman a classic Ottoman conqueror, a man of destiny comparable in the eyes of his people to the legendary Mehmed.

He was also to prove himself an Empire builder of skill and wisdom.

Christian nobility in eastern Europe — Hungary, Moldavia, Transylvania (Rumania) — was infamous for its mistreatment of peasants, taxing them to starvation and slaughtering them as casually as sheep or goats. Resolved to incorporate these fertile lands as an integral part of his Empire, Suleiman was to place a commoner, John Zapolya, on the Hungarian throne and he gave orders that the countryside and peasants be well treated. His diary revealed how well he enforced his orders. "Near the village of Kemal, a soldier is decapitated for trampling down the har-

---

1.   Time proved them correct, for Charles subsequently gave Malta (his personal property) to the Knights where they built a fortress which was to cost Turkey many ships and thousands of lives.

vest." Another day, "Two soldiers who stole horses have heads cut off..."
and again, "Two sword bearers lose heads for pasturing horses in unhar-
vested fields."

The Turks, by comparison with the Christian aristocracy, were sunshine after rain.

The first of these campaigns was highlighted by one of the key battles
of the 16th century — a warning flag of the fearsome threat to central
Europe that Turkey now represented. With the Turks approaching, the
Hungarian king, Louis (a cousin of Charles) who suffered from the hu-
bris common to the Hapsburgs, declared, "God will be on our side!"
and, scorning the assistance of infantry commoners as well as a natural
defensive position behind a river, chose to meet the Turks on an open
plain with mounted, armored knights — noble aristocrats all.[1]

Almost within sight of Budapest, in one day of heavy rain, the Turkish
short bow and the fearsome Janissaries effectively destroyed the male
half of Hungary's ruling class.

In the third person, Suleiman's diary recorded the grim statistics of
the victory: "The Sultan rests at Mohacs ... twenty thousand Hungarian
infantry and four thousand of their cavalry buried ... massacre of two
thousand prisoners ... the Sultan, seated on a golden throne, receives
homage ... rain falls in torrents."

Louis himself was among the casualties — borne down by his heavy
armor to smother in the mud. Bemused with the stupidity of the young
Louis and, in a way regretful, the Sultan surveyed the mud-soaked scene
of carnage — his own tents huddled among huge cannons like bedraggled
birds — and said to Ibrahim, "It is true that I came in arms against him,
but it was not my wish that he should be cut off while he had scarcely
tasted the sweets of life and royalty."

Having said that, he had a special pyramid of a thousand noble heads,
complete with beards and helmets, piled next to his tent.

These campaigns reached a climax at the end of the decade when, like
the thunder of a summer storm, the legendary Turkish gun trains rumbled
westward toward Austria and its capitol Vienna, the final obstacle remaining before the heartland of Europe. Thousands of volunteers from

---

1.   The expense of individually fitted armor, the years of training and, not least, the
     unique concept of bravura that surrounded Knighthood, meant that only nobles
     were Knights.

Suleiman goes to war (note siege gun).

a half-dozen Christian states had gathered in Vienna and the defense of the city was entrusted to Count Nicholas von Salm, a professional soldier.

The Hapsburg Kings chose to wait out the battle some days distant at Linz.

With Europe in an agony of suspense, Christian prayers must have been heard. Not only was Von Salm a good choice — he destroyed hundreds of wooden buildings that might catch fire, leveled all outlying stone structures of potential use to an enemy, completely encircled the city with twenty foot earthen walls, mercilessly evacuated non-combatants to conserve food supplies, and once engaged, employed his men brilliantly — but rain and cold set century old records, delaying the Turks for weeks and miring their heavy guns beyond rescue. Suleiman captured the border city of Guns and ravished the Austrian countryside in a complete encirclement of Vienna but, between the time lost at Guns and the absence of his heavy cannons, he could mount only a short lived siege of the city itself.

Repulsed, frustrated, sick of the slate-colored hills piled under the gray rain of an Austrian autumn, the Turks retraced their long path down the Danube. It was snowing when Suleiman reentered Istanbul on his gold-accoutered Arabian.

To Europeans, Vienna was the salvation of Christianity. Prayers rose from the countryside like a winter fog, church bells rang, bonfires were lit and barrels of wine breached. The Terrible Turk had been denied.

But the Hapsburg Kings whose states lay close to the action were well aware that the margin of victory at Vienna had been slight and, mindful of other seasons to come, agreed to a treaty ceding to Turkey all territory already in Turkish possession, effectively abandoning Eastern Europe to Islam. Further, Charles' brother, Ferdinand of Austria (one of those who sat out the siege at Linz) was forced to address Suleiman "as a son to a father" — a phrase inordinately pleasing to the Turks.

While Vienna itself had eluded Turkey, from Istanbul's point of view, the campaign was not a failure. Casualties had been light and enough spoils had been taken to pay expenses — the prime objective of Ottoman aggression. To insure that his people perceived the campaign as a success, Suleiman demonstrated another skill, that of the politician.

He declared Vienna to be a Victory, rewarded the Janissaries out of his own purse and had his three sons circumcised as the centerpiece of a three-week national festival. His reputation as a brilliant, brave, and lucky conqueror remained unsullied.

But circuses or not, treaty or not, Vienna taught him a lesson. Austria was about as far as Turkey could stretch on land.

Wars were fought only in the summer, and although Turkish armies could be moved at a rate of eight miles a day (double that of Europeans), nine hundred miles over a route denuded of forage and harassed by partisans, past walled cities willing to defend themselves, in a climate known for early frost, was the limit dictated by 16th century logistics.[1]

Turkey had also suffered at sea. Andrea Doria, now sailing for the Spanish, had been hired to take pressure off Vienna, and he had chosen Turkish ports in Greece to wreak his mischief. He captured the city of Patras, the port of Coron, and the two forts commanding the entrance to the Gulf of Corinth. When the Turkish Admiral-General, Lufti Pasha, set out in challenge, Doria handily took his measure, sinking half the Turkish fleet in one afternoon.

Not only had Suleiman's armies reached their logistical limits, Turkey's maritime capabilities had proved wanting.

The Ottoman problem at sea was a matter primarily of quality and skills. During the 15th century, the land oriented Turks had acquired maritime properties more or less incidentally as they overran the Greek archipelago and Balkan shorelands. As conquerors, they had benefited from the maritime skills and traditions of these peoples — especially the Greeks — but they had lavished little attention of their own on the sea.

Their one major effort had been counter-productive. At the turn of the century, with a hodgepodge fleet of pirates, paid Egyptians, Syrians, and other foreigners — most of whom acted only as their mood and enthusiasm dictated — Turkey had prevailed in a sea engagement with Venice.

Dragut, the only native Turk among the reis in Barbarosa's inner circle, reviewed Turkish maritime history — including this affair.

"We first used galleys when Mehmed stormed Constantinople less than a century ago — and the performance was so laggard that he personally bastinadoed his chief Admiral. Then forty years ago, Bayazid challenged Venice at Lepanto but, although the Venetian fleet collapsed, Turkish ships

---

1.   Camels, a major element of Turkish transport, became unusable with the first frost.

weren't worth the sweat on a fat slave. The master builders thought big was good. Their two main ships were eighteen hundred tons, carried a thousand men each, and boasted sixty-foot high platforms mounted on mainmasts of five trees bound together — large enough to hold forty sharpshooters. No wonder they burned themselves up when they tried to use Greek Fire."[1]

The Turkish victory in this battle, he said, was actually gained through Venetian cowardice and ineptitude — and by the Turkish army which captured the nearby port of Lepanto. He felt that in the long run the battle had done more harm than good. "Turkey's large ships were nautical failures. Bayazid's ship-building foremen did not possess the skills to duplicate Venetian ships and we have never, in my lifetime, made any real effort to improve our fleet."

Nevertheless, the Ottoman Empire had a large residual capability in ship building that could be organized and developed. Gold was no problem, Turkish carpentry and metallurgy were the best in the world, and timber for ship construction was practically limitless. Turkey needed only a master builder who could design proper war ships, an organizer who could assemble a shipbuilding program, and a leader capable of commanding the ships in battle.

Barbarosa and history were approaching marriage.

In the fourteen years since his appointment as Beylerbey of Africa by Selim, he had earned a solid reputation within Istanbul court circles. Supporters undertook to advance him to the Sultan and a relatively small battle gave them their opening. Andrea Doria raided the city of Shershell, west of Algiers where a squadron of Barbarosa's newer galleys surprised him. The Corsairs sunk eight of Doria's twenty galley fleet, killed six hundred of his men and took nine hundred more prisoner.

Barbarosa said little about Shershell. However, he found it necessary to ship the Christian slaves from that battle all the way to Istanbul. He may not have realized that several hundred of Doria's Christians in the highly visible bagnio of the capitol city would be a daily reminder of his qualities as a Galley-King, however, as Ochiali observed one day, "Its

---

1.   In this battle, the Turks gained their first naval hero when a brave commander known as Borak reis went down with his burning ship. Attempts to duplicate the lost recipe for "Greek Fire" — probably naphtha or pitch added to quicklime or phosphorus (which burned in contact with water and impressed the superstitious) — were always futile and frequently fatal.

possible that it never occurred to the old man, but if you can believe that, you can believe that a camel has a sweet nature!"

Whether or not Suleiman noticed the slaves, he dispatched an order to Algiers, commanding the Beylerbey of Africa, together with such of his officers as he chose, to present himself at the Sublime Porte. It was a signal honor; a command which no Muslim could refuse.

It was a message Barbarosa had been waiting to hear since the death of Isabella.

He let the news be known almost casually at a meeting. "For those who live by The Book, rewards shall be given," he said. "The Lord of the Two Worlds has issued a ferman[1] requiring my services, and those of any others I might find useful."

His pronouncement brought instant and full attention.

Everyone waited expectantly for him to continue, but he turned to study the harbor, apparently not intending to say more. Finally, Dragut breached the silence. Picking up Barbarosa's turban where it lay on the table, he said, "We're all on a lee shore waiting for your wind, o younger brother of a red bearded king. But we can't wait all day for your Greek games. This turban would look good on that donkey I saw outside the gate a few minutes ago."

Barbarosa joined in the general laughter. "All right, children, if you want to know, the Sultan plans to build a new fleet of one hundred war galleys."

Dragut beamed. "A real Turkish fleet! Things have changed since I left Egypt."

Barbarosa continued with his news. "I am to have charge of the building of this fleet at the Golden Horn and, when it puts to sea, am to be the Kapudan Pasha, free to choose my officers. I wondered which of you might be willing to join me."

With a twinkle in his eye he waited for the easy-to-predict answers. After years of operating on the fringes of law, dependent upon their own strengths for security, the opportunity to walk through the streets of the greatest city in the world as men of consequence, secure in the status of a respected official, would be the personal fulfillment of a lifetime for any pirate-corsair, no matter how rich.

---

1.   Imperial proclamation, order, command.

Sinan the Jew was the first to find his voice. "I have not seen Smyrna for years."

"I have always wanted a home on the shores of the Bosporus." Salah added.

Aydin: "Why not have the Empire build our ships for us?"

Dragut. "I'd like to see the Greek islands again."

Piali, not yet a full reis, sat by the door. A Balkan waif absorbed in a devirsme. Intelligent, able, brave, he had excelled in his training and had caught the eye of no less a sponsor than the Sultan himself who had dispatched him to Algiers two seasons ago for education in matters of the sea. His smile supported those who were senior enough to speak their minds.

Ochiali had a practical concern, "Can we take along our women?"

That question energized Salah. "Our hero of the carpets would lose his appetite and waste away without the daily exercise of the two backed beast."

"Better my stable of mares than a harem of boys!" Ochiali retorted.

Barbarosa considered Ochiali to be his most able commander — next to Dragut — and there would be a great deal of use for him in a large fleet. He answered the question, "Friend and great warrior of the sleeping rooms, I plan to leave my women with Hassan Aga, but you are welcome to bring all the companions you can carry in one ship."

Having heard what he expected to hear from the group, Barbarosa then announced, "My son Hassan will remain here. I plan to have Hassan Aga appointed in my place as Viceroy." He added a comment he intended to be heard by every ambitious man in Algiers — an announcement that eliminated any thoughts of opposition. "I have given into Hassan Aga's hand the sword of my friendship."

Choice of the eunuch surprised no one. He was popular and, when young Hassan was ready to follow in his father's footsteps in a few years, could be trusted to yield the post gracefully.

Weeks were used in deciding on tribute gifts for the Sultan and more weeks in preparing for departure. It was not until late August that the Algerian fleet sauntered eastward.

The trip passed uneventfully, calm summer weather held for the entire voyage. On the day of arrival in Istanbul, the air had been left cool and clear by a relatively benign cold front that had passed in the night, and a light breeze fluttered pennants and flags. Sparkling in the morning sunshine and clear of debris, the sea matched the blue of the sky, quietly enjoying the dappling of sun on its face by an occasional adventurous cloud.

The constant cool water of the Black sea flowed through the Bosporus and into the Marmara rapidly enough to make the progress of Barbarosa's fleet past Seraglio Point appear stately. With the first ship flying a long green banner with gold calligraphy repeating the name of Allah thousands of times — a copy of the treasured great banner of Mecca — thirty nine ships flying the moon and star of Turkey made their deliberate way, stroke by stroke, into the Golden Horn.

It was an impressive sight, fit for a Roman Pro-consul.

First came three large galleys in a vee. With synchronized strokes, the ships moved as one, making incremental course changes in perfect unison. Sixty oars in each ship (with three men on each oar) dipped as one, pulled as one, then raised and swung back as one.

Holding fixed stations on each wing of the leading trio, eight forty-oared galleys minced along in short oar strokes. They too were black-hulled, but richly decorated in a riot of colored sails, streamers and pennants. Like those in the leading vee, the rowers wore white trousers, sleeveless open vests, and round hats known as Fez after the Moroccan city where they were made — clothing that announced them to be free men.

Then came eighteen great cargo galleys, each rowing at its own count, but maintaining strict spacing. Having been Christian in earlier life, some still operated with oars in banks and they varied in appearance, but none displaced less than four hundred tons. Once they came within easy eye range, shaved heads and chains marked the rowers as slaves.

Even more impressive than the fleet itself were the tribute gifts it carried. Public spectacle was hardly new to Istanbul. Pomp sparkled with glory in Suleiman's court; ceremony and ostentation marked all public events. But even in this ocean of wealth and power, the parade that made its way through the old city became celebrated.

Barbarosa's own delight in martial music was expressed by a thirty-five member Janissary mehter — a martial band of drums, cymbals, suspended bells, brass horns, and piercing reed instruments. Fully as striking as their music were their costumes — brilliant jackets trimmed in white, leather-edged cardinal trousers tucked into knee high black boots and square dress turbans.[1]

Following the band were animals intended for the private zoo which Suleiman, like many rulers of the day, maintained. Slaves carried hooded falcons on gloved wrists and brightly feathered birds in small cages. Giant snakes were somnolent in large wicker cages suspended from poles. Escorted in pairs were zebras, wildebeests with their strange goatees, leashed leopards, hyenas and tigers in their own cages, and a single giraffe for which Barbarosa was to apologize, its mate had died enroute. Uncaged and pacing sedately on chains beside African trainers were eight lions.

Intended for the Sultan's ceremonial guard marched fifty exceptionally tall black pikemen whose distinctive narrow heads and scarred cheeks marked them as Nubians — men of the same African tribes that Hannibal had led into Italy sixteen centuries earlier.

Then came the breathtaking stars of the parade: two hundred girls ranging in color from alabaster to ebony. With the exception of the Abyssinians, their waist length hair was gathered at the neck with jeweled clasps. Long strides in slight sandals emphasized their youth and spirit. Carefully chosen for beauty, they were dressed in opaque blouses, gossamer harem pants and colored slippers — and each carried on her shoulder a silken cushion with a basket of golden coins.

Finally, with a brilliant caftan flowing behind him in the slight breeze, followed by eighteen galley reis in pairs, came Barbarosa Hayreddin, the King of Algiers.

The spectacle made its way through the city and up the hill to the open center of the ancient Byzantine chariot hippodrome where the Sultan waited on a golden throne, framed by rows of brightly costumed Janissaries and court officials.

"He has come to rub his face against the royal stirrup," observed a Venetian diplomat viewing the procession from a section of the stadium set aside for foreign dignitaries.

His companion agreed. "He could rub his face against anything in Europe for that kind of admission fee. My God, money could hardly buy those women. Look at that pair of tall Abyssinians. One could hang by the chin on their breasts!"

---

1.   Military bands were an Ottoman innovation. They inspired attackers and terrorized enemies. "The noise of them presses men's brains out of their mouth…"

"Perhaps that could be accomplished by a man of your short stature," answered the diplomat, "but more to the point, they say each of those small baskets carries five hundred gold ducats."

"If you would prefer gold to those beauties, life here in the East has aged you."[1]

That winter, with the resources of the world's greatest Empire at his disposal, the son of Yakub displayed a facet of his genius heretofore unrecognized. Within weeks of his arrival he had the existing shipways reorganized and had built a large new one. With these, out of whole cloth, in one winter, he designed and created a fleet which bid fair to equal that of Venice — the world's greatest galley fleet.

His subsequent fame in Turkey would have been secure for this performance alone. An artist, an engineer, a draftsman, and a creative carpenter, he embodied the skills of a master shipbuilder with those of an organizer. With no family, eschewing wine and women, and eating barely enough to fuel himself, he lived the life of a monk, concerned only with his work. Throughout that long winter, in all weather, from one end of the shipways to the other, his broad frame could be seen daily, explaining, urging, inspiring, correcting, disciplining — and praising. Nights he spent under lanterns in one of his offices, checking design, arranging schedules, issuing orders, and evaluating people.

One man can be said to have created a new Turkish navy in less than one year.

Suleiman judged the capabilities of his new Admiral in a series of personal meetings — frequently coming to the shipways himself. On an early evening visit in November, the Sultan arrived at the larger dockyard with a Janissary escort and his ever present pair of mutes. The silent giants preceded him into Barbarosa's office and, satisfied, stood aside, bowing as the Shadow of God entered.[2]

The physical contrasts between the Sultan and his Admiral were

---

1. The magnificence of this affair is a matter of general agreement between Christian and Muslim historians. Some later portraits credit Barbarosa with a pet lion on leash which accompanied him around Istanbul, but they are surely embellishments.

2. Suleiman's personal interest in shipbuilding was inspired in part by his own craft skills. Ottoman princes were required to obey the Islamic admonition that a man should learn a trade at youth, and he was a skilled goldsmith.

A Sultan in his bath (as imagined by an envious artist).

marked. Barbarosa was fifty three years old; Suleiman only in his thirties. Barbarosa was large and muscular, the Sultan a slender man just over average height who appeared almost delicate in his ornate robes. Barbarosa's tanned face was decorated with a gray beard and a handsome mustache; his open, homely countenance often alive with a smile. Suleiman's thin, sallow face was poorly complimented by a sharp, overlong nose, and a wispy, drooping mustache. On his dark countenance, the wrinkles with which humor frequently endows a face were not to be seen.

But opposites apparently attracted. The men had become friends.

Suleiman's dress always proclaimed exalted position; on this night he wore a brilliant jeweled turban so high as to be a rectangle on end, a black silk caftan emblazoned with golden calligraphy, and short, slipper-like boots whose fur trim matched the ermine stole draped over his shoulders. His only personal weapons were the two hovering mutes. Impassive and incurious, they existed solely to protect the Sultan and to carry out his slightest wish — including the instant dispatch of anyone who offended. Purposely mutilated, unable to read or write, solid, noiseless shadows, they accompanied him everywhere, even to his bedchamber where, to avoid royal insomnia, they carefully extinguished and relit candles as he turned in his sleep.

Whether they remained during connubial pleasures was not known.

Barbarosa was dressed in expensive but simply cut clothing; his one concession to high Turkish rank a tube and feather on his Turban. Over light Persian silk he wore a heavy soft wool robe of rich red. In the presence of the Sultan, he presented himself unarmed.

In describing his activities and plans, Barbarosa spoke directly and, considering the audience, with extreme informality. "As long as I have sailed, the greatest shipbuilders in the Mediterranean have been the Venetians. They are able to produce two heavy galleys per day.[1] We'll need to approach that figure within months if we are to float a hundred new ships by next spring. Their arsenal, which is what they call their dockyards, has fifteen hundred carpenters, seven hundred caulkers, five hundred iron workers, two hundred oar makers, two hundred various specialists, and five hundred laborers. I am aiming at essentially the same numbers, especially carpenters able to shape a forty foot timber of twelve-inch larch close enough for fitting exact joints. I expect to pay them four aspers a day, and such men will probably be working on Mosques or in the Palace where framing and bracing with large timbers is required."

He left unsaid his request, but the Sultan understood — poetically. "The waves of God's seas distribute their attentions evenly, caressing the rock no less than the sand. The mosques honor God. The ships will be God's sword. You will have all the carpenters you need."

Barbarosa bowed in acknowledgement and went on, "For larger ships we require a wide selection of woods. One can say that a war galley is an orchestra of the forests, a song of wood. Larch is used for hull planking, interior bracing, and bulkheads. Oak for keels, knees, ribs, and main shipmembers. Spruce is best for masts. Either elm or walnut is needed for blocks, capstans, and rudders. Beech or ash for oars — a surprising amount of it. Ships lose or break many oars, and I've known reis stranded in cold weather forced to burn oars for warmth."

"Do you have all these types of wood?"

"Yes, although oak presents a problem. Its very important in ribs, knees,

---

1.   Once launched at the Venetian Arsenal, a basic galley hull was towed from station to station for fitting and equipment installation, an early version of the modern assembly line.

or other curved pieces, and we do our best to find trees growing that way. Picking the right tree and cutting it to be transported is a skill in itself. We have enough to start over fifty keels — and by the time layout is done, Black Sea timbers should be arriving. I have already dispatched teams to the Rumelian mountains.[1] Oak also takes time to work, for it must not only be seasoned like all woods, but soaked in water before cutting. An adze is harder to control and a saw becomes useless in only minutes on dry oak."

"Must all woods be cured?"

"Surely. Green wood will warp or shrink, a condition that will be unfailingly discovered by the sea."

"How long must you cure?"

"Aging varies. For larch and spruce I like one year; somewhat more for hard woods such as walnut or ash, but I can shorten that time by using heat from the iron foundries."

"Speaking of foundries, do you have the metals you need?"

"Yes. In abundance. Especially brass, of which I had little in Algiers. We also have plenty of worked cotton or hemp for caulking our caravelle hulls."

"Caravelle?"

"There are two main types of hulls: caravelle and clinker. Caravelle butts the planks evenly, one on top of another, fastened with vertical wooden dowels which marry top and bottom edges. In clinker, each plank overlaps the one below and is commonly fastened with iron nails. Some Christian galleys are clinker, but since we were short of iron in the west, I built only caravelle and have grown to prefer it. The hull planking is smoother, fits the ribs better and is stronger. I also believe it to be faster — although others differ."

"What size ships do you plan?" The Sultan asked.

"A war galley seems to be most efficient between one hundred and thirty and one hundred and fifty feet and needs from one hundred and fifty to two hundred men to move it at its best speed. Our ships will be somewhat lighter than Christian ships — about one hundred and forty feet and we will use one hundred and eighty men, three per oar on

---

1. Forests were a critical state resource, but large timbers could only be moved by water, and often came from very long distances. It was said that the shock of Turkish rams engaging at sea could be felt in the mountains of Albania.

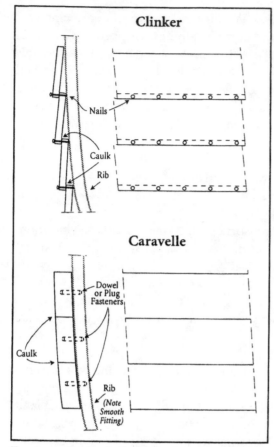

Clinker

Nails

Caulk

Rib

Caravelle

Dowel
or Plug
Fasteners

Caulk

Rib

(Note Smooth Fitting)

Two types of galley hull construction. Iron nails were expensive, precious. Venetian law hung a chain of nails around the neck and "whipped though the arsenal" any shipbuilder caught concealing them when leaving the yard.

sixty oars. I'd like to claim the idea of several men on an oar for myself, but the system is coming into use everywhere. The Spanish even have a word for it — scalaccio."

Suleiman pointed at a sketch on the table. "What are those narrow boxes with the handles on top, located on either side of the ship?"

It took Barbarosa a few seconds to realize that he was asking about the bailing pumps. "These are called Archimedian screws after the ancient Greek who designed them. They contain long metal sheets bent in a spiral that reach down into the bilges — the bottom of the ship — to bring up water and pour it overboard. They are turned by the handles on top. The Arabs build these entirely out of wood, but metal lasts longer. We also use a great many buckets."

He straightened and stretched his shoulders. "Back to hulls for a minute. After the caulking is completed — a task requiring as much skill as ironwork or carpentry — we cover the underwater hull with pitch, or a thick tar from the Syrian burning pits to prevent teredo worms from eating the wood. These worms, if left unattended, can eat the inside out of a ship's timbers in a season.

"Last of all, we rub tallow over the underwater portion of the hulls to make the ships move easily. There is enough mutton fat in Istanbul to grease all the ships in the world!"

Barbarosa summarized the cost. "A basic galley is cheap enough, around two hundred sultanins, but gunpowder is changing war at sea and we'll have to spend a great deal on ship's guns. I haven't set a cost on armament yet, for there are still some decisions to be made, but it may be more than the ships themselves."

The Sultan nodded. "Ibrahim is gifted in military matters, and he speaks with my voice. Talk to him if you need any help on guns." He changed the subject to navigation. "What devices help men find their way at sea?"

"We have three: the compass which tells us direction in a general sense, the astrolabe which gives us some idea of our location, but which requires a steady platform and an exact time. And we have the simplest and most commonly used — al kemal. It measures location by using Polaris, the North Star. Unlike other stars, Polaris remains constant all night long; its position and height unchanged. Naples and Istanbul are about equally far north, and if we draw a line between them — such a line is known as latitude — any place located on that line will see the star at the same height."

"How do you perform this measurement?" As he spoke, the Sultan signaled one of the mutes and ordered fruit. The man disappeared through the door as though blown smoke.

Barbarosa handed Suleiman a flat square of thin wood about the size of two spread hands with a four-inch vee cut into one side and a yard-long twine fastened to its center. "This simple instrument was in use among Arab captains long before I went to sea. It requires clear skies or a moon in order to see the horizon, but most nights in sailing season satisfy that need.

"With your permission, let's step outside and navigate a bit."

Once teacher and pupil had accustomed their eyes to the night sky, Barbarosa continued, "You will see Polaris just over that minaret. Hold the plate, flat side facing you, so that the star is visible in the notch, Supreme One." He waited until the Sultan had done so and added, "Keep it in the notch and move the plate to or from you until the bottom of the plate is even with the horizon."

Suleiman caught on quickly. Once he established the right position, he commented, "We now have two points of our triangle. Much like an artillery problem. We need to measure the third."

"The distance between your eye and the wooden plate is the third leg of the triangle. Keep the plate steady and pull the string to your nose. Tie a knot at that exact point. As I said before, Istanbul and Naples are on approximately the same latitude, so the knot you just tied here in Istanbul can also be used in Naples."

The Sultan complied and, with no change of expression, asked, "In the case of some whose noses are too large, might some other feature be used?"

Barbarosa, who shared a generous nose with his Greek ancestors, gravely replied, "Your point is well taken, Light of Two Worlds, I use my forehead."

The Sultan turned the wooden plate over in his hand, "Does each captain have his own kemal? And does he tie the various knots only by visiting various known places and taking measurements himself?"

"That was common. For many years a collection of knots was a secret known only to the reis who tied them. But one of the first orders I issued was to develop a standard kemal, together with charts that show ports and landfalls. These will be issued to every reis and I will require deck masters on each ship to be familiar with them in case the reis is lost."

"Then your measurements are no longer secret?"

"Far from it. But then, they never were; one simply hired a reis who had his own measurements."

Suleiman led the way back into the office. The fruit had arrived and he picked up a tangerine. "Now, measure east and west for me."

"You've stated our major need. We have only the astrolabe — a disk marked in degrees with a hinged arm called alidad, which does the same thing as al kemal in a more detailed way; it measures the angle from horizon to various stars to get what we call cross-bearings. It can be used on the sun or many different stars, but they all move, so one must know the time exactly within the smallest fraction of an instant, and no time keeping device remains sufficiently accurate at sea. Also, the instrument is very sensitive and works best if it is fixed rigidly without movement — something nearly impossible to do on shipboard.

"We could do quite well if we could measure the distance traveled

Barbarosa's personal battle flag. (The Star of David and the four caliphs).

though the sea, but we can't." Barbarosa's broad hands smoothed the map. "Two English slaves, whom I purchased and freed, claim that the English have a device called a 'log' which they tow behind their ships to record progress . Their knowledge of it was sketchy, but it seems that its some method of counting revolutions of a small water screw. We are at work to develop one, but have made little progress."

"What would be the value of an instrument that would measure east and west?"

Barbarosa threw up his hands, "With accurate navigation, warships could surprise any enemy, a force could gather in secret, prize crews could avoid areas of known risk. For example, the circumnavigation of Sicily out of sight of watchtowers would be of small moment."

The Sultan drew from his caftan sleeve an amulet worked in gold. "This keepsake was made by me and bears my signature. You may use it to reward the man who discovers such an instrument, and you may offer from my treasury whatever additional gold you think such a discovery is worth."

Barbarosa bowed. "The privilege of owning your personal tugra would be ample reward for any True Believer."

"Experience has taught me that while men may covet honor and recognition, there is no lasting substitute for gold." The Sultan rose to leave.

Barbarosa instantly stood and took a breath. "Light of the Two Worlds, I have one other request. Shall I mention it now?"

"State it quickly."

"Biscuit is as important as oars, Not only is the dry food needed to operate, it is expensive — about a quarter of the overall cost of operation. I need to control the manufacture and supply of all corn products. The Peskimet-emini should be made directly responsible to me."

"To whom does he report now?"

"Iskender Chelebi, your treasurer."

"Can't Iskender do the job?"

"I do not charge him with anything other than a small mind. He will, I'm sure, object, but I consider it so important that it deserves your personal tugra."

Barbarosa was on dangerous ground. To question the royal treasurer was to imply, at least indirectly, suspicion of his honesty.

The Sultan looked at Barbarosa for a thoughtful moment. "You must consider this issue important. I'll talk to Ibrahim."

He turned and strode out.

Barbarosa may not have cared if he made an enemy for himself, but he had certainly done Ibrahim no good, for Iskender Chelebi was to blame the Vizier for the organizational change that took the biscuit supply of the fleet — and its gold — from his control.[1]

---

1.   Peskimet-emni: literally — Attendant of the Biscuit. Food, which equated to fuel, became the Achilles heel of galley fleets. Between 1520 and 1540, biscuit increased in price from about one half asper per pound to nearly two. When added to the increased manning of the new galleys of the 1530s, the overall cost per galley increased six to eight hundred percent. Ironically, this became a Muslim advantage, for only Turkey could afford such cost for any period of time.

11

A FLEET

1533

I brahim grimaced, "Your biggest difficulty will be the Lufti Pasha
men, the Old Navy. They won't openly resist you for fear of exciting
the Sultan, but they'll not lift their tent flaps until you pull down the
tent pole. Count on them to watch the garden grow without water."
He had just arrived at Barbarosa's dockyard office and had spoken while
seating himself. As promised, the Sultan had instructed him to give
Barbarosa administrative assistance, and the two had been holding a series of meetings. Today, Dragut was included.

Within a month Ibrahim and Barbarosa had become at ease with one
another as though friends for years. They were both devoted to the Sultan, they shared Greek ancestry, and each had risen from unpromising
beginnings through his own abilities. Nor was the friendship of the two
men burdened with competition. Their interests and spheres of power
swung independently of one another.

Their one difference was in Turkish foreign policy.

Barbarosa, concerned with making Turkey a maritime power, saw the
strategic need for a chain of shore bases to support the notoriously short
legged galleys, and Venice, which maintained the Mediterranean's most
extensive system of ports, seemed to him a likely market in which Turkey
might do some shopping. Ibrahim, however, valued the economic benefits accruing from tariffs and trade relationships with Venice. Also, like
other Turkish land oriented leaders, rather than war at sea he favored
land warfare which produced new territory for the Timar lords and Raya
land holders.[1]

---

1. The two main classes of Turkish land owners whose birth rates required more land
   constantly.

But such difference in opinion never caused conflict between the two. In the first few years Barbarosa remained too busy at sea and, later when differences might have mattered, Ibrahim was occupying a grave in Istanbul.

Barbarosa answered Ibrahim's comment about men of the Old Navy. "I'll deal with them when the time comes. Right now I'm building ships."

"Very well, no more advice. I believe we were going to talk arms today. Are you ready to tell me how many Christians you plan to circumcise with a rusty knife?"

Barbarosa made a deprecatory hand motion. "Today Dragut and I will talk about muskets and cannons." He motioned the servants to serve tea and sweet cakes and, as they carefully moved aside drawings and charts to clear space, went on, "Our most important need is cannons. They are fast becoming dominant at sea. Our battle tactics and ship design depend on them."

Ibrahim sipped his tea and nodded.

"But in our little talk today, we'll save cannons for later. First, Dragut is going to show you a new musket."

While Dragut uncased a short, bulky musket, only two thirds as long as the six foot arquebus, Barbarosa went on, "The arquebus is a remarkable development, but in battle little better than the crossbow.[1] Neither packs enough striking power against armor. With The Religion now established on Malta, sooner or later we'll have to deal with armored knights, and the only way to stop them, as you know, is with shock."

Men in armor were extremely dangerous fighting machines in hand to hand battle. Together with its wool or felt protective undergarments, a suit of individually designed body armor with articulated joints at every body-junction weighed as much as eighty pounds, but the weight was distributed evenly over the body, allowing good balance and expenditure of strength. Escorted by men at arms in quilted or leather protectors who acted as expendable flankers and screeners, an armored Knight represented a battle unit, a centerpiece of unmatched force. Practically impervious to hand-held weapons, a dozen armored knights could turn a

---

1.   When invented, the crossbow was so effective it threatened established arms. In 1139 the weapon was outlawed by the Roman Church except against "infidels". Constantly improved, it remained useful well into the 16th century. Columbus considered it practically interchangeable with the early arquebus, requesting 100 each for his 2nd voyage to the New World.

battle against hundreds of unarmored opponents.[1]

Barbarosa indicated the heavy musket Dragut was placing on the table and added, "We captured several of these muskets from a Spanish merchantman. It's worth looking at."

Dragut passed the gun to the Grand Vizier and explained, "This musket can handle a larger powder charge and a ball four times heavier than the standard arquebus." Nodding to Barbarosa, he added, "You remember how much a single arquebus shot meant the day Portundo's galleys were captured — and that was from a distance of not more than a hundred feet with a half ounce ball. This weapon delivers a two ounce ball that can cut through body armor at two hundred yards. Its hitting shock alone will knock a man down at three hundred."

Ibrahim asked about the firing mechanism and was told that the weapon used a match sparked from friction to fire the powder — an improvement over the slow fuse of the arquebus. "This weapon is easier to use — although rain will generally put it out of business as quickly as the old fuse type."

The next question dealt with economics. "How much do these brutes cost?"

"About double the arquebus, with more for the finely grained powder it needs. If they were five times as much, we'd want them."

"It must have a drawback."

"It does. It has a strong kick that can break men's shoulders, but in ten years you'll be replacing the short bow of your Sipahis with this weapon."

"Ah, you've been into the kef today! It will rain in the desert all year when I take short bows away from my army!"

"I agree that the short bow is the best, but I'll have upwards of twelve thousand fighting men at sea, not more than a few hundred of whom are skilled in the bow. Unlike the bow, any strong man can be taught to use this musket in a week." Without thinking, he went on to lecture the Grand Vizier — a distinguished general in his own right. "Sooner or later, you'll have the same problem with your Sipahi cavalry. As the Empire grows, you will run short of country horsemen who were born with a short bow in their hands."

---

1.   During the siege of Malta in 1565 when accurate records were kept by the Christians, the casualty ratio was 40 knights and 180 men at arms to 2100 Turks.

Ibrahim didn't mind being lectured. "You may be right, if we have many more affairs like Rhodes ten years ago." He lifted the weapon appraisingly and sighted down the barrel.

"Would you like to have it fired?"

"Not now. Something as good as you claim should receive a full trial with our arms and foundry experts. I'll have a test set up. I'll let you know. You're sure this gun will do what you say?"

"As the sun rises and sets, as men thirst for water in the desert, as an Arab will bargain!"

Ibrahim nodded agreeably. "If the tests prove out, you'll have them by sailing season."

The subject of muskets concluded, Dragut opened a discussion of cannons. Addressing Ibrahim, "Pasha, your armies use cannons against city walls or massed groups of men where throw weight is as important as accuracy. But a galley is a small target and a close miss does no harm to the water. Pedrero stone throwers are great for siege, but couldn't hit a camel in the backside if the animal was leaning against the muzzle. We need the accuracy of guns that throw iron balls."

Barbarosa added, "Your armies haven't had to worry much about weight either. You can always tie another mule or two on to a gun train. But galleys carry little weight."

Ibrahim saw where they were headed, "You want some of the new culverins."[1]

"I bow to your perception." Barbarosa offered the Vizier a sweet candy. "Can they be had?"

Now was Ibrahim's chance. "Its your turn to be lectured. You know very well that the new guns are in worse than short supply. That's why you brought me here and put on this little karaghuz play."

Barbarosa colored slightly and raised his hands in apology.

Ibrahim closed his eyes and thought out loud for a few moments, "...we are casting heavier...maybe more pits for lighter gun output...

1. Once the bombard disappeared, large guns could be roughly grouped in two categories, the pedrero, an early, poorly cast, iron weapon that fired stone balls — and newer versions known simply as "cannons." There were dozens of specific types and names, e.g. bas topu (main cannon) but perhaps the best known were culverins of different lengths — a gun that could withstand the heavy charge demanded by iron balls.

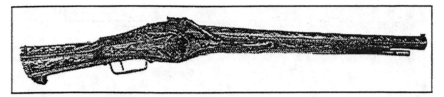

Musket. Successor to arquebus.

iron balls are cheaper . . . some of the new brass fire as well as bronze . . ."
He looked up and said, "How many and what size? Be specific."

"One hundred galleys. One thirty-pounder and four ten-pounders
per ship. The thirties weigh up to three and a half tons and must be
centered on the rambade deck. That means we have to move our fore-
masts to the side in other to provide for the recoil track."

Ibrahim thought for a minute, "The gun trains are being readied for
Persia, and casting pits have been built for somewhat larger molds. I can't
give you exact figures without checking, but I think I can get you two
dozen thirties this winter, and all the smaller ones you need. In the mean-
time, build your ships to accept them."

Barbarosa had expected to settle for less.

With Barbarosa's quick acceptance, Ibrahim added a modifier. "Most
of them will be brass. We have enough copper to pave the Mediterranean, but are currently short of Iron."

"As long as quality and weight are not compromised."[1]

B arbarosa's friendship with Ibrahim and his increasing intimacy with
Suleiman drew curiosity from powerful men in Istanbul. This pirate king who had risen like a crocus in the spring became a prime
subject for gossip. One such occasion occurred when two Ottoman officials, old friends, settled down in privacy for a relaxed social visit.

The scene: An unusually large, light, room, occupying most of the
second floor of a secluded yali on a hillside above the Bosporus. It is
furnished in the Persian style: low couches, cushions, silk carpets over
white marble floors. Three walls are hung with tiles, gold scrolls, and
porcelains. The fourth is largely of glass and opens on to a terrace com-

---

1.   Altough brass was softer, there was little performance difference.

Suleiman and Barbarosa. Famous 16th century miniature whose style is meant to demonstrate (1) the intimacy of the two (Barbarosa is seated) and (2) the unequalled status of the Sultan (he is higher than Barbarosa).

manding a spectacular view. South, directly across the Bosporus, can be seen the minarets of Scutari, its indistinct waterfront shouldering aside the dark Sea of Marmara. West, to the right, over the crowns of nearby pine and cedar, the Golden Horn prostates itself before the architectural cornucopia of Old City — a thousand years of Byzantium structures overlaid with a century of Ottoman palaces and Mosques. Irregular paths of boat lanterns streak the darkening water. Ashore, a carpet of city lights flickers its dainty challenge to the growing dusk.[1]

February weather is months ahead of season; no fires are needed.

There are four people in the room. Two are men, one of whom is the host — a slight, olive skinned man whose graying black hair reveals him to be in his fifties — the other is his guest, a burly, powerful, man at least fifteen years younger and, in the manner of the Turkish military, beardless. Both wear light caftans; neither wears a turban.

The men are enjoying the company of a pair of provocatively attired

---

1.   Yali – Seaside villa, popular among the wealthy of Istanbul.

girls trained as companions, and property of the Governor. The taller of the two, wearing a light jacket of rose colored silk with matching harem pants, is a voluptuous Mediterranean type of perhaps twenty with waist length black hair and eyes heavily darkened in the Turkish style. Her bearing, verified by an expensive jeweled girdle, indicates she is accustomed to the indulgence of a favorite.

Her companion is hardly sixteen — slender, petite, with the graceful movements of a dancer. Likely a Berber girl from the desert. Her dark eyes, flashing ivory teeth, and dark curly hair are almost central African, but her facial features are not as coarse. A vibrant, nubile girl-woman, her glowing health and youth need no cosmetic enhancement. She is shy, and less assured than the older girl.

The guest is talking about his host's name. "The name Mehmed must have been given you as a devirsme boy."

"No, oddly, I was not given a new name, I was permitted my own choice. Since I was born an Israelite, and Mehmed is the name of The Prophet, my choice was a public declaration."

"When you finished your training as a man of the pen,[1] you were sent to Adrianople thirty or more years ago by Bayazid, weren't you? I know you were there when young Suleiman became Sanjakbey of Erdine. And weren't you secretary to Ibrahim for a time?" The thought of Ibrahim reminded him about gossip, and he continued without a break, "How about Suleiman and Ibrahim? Did they stand behind one another in the baths? Its known they shared a bed."

"When boys, its true that Suleiman and Ibrahim slept in the same room — and it is rumored that there was love. But, even if I thought so, I'd keep my mouth closed. The Sultan's mutes are quick with their bowstrings. Also," he added with a grin, "I've never married and have no sons myself."

His guest shook his head. "You like women too much to be a male goose."

The guest was a native Turk. Muscular and so broad as to appear short, he gave the impression of vital, elemental, energy. Even without his formal black turban, he appeared to be exactly what he was, an Agha[2] of

---

1.   Term for devirsme trainees chosen for government. Janissaries were "Men of the Sword."

2.   General, very high ranking official.

Sipahis — the cavalry called up periodically from Turkish landholders. As an official in Ottoman government, he was a rarity. In keeping with Ottoman policy of a government that owed loyalty to the Sultan alone, native Turks were forbidden high office, military or civil. Exceptions required the personal approval of Suleiman and there were not more than a handful in the Empire.

Of the two, he was an "outside" man — used to the exercise of armies.

His host was an "inside" man, a career bureaucrat risen to become governing Bey of Istanbul. The two had been friends for the past twelve years — since shortly after Suleiman had brought his entourage to Istanbul to become Sultan.

The four had dined and the men's conversation was desultory. They touched on the recent Danube campaign and the unrest among the Shiites in the eastern mountains, admired the wealth and charities of Suleiman's Seraglio and approved the recent kanuns.

The Agha was first to raise the subject of Barbarosa.

"Regarding the new fleet: from what I hear, this Barbarosa Hayreddin is about your age, so he should be a set-in-his-way old sea dog. This man grew up with simple rowing galleots — what is it the Venetians call them — alla sensile?"

The Bey replied, "Like most military minds, you are only half right. The term alla sensile, doesn't mean light or little. It has to do with the number of oars and how they are manned. Barbarosa did grow up with small galleys, and still prefers ships somewhat lighter than the Christians. He thinks the Christians put too much weight into their construction and accommodations."

Ignoring the Bey's comment about the mindset of military men, the Agha asked, "Will they carry cannons?"

"Probably their most important feature. I don't know much about guns, but I understand the new casting methods make them stronger, and the new gun powder should make them lighter." He reached up and in the absent-mindedness of long habit, casually swept his raven haired companion on to his lap.

The Agha agreed. "You are correct about the new powder in grains.[1] It has double or triple the force. We are now casting field guns that throw a

---

1.   A type of gunpowder invented in the East, but improved and developed by the British who referred to it as "corned". It burned slowly and evenly, driving balls with a smaller charge.

fifty pound stone but are still light enough to be pulled by two oxen or four mules."

"Now that there are sea going cannons, he says that galleys can't really defend themselves. The guns are important, he says, not the hull. Barbarosa learned about ship's guns very early when his brother was taken by The Religion and chained to an oar for two years."

"Does a brother figure in our new fleet?"

"No. He was killed by the Spanish fifteen years ago."

Curious at the depth of knowledge of Barbarosa displayed by his host, the Agha asked, "You seem well versed on the man. Are you acquainted?"

"He's the best sea warrior in the Mediterranean, a superb strategist, and a great innovator." Apparently not intending to expand on his description, the Bey turned his attention to his fragrant companion.

Noting that his host had not answered the question, the Agha opened a new subject. "How about those pirates he brought with him? Can they command galleys in war?"

"They are some of the most able men in the Empire. Dragut, who has been with him for years, and Ochiali, who is younger, are the best..."

The Agha interrupted, "I respect them as fighters, but most of them are renegados. None of them is a Turk, as far as I know."

"Only one is — the man Dragut I just mentioned. As I was going to say, a galley depends absolutely upon the skill, bravery, and judgment of its reis. A natural talent and years of experience are required, and these sea-ghazis are the best. The Spaniards offer a special bounty for one of them — even from the smallest galleots — and when they have one, execute him immediately.[1]

Determined to smoke out the Bey's personal acquaintance with Barbarosa , the Agha returned to the attack. "They say that your friend does not observe many of The Laws."

Ignoring the word "friend", the Bey continued, "Although he seems to have developed a private communication with God since the loss of a favorite wife a few years ago, he has never been noted for devotion. I doubt that he will ever recite the great book, he loves the juice of the grape, I'm sure he doesn't pray five times a day, and I'm positive he will never take the time to go to Mecca."

---

1. Ghazis were fierce, cruel cavalrymen who served for spoils only. The term when applied to corsairs was meant as a compliment. The Spanish reward for a pirate reis was 500 ducats. (A Spanish cavalryman, with his own arms and horses, could be hired for five ducats a month.)

He still hadn't explained.

The Agha changed tack. "Our new Admiral's ships will require fifteen or twenty thousand rowers. In my experience, just to support that many men on the march takes a field train of two thousand men and five hundred camels — and that means still more rowers. Where will he get them?"

"He dislikes to use slaves, but does if necessary. He brought two thousand True Believers with him from Algiers and they will form the nucleus of the fleet. All he needs is a few old hands on each ship to act as drill masters for new men — and one man on each oar who can teach the others. Also, he has asked the Sultan for Janissaries."

"Yes," was the Agha's comment, "But he won't get many. The Sultan needs those pretty pike carriers to hold up his balls from the cold ground while he sleeps."

The Agha's Sipahis were free horsemen disdainful of the Janissary infantry. Well aware of the rivalry, the Bey was amused. "I'm sure you know of the new policy of devirsme recruitment. Nowadays they take only Albanians, Bosnians, and Serbs — tough mountain men who prefer fighting to parading. It takes a real man to be a Janissary!"

"May your bowels pass thorns and your teeth remain in your soup! You may have those tall turbaned, heavy footed court attendants and I'll stick with free men on horseback!"

Having said his piece, still unable to pry from the Bey any information as to his source of knowledge concerning Barbarosa, the Agha turned sideways, put his hands around the small girl's waist, lifted her as one would a toy, and held her aloft to admire her. "Friend, you have remembered my taste for a woman I can strap on and carry around. How much does a jewel such as this bring in today's market?"

"She is yours."

Much as a man of ordinary strength might do with a bouquet of flowers, the Agha lowered the lean girl to his face and inhaled the fragrance of her flat abdomen, then set her down, and answered, "Aha, I apologize. I didn't mean to burden you with the obligation of a gift. I am no guest, I am your brother."

Watching him, his host answered, "Brother, I gain merit by giving her to you. Keep her for the winter, and when you go to the field, I'll guard her until you return." He thought for a minute. "Better yet, give her a horse and take her along."

Companions and camp followers were strictly forbidden in Suleiman's armies, and the Agha smiled at the thought. He gently placed the object of his approval astride his knees, and addressed her affectionately, "Little flower, would you be happy to share the winter of a rough soldier?"

Excited by his prodigious strength, she also realized that as the favored companion of this vigorous man she would be given more attention than she could hope to find in the house of the Bey who was, after all, getting on in years. She answered shyly, "It would be a privilege, father."

"Very well," said the Agha, speaking to his benefactor, "Some give because it is written, some give to experience joy, some give in order to be praised. Who am I among the needy to say which gift earns merit?"

The subject of gifts exhausted, he decided that the time had now come to expose Mehmed's acquaintance with Barbarosa. "Good friend, avoid me no longer. How come you to know this pirate King? Have you had investments in his ventures?"

Mehmed raised his wine glass in a mock salute, "For a Turk who spends most of his life wading around in horse dung, you are an observant creature. I do know Khizr, and I have a great affection for him."

"I note you call him by a Persian name."

"Khizr was his birthname, son of Yakub. Barbarosa is a nickname. The title Hayreddin was given him by Selim."

Finally getting the information for which he had been probing, the Agha lifted the girl from his knees and set her aside. "I can see that you must have had dealings with him in your criminal past, but you explain yourself like an Arab caught stealing. He has had no court training. Suleiman never met him until that Roman spectacle sailed around Seraglio point last summer. I can't believe he would have won such an important post without friends in the Sublime Porte."

He settled down against his small companion to listen.

His host admitted, "I have known him for many years." He handed the Agha a worn amulet. "Untie the string and read the signature. This was my name before I was known as Mehmed."

The Agha took out the porcelain signature piece from the leather pouch and read the script. "Boaz. That's an ancient name from the Hebrew tribes."

"As you know, I am descended from those tribes, and lately I've become convinced I'm ancient. Barbarosa, when he was known as Khizr, and I, when known as Boaz, shared a youthful adventure or two in the sin quarter. One night he saved my good looks, if not my life, with a spectacular display of strength. For more than thirty years I have been in regular contact with him."

The Agha understood friendship, "Inasmuch as he has been your brother for thirty years, is he as good as he seems?"

"I'll try to give you a fair description." Boaz absently caressed his couch-mate and thought for a moment. "Implausible as it may seem for a pirate King, he is a man of intellect and training, much of it self obtained. He has a love for music — you will find musicians in Turkish fleets from now on. He speaks every major language fluently as well as several dialects and he knows more history than most scholars. At the same time, he is as fussy as a woman about his dress and appearance — foolish really — and he loves wine, sometimes to excess. Women are a pride and major occupation of his life — fortunately he is not subject to the sexual perversions so common to you Turks ..."

"Now wait a minute, you skinny keeper of books," the Agha interrupted, "I want a description of him, not Turkish habits!"

Ignoring the interruption, the Bey continued, "He had an unusual childhood. His father was a Janissary, but his mother was the widow of a Greek priest who abandoned neither her native language nor her Christian religion, and the customs of his youth were Greek. From all reports there was affection between his father and mother, and family bonds apparently made him easy-going and tolerant in matters of women as well as religion. To attribute his nature to his home life is fanciful, even so, there is no doubt that his childhood in Mytilene had an effect on his character."

"In short, he is Greek." Observed the Agha.

"I can best introduce you to the character of this man by telling you a story. One of his best captains, Dragut — the one I mentioned earlier — was almost as much feared by the Christians as Barbarosa himself. He was also Barbarosa's closest friend. Some years ago, attracted by the report of a rich cargo, Dragut took a flotilla of galleots to Corsica. It was mistreated by the Genoan nobles who owned it and spies were easy to come by. Owing to the treachery of one of these agents — and partly, let it be said, to his own overconfidence — he was captured by Giannatino, a cousin of Andrea Doria, in a neat trapping maneuver when he tried to run under the guns of a harbor fortress. This Giannatino was an infamous "al maful"[1] as the Arabs say and, in view of the reputation of this creature, Dragut was humiliated as much as angered."

"I can sympathize." Commented the Agha:

"Dragut's capture was well known, and on a state visit from Malta the Grand Master of the

Caftan. Silk and brocade woven with gold threads for one of Suleiman's sons. On display in Istanbul.

Knights went out of his way to visit the famous pirate. He greeted Dragut cordially — the Knights always accorded a sincere respect for Barbarosa's men — and sympathized with his condition. 'It is the custom of war that you find yourself so, Senor Dragut.' He then asked for the prisoner's health.

"They say that Dragut, even though chained, naked, dirty, and badly burned by the sun, casually responded to the Grand Master and the party of dignitaries as though he was on his own quarter-deck. He assured the Grand Master that his health was good, and looking directly at Giannatino added, 'What am I, slave to a catamite?'

"But the point of the story is Barbarosa's behavior when the news reached him. To make a long story short, he willingly paid a backbreaking ransom for his friend. At the time he had not reached the wealth he later commanded. Some say that he had to place himself in the hands of the gold merchants, but wherever he raised the gold, it was exceptionally

---

1.   A man who preferred to submit himself sexually to other men.

generous. Brotherhood to this man is as important as power to most."[1]

A Muslim and thus a believer in brotherhood himself, the Agha was impressed. He was also interested in loan procedures. He asked, "What guarantees such loans?"

"The future, friend, the future. Kings can borrow at a somewhat lesser rate by allowing special trade privileges, or entailing their taxes and giving lenders the right to collect them — Spain is said to have obligated half a lifetime of State income to the lenders — but lesser men must have a record and must be believed at the outset." He concluded, "My praise of Barbarosa is indeed rich."

"And you peddled him to the Grand Vizier."

"If I was helpful in arranging the marriage of this man and the Ottoman fleet, I have done a great good."

The Agha nodded, "Some days I think you are an asset to the Sultan — but I'll keep it a secret."

By now the evening was mature; the slight warmth of the afternoon had disappeared. The host, realizing his obligations — as well as the hour — stood and informed his friend, "You men of war are impervious to fatigue, but we slaves of government must have our rest. The room on the left and this small desert dancer are yours."

They rose and embraced. The brawny Turkish warrior held the slight Boaz at arms length and said admiringly, "The pleasure of your presence has shortened the passage of this day. To be your friend is a privilege, to be your brother is an honor." Indicating his companion, he added, "Your gift of this ninety pounds of beauty and pleasure has earned you merit."

Boaz, savoring the surprise he was about to unveil, spoke slowly, "Don't thank me, dear friend. Thank Barbarosa.

"He gave her to me."

During his later years while still in Algiers, Barbarosa had often thought of Tunis as an apple that might be easily shaken from the North African tree. With the death of Muley Mohammed, his grandson Muley Hassan had solicited Spanish support and murdered

1.   One historian claims that the ransom was 30,000 ducats, but details (the time and place) vary, and the actual amount is not known. It is, however, generally agreed that Barbarosa "impoverished" himself for no reason other than obligation to a friend.

his way to the throne over the corpses of forty four of his own brothers — a record even by Arab standards. Chiefly noted for maintaining a harem of more than a hundred pretty boys, his mistreatment of his people had inspired a personal plea to Barbarosa.

> *"Hayreddin Pasha, hear us. O noble prince and defender of the faith, hear our plea. Muley Hassan, King of Tunis, a tyrannical and avaricious Prince, being abhorred by a great Part of his subjects, more particularly by the Citizens of Tunis, whom he has most oppressed, having sacrificed to his revengeful Humor many of the wealthiest and best esteemed among them, their surviving Friends, under hourly apprehensions of being the next Victims, secretly, and with the utmost Caution, do entreat you to raise the greatest Force you conveniently can, and to free them (us) from their (our) Tyrant. We fully Promising that if so done the sovereignty of our City and the whole Realm will be yours to hold with our loyalty. As thee, in your younger days, while residing here with your brother Barba Rossa Aruj, hath become very well acquainted with all those that figure in this Invitation, this is a proposal that cannot therefore in any wise be rejected. We entreat thee to raise a Power sufficient to render us effectual service."*[1]

Barbarosa had kept this document and he showed it to Ibrahim. "Muley Hassan," he said, "is like donkey shit, shiny on the outside but rotten in the middle. I can gain his city without the loss of a man."

A visit to Tunis would also allow Barbarosa to take care of personal affairs. Since the death of Isabella, the addition of one or two women every year to his Algerian household had seemed to occur more or less in the natural course of events, and these women were still there. Also, he wanted to see how well Hassan Aga was conducting his stewardship for the eventual promotion of young Hassan.

Not least, his slaves and property could be converted to specie.

Suleiman also viewed Tunis and its strategic harbor as a desirable Ottoman acquisition and it was little trouble to have it placed on the agenda for the first cruise of Turkey's new fleet. First, however, the Sultan required a tweak of Charles' beard. The Kingdoms of Naples and Sicily — major sources of Charles' personal income — were to have the pleasure of entertaining the new Turkish fleet before anything else. Later, there would be time for Tunis.

---

1.   Taken exactly from a 17th century translation

Before departing, Barbarosa asked Piali, whom he had grown to trust, to remain in Istanbul as his personal representative. "There is no one who can do better with the crowd in the Sublime Porte[1] than you. You have the protective color of a court official — you have learned the importance of dress, and your three languages are perfect. You have the ear of Ibrahim, and the eye of Suleiman. Fill your mouth with food rather than air, open wide your mind, and fly your ears like a hungry donkey. I may not be back for two seasons, and I need to know who are friends and who are enemies."

Piali, rapidly becoming established as a court favorite, had no objections.

In late April, with musicians playing, decorated in green streamers, a fleet of eighty new war galleys left the Golden Horn, sailed west through the Marmara, south down the Aegean, around the Peloponnesus, and west again, toward the great boot of Southern Italy.

---

1.   Literally, "The Sultan's Gate."

12

A Win – A Loss

1534

At sea when the breeze was a friend, Barbarosa could spend hours leaning against a bulwark or slowly pacing his after-deck, admiring his creation, a great crescent of black seabirds effortlessly skimming the sea, bright sails enfolding the gift of wind. When nature's friendship was withheld and sails were furled, these seabirds became graceful water-bugs, long legs striding steadily in perfect unison over smooth, unhurried water. In the peace of a quiet sea, one might faintly hear the regularity of tambours, but the painful lament of oar looms and chains was obscured by distance — and the straining men could not be felt.

On ships nearby — within an arrow shot or so — he could admire details of his own creation such as stanchions on which battle shields for the rowers could be fastened, or the protected stations at regular intervals along both gunwales for the bowmen, most of whom now had muskets. The stern mounted rudders were his personal design and, although he had stolen the idea from the Portuguese, when the breeze was being used, he was proud of the new foresails holding the ships into the wind.[1] While not visible, in his mind's eye he could see the new bottom-tanks of drinking water he had installed to serve both as ballast and as comfort to the rowers sweating in the Mediterranean sun.

Each of the flotilla lead ships (twenty five had been so designated) mounted one thirty-pounder culverin that fired iron balls — cannons

---

1. Lateens approached the efficiency of modern sails, but the danger of submerging gunwales and oars when the ship heeled (as well as the lack of real keel) prevented galleys from sailing into the wind with any real degree of success.

which Ibrahim had worked wonders to provide. Most of the other fifty carried lighter guns of about the same caliber, but with shorter barrels. All ships sported two twelve-pounder forward-firing, and four five-pound mankillers.

A proud parent, he delighted in his children.

Throughout the winter's training of crews, Barbarosa had insisted on intership communications to a degree previously unknown. And now that the fleet was at sea, things had not improved. Several times each day the Admiral called for a fleet flag drill — and he could read the flags as rapidly as any signalman. New officers forced to repeat flag drills for the hundredth time were convinced that the Admiral had been in the sun too long. A common description was, "A tough Pasha with odd ideas. Music every day, same food for slaves as fighting men. Whips ain't used. Any man can speak to him and get an answer. But them flags and horns forty times a day, even when secured, is enough to dry a man's brain!"

Two weeks, and the smoky green hills of southern Italy raised their verdant dignity from the horizon.

Late in the day,with Sinan as an audience, preparing to enter the narrow passage between Italy and Sicily known as the Strait of Messina, with the ships moving slowly to insure a night arrival at Reggio di Calabria, relaxed in his cabin, Barbarosa indulged in a bit of philosophy. "When I'm at sea, the blood of my mother often shows, for I think of the great Greeks. Jason and his men on the Argonaut searching for the Golden Fleece were pirates little different than my brother and me on Mytilene. This passage we enter today is said to have been visited by Ulysses who described it as a choice between Scylla and Charybdis.[1] I've made it many times and have found neither dangerous whirlpools nor many-armed beauties — but, Ulysses or no, as we carry our flag west, this strait will be important to Turkey."

Known to the ancient Romans as Rhegium, Reggio had last been captured by Dionysius, four hundred years before Christ, and it was here at this rich city that Barbarosa intended to make the first announcement of Islam resurgent. Reggio not only dominated the Straight of Messina, its capture was meant to be a signal to Christianity that the unsheathed Sword of Islam was at sea.

---

1.   As in the case of Djerba, modern historians feel that Ulysses' famous passage of danger and temptation was somewhere other than Messina.

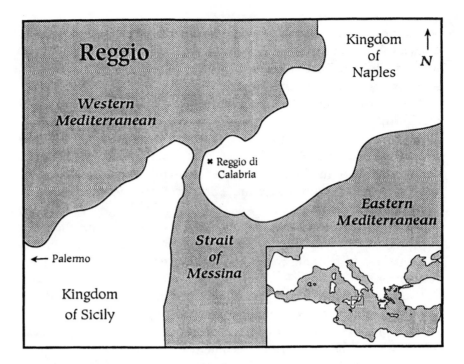

The surprise was complete.

Arriving unexpectedly, bypassing unmanned and unsuspecting fortifications, Barbarosa's fighting corsairs and Janissaries stormed ashore in darkness and took the city with ease. In the confusion, Reggio never asked for conditional surrender and when the short-lived fighting ended, the men would ordinarily have been entitled to the traditional three days of looting. However Barbarosa forbade burning or destruction. Valuables that could be easily uncovered were confiscated, several hundred new rowers joined the fleet, and Ochiali had a king's breakfast, as he put it, of tender maidens from which to choose.

But, with little physical damage, Reggio was free to commence restoration upon their departure. It was to be a Turkish crop planted for future harvest.

Reggio provided the first major event of a season of unprecedented Muslim attacks on Christian territory. No existing Christian fleet could deal with eighty war galleys. Flight offered the only defense for coastal inhabitants, but even that was rarely possible, for fleet elements were detached to approach the next victim even while a current captive city was being stripped. In four months the new fleet ravished towns and cities all along the west coast of Italy, Sardinia, and the Balearics. Then, turning south to Sicily the fleet took another leisurely month circling its rocky coasts to pick out rich morsels.

Traditionally secure from light Corsair ships, the larger towns had never previously been victims, and organized plunder by thousands of trained fighters backed by ship's cannons was an entirely new and frightful experience. That summer Barbarosa returned treasure to Istanbul worth double the cost of his fleet and enough Christian slaves to create a market glut. Istanbul bagnios were to report that Christian slaves brought "only one large onion a head".

Before the season was over, wailing rose like evening smoke along the ravished coasts; it was claimed that the only women left to press oil from the olive crop were under twelve years of age; the only able bodied men over thirty.[1]

War at sea for the Turks was proving as profitable as war on land.

The bonanza in slaves allowed Barbarosa to be generous with his captains. Captives retained as rowers became the personal property of each reis, divided in the same manner as other treasure. Ownership of slaves by ship captains was common in Christian ships, but the system was flawed, for a slave's death was a Captain's (or ship-owner's) loss. In Barbarosa's fleet, slaves were charged against the reis only if lost through ill treatment or poor seamanship.

In late September, with his holds full to overflowing and his ships crowded with men, Barbarosa was ready for Tunis. Pausing to clean and tallow his ships on a Sicilian beach only seventy five miles across the strait from Cape Bon, he outlined his plans. "Doria leveled the fort on the Goletta when he recaptured the Lomellini galley fifteen years ago, and it's not been rebuilt. We'll move to a standard line abreast formation in the outer bay, and will exercise a few of our new culverins. I don't expect any resistance. Just the sight of us will give loose bowels to that Arab child-eater."

His prediction proved correct. The Turks had only to skip a few cannon balls into the lagoon to announce their intentions, and Muley Hassan

---

1.   Some of the Torre di Guardia (outlook towers) of an elaborate Italian coastal warning system built as a result of Turkish raids in those years, may still be seen — a few incorporating Barbarosa's name.

Charles I, 1500-1588 – King of Spain, who was also **Charles V,** Emperor of the Holy Roman Empire. Withdrew from power in 1566 in favor of his son, Philip. A man of unsuspected and erratic abilities as well as behavior, he was a food glutton and closet lecher tortured by his conscience since the early death of young Isabel of Portugal, a state marriage that had matured into deep love on his part. At the same time he was a religious zealot whose thoughts were rarely far from his duty to Christ.

took such of his boy-harem and treasure as could be hastily loaded, and departed for Kairouan, the ancient Islamic fortified capital in the southern hills.

Once ashore, Barbarosa planned to spend the winter in Tunis. Maintaining the entire fleet would reduce his profits, so he kept only a carefully selected fifteen galleys with non-slave crews. The rest of the fleet, loaded with treasure and slaves, was sent scudding eastward to the Golden Horn.

Then he turned to his own affairs.

Over the years Barbarosa had acquired an enviable collection of female companions in Algiers. Thinking of the example of Mohammed — who had provided a separate dwelling for each of His fifteen wives and had adhered to a balanced schedule of connubial visits[1] — Ochiali commented, "Like The Prophet, the old boy doesn't have to plow the same ground any two nights in a week!" However, resolved to give Turkey a fleet in the shortest time possible, Barbarosa had left his women in Algiers

---

1.   Mohammed occasionally favored a teen age favorite with extra visits (Aisha, the same girl he forgave for spending a night in the desert with a handsome young man) but his treatment of all women was kind and generous; he set an example for Muslim men to follow.

Isabel of Portugal *by Titian*

when he journeyed to Istanbul. With over a year's absence, his heart had grown markedly fonder.

The first shipment to Tunis were these women.

His second movement of people was to prove a mistake of great consequence. He ordered all of his slaves in Algiers sent to Tunis for work on city defenses and the fort on the Goletta. When added to those already in the the city bagnio, there were eight thousand men — too many to be safely guarded in existing facilities.

For the winter and early spring all went well in refurbishing Tunis. New wells were dug, streets paved and buildings that might interfere with defensive military positions removed. The slaves completely rebuilt the fort and made a first class fortress of the city walls. The city market was rejuvenated, foreign trade welcomed, and the citizens were pleased with their new government.

By the time spring flowers greeted the sun, Tunis was recognized as an established Ottoman city.

But as these same flowers blessed Tunis, storm clouds were maturing in Spain.

Not only had Charles' holdings in Sicily and Naples suffered unprecedented damage from Barbarosa's tour the preceding summer, but with the capture of Tunis, Spain's vital corn supplies were threatened. Major Sicilian ports such as Trapani were now within a day's row of Turkish ships. Tunis loomed a threat that could no longer be ignored.[1]

By now, Charles was an experienced and capable King and Emperor. He had made himself fluent, perfect, in the Spanish language, and very much the complete master of his realm, toiling his endless hours with the flood of paper that arrived in Madrid from a world empire in which only his decisions were final.

---

1.   Charles recognized Barbarosa's depredations in the western Mediterranean and capture of Tunis for exactly what it was: the opening of a new front in the old war of religions.

A man in whose blood the poison of insanity ran — his mother spent the last quarter of her life gibbering under restraint, and his grandson boiled and ate his own shoes — Charles' skill in planning was exceeded by no King alive, and despite his unprepossessing presence, he rightly deserved admiration for his courage in battle. No less an authority than his lifetime enemy, the King of France, considered Charles' presence in battle ". . . worth five brigades of cavalry".

Now in his late thirties and aready showing signs of the corpulence and gout that were to cripple him later in life, he decided that the discipline of a campaign in the field would do him good.[1]

He announced that Spain would recapture Tunis for the sake of Christianity, and he promised to don his armor and lead the way.

Although Spain would provide the bulk of ships and all of the money, Charles welcomed support, and three participants joined: a contingent of German soldiers from the German states of the Holy Roman Empire, a papal squadron from Rome, and two ships from the Knights of Rhodes — now operating out of Malta.

Charles flagship, under construction in Genoa, left no doubt as to his sincerity. Worthy of his royal presence, it measured one hundred and eighty feet by forty and moved by courtesy of sixty oversize oars with

Anchored galley with awnings supported by oars.

---

1.   After Isabel's untimely death, he comforted himself with food. His morning eye-opener before prayers — and breakfast — was a beaker of strong beer and a plate of sweets.

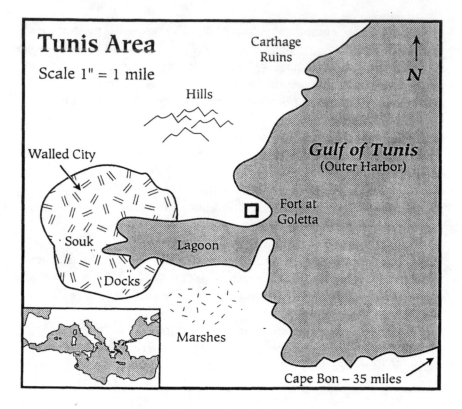

Tunis Area

Scale 1" = 1 mile

Carthage Ruins

N

Hills

Walled City

Gulf of Tunis
(Outer Harbor)

Souk

Fort at Goletta

Lagoon

Docks

Marshes

Cape Bon – 35 miles

seven men on each loom. Decorated with lavish carvings, brocades, religious artifacts, and comfortable furniture, within the hull were enclosed cabins and a kitchen for use at sea.[1] An emperor's gig swung on davits from the aft deck. It had four large and four small cannons on the bow, four on the stern, as well as a half-dozen lighter side guns mounted on small platforms built above the rowers.

In June, Christian ships began to leave Barcelona, Genoa and Malta for rendezvous in Sicily. Twenty thousand soldiers and twenty five thousand rowers, plus ship's crews, excited supply and contract cupidity all over Europe. One week of food and water alone for such a force meant that seven hundred Venetian tons of stores would have to be at sea. Nothing like it had been seen since the days of Rome — and Rome didn't have cannons.

---

1. Fires aboard Barbarosa's galleys were ordinarily forbidden but on large Christian ships were common — and occasionally regretted.

With most of the Turkish fleet in Istanbul, Barbarosa was going to have to defend Tunis with whatever resources he had at hand. The Sultan and Ibrahim were both with an army in Persia, and without decision-making authority in Istanbul, no additional forces would be forthcoming.[1]

Nevertheless, he was confident. "Sinan will take our fifteen galleys to Bone and he will leave us all the men he can spare. The cross-kissers will need a month or more to reduce the fort, and as long as it remains they can't get into the lagoon. That month will use up a good deal of their strength. Once the fort is no longer defensible, we'll bring the garrison back to the city, and counting Sinan's people, we'll have close on six thousand fighting men. If we can't defend against four times our number, we don't deserve to be called fighters. It would take those violators of sheep six months to dig us out of the city, and they can't remain off shore once winter blows. By next season we'll have help from Istanbul."

On the 13th of July, 1435, three hundred Christian ships began to leave Trapani in southern Sicily; two days later, three hundred Christian anchors tasted the mud of outer Tunis bay.

The stars of this armada, the two new ships of the Knights floating just out of reach of the fort — ships which the defenders saw for the first time — were a new concept in sea-borne siege, and stomachs churned as they were studied from the city.

Borrowing from European experience in the Atlantic, the Knights had built floating forts whose six-ton culverins fired fifty pound iron balls nearly five hundred yards — with a fair degree of accuracy.

As they were subsequently described by Barbarosa, "The Religion called them carracks. They were more or less newer versions of the Galleasse they were using when Aruj was taken prisoner thirty five years ago, each large enough to carry several hundred men for months. The hulls were at least two hundred fifty feet long and sixty feet from bulwark to bulwark. About forty oars were placed midships, useful only for making port. At sea they would have to depend entirely on sails — and they had three masts sixty feet high. Eight decks, some for men, some for supplies, some for managing the ship   and some for their long cannon which fired from the waist. I counted twenty on each side. They remained

1.   Turkish government was mobile. Whenever the Sultan took to the field, his cabinet (divan) accompanied him on horseback.

out of our range, but their sides appeared to be sheathed in what must have been ten inches of oak, and I don't believe one of our balls would have penetrated if we could have reached them."[1]

They were the reason that the fort — the Golatta defense that was to hold for a month — crumbled within three days. "That much iron striking dead on to sandstone", reported the fort commander after the first day, "is opening up these walls like a monkey eating a banana."[2]

Late on the third day, with the Tunis fort in shambles, the Knights put armored men ashore and only the dark of night saved the garrison from annihilation. With the next day's planning, Barbarosa's choice was either to sacrifice the remaining men in the fort, or risk a rescue force outside the gates.

His personal sense of obligation made his decision.

During the night he ordered the slaves moved to a series of dungeons where powder kegs could be ignited and dropped through the gratings in case of an uprising, and he left two renegados with a Berber detachment in charge of them. He detailed his small force of Janissaries to hold the armory.

Every other fighting man went outside with him at daybreak.

At first, the gamble appeared successful. The sheer weight of muslim numbers stymied the knights long enough to allow the men in the fort an orderly return to the city. But the early success turned to ashes.

The city gates had closed behind them.

The slaves had managed a carefully planned and brilliantly led uprising. The renegados in charge of the powder kegs had not fired them and, by the time Barbarosa's force returned, the slaves were in control. They had only makeshift arms — the armory was apparently still held by the Janissaries — but with eight thousand slaves loose, it was only a matter of time.

Barbarosa was unaware of this development until the first of his men reached the gates and were unable to enter. There was a great deal of confusion at first, but as correct information finally spread, some of his Arabs began to think for themselves, heading piecemeal for the low hills

---

1.   These carracks were not unusually large by some European standards. Twenty years later Henry VIII commissioned a galley of 207 cannons and 1000 fighting men.

2.   Heavy guns that threw iron balls were revolutionizing fortification design. Before the century was out, every occupied fort in the world was rebuilt.

to the west. He refused to believe the reports, and he spurred to the city gates to call for his renegados, but they were either turncoats or dead. He found only one ray of hope; the Janissaries must still control the armory, for the hostile men on the walls had no arms. If he could rally his men, he might regain the city before the Spanish fleet could enter the lagoon. He galloped to the head of the retreating stream of men and halted the movement. "They don't have weapons! The armory's secure! We can re-take the city!"

But while he was still persuading, the cannons on the city walls, aimed at the sea, began firing blank discharges. The slaves were letting the Span-ish know that they were in control.

Even his Corsairs lost interest.

In frustration and unreasoning anger, he became a man possessed. He would go himself.

He cast off his Turban and unsheathed his sword. Entirely without thought of his own safety, his battle cape streaming over the hindquar-ters of his horse, he was a vision of insane recklessness as he galloped back to the city gates. Screaming threats to traitors, he dismounted and assaulted the gates with his sword and bare hands. He cursed, threat-ened, promised, reminded the renegado leaders of past kindnesses, his voice hoarse in anger and frustration as he tore his clothing and beard.

His courage was admired; his message unheeded. The men on the walls still had not obtained small arms, and their threats remained only verbal, but with the cannons mastered, it could only be moments before arquebuses and bows began to appear. Several of his men risked them-selves to follow, overpower, tie him on his horse, and carry him back to safe ground.

His pride, shame for his error in judgment and his inability to affect the course of events combined to overwhelm him. Near hysteria with rage, distraught, clothing awry, his features distorted with tears, he rec-ognized Ochiali standing before him. "I am ruined! Those sons of dis-eased whores have taken my gold, my women, my city!"

Ochiali spread his hands in hopelessness and sympathy, but said noth-ing until Barbarosa quieted, whereupon, still without speaking, he mo-tioned the men to loosen the restraining ropes. Untied, Barbarosa asked his friend, "How can I face the Lord of the Two Worlds?"

Ochiali assured him that the loss would be of little moment to

Suleiman. Tunis, he argued, might be a valuable port, but in the final analysis it was not much of a city in comparison with Belgrade, Budapest, Baghdad, Adrianople, or many others. He added, "Suleiman has been occupied for over a year on a campaign against Tabriz that he considers important enough to justify an army of more than a hundred and fifty thousand men. A loss of this small city will be of little moment to him.

"Old friend, in this business, sooner or later we all lose something. No one could have foreseen those carrack guns — I hardly believe them myself — and your effort to save your men does you credit."

The encouragement reminded Barbarosa that he had a duty to his men and a debt to repay. He collected himself and said, "Scaly Head, you are a treasure — if you see me go overboard again, hit me with the flat of your sword. Would you get together as many captains as you can find?"

In fifteen minutes Ochiali had gathered a half-dozen senior reis.

Barbarosa's instructions were brief and to the point. "We have ships in Bone. If we can get there before those bastards of Satan, we have the great sea waiting. Load the few horses with anyone who is hurt; others will walk. Each man will carry only such rations and water as he needs. Leave everything else."

"Muskets too?"

"Aye. We can save ourselves only if we get there first."

Within the hour two thousand loyal Turks and Corsairs had melted into the sandy hills to the northwest, everything of weight abandoned on their frantic race.

Charles' victory dispatches to Europe triggered international joy to the level of delirium. The Turk had been defeated! Christ was in his glory! Bonfires were lit, bells rung, masses held, and artists vied with one another to create the definitive painting of Charles' triumph.[1]

But Charles threw his victory away.

Notorious for outrages in conquered cities, the Christians outdid themselves in Tunis — robbing, plundering, torturing, murdering. Men were strung up by the genitals, pregnant women sliced open, live prisoners flayed and their skins stuffed, young girls impaled on poles. Those caught praying to Mecca had their feet amputated on the spot. The elderly were blinded. Babies too small to serve as slaves had their brains beaten out

---

1.   While Titian, Charles' favorite portrait painter, failed to accompany him to Tunis, at least two of his versions of the victory hang today in the Prado in Madrid.

Light galleys, or galleots.

against stone walls.

There was one ray of cheer for the inhabitants. When the Christian slaves who had escaped the dungeons had the poor judgment to appear, Charles' soldiers slaughtered those carrying treasure.

Afterward, Muslims claimed that the Christians murdered seventy thousand people. By Spain's own count, the dead totaled twenty thousand. But by whatever measurement, Tunis was a stain on Christianity, and it bore two offspring. The first was a new, more intense level of Muslim hatred that, reinforced by Charles' subsequent decision to reinstall Muley Hassan as King of Tunis, would materially contribute to a permanent Turkish recapture of the city a few years later.[1]

The second result of the Rape of Tunis was sufficient time for Barbarosa to reach his ships in Bone. He and his fighting men made the trip in three days and, once there, put to sea in about the same number of hours.

His first stop was Algiers, where he picked up a half dozen corsair galleots, rearranged the manning of his ships (including some slave row-

1.   One might compare Christian behavior in Tunis with Muslim behavior in Tabriz that same year. After capturing Tabriz — a traditional enemy of Turkey — Suleiman carefully protected women and children, no structures were damaged, and captives were released on their own pledges.

ers) secured more supplies, and took on his son Hassan. Then the Sea swallowed him up. He intended to teach the Spanish something about the use of Sea Power, and he wanted to conduct the lesson in a Spanish classroom.[1]

The city of Mahon on the island of Minorca, the chief Spanish port in the Balearics, had been a major contributor to Charles' expedition, and the inhabitants thought it only natural that they should have the first opportunity to welcome the returning victors. When a galley fleet flying Genoan colors appeared over the horizon, it was welcomed with open arms by the city — as well as by a pair of visiting Portuguese merchant galleons.

In one afternoon, Barbarosa not only took the city, he captured the Portuguese ships — a feat he would have had a great deal of trouble duplicating at sea. The treasure was particularly rich, for the inhabitants were unsuspecting. Neither people nor goods were hidden. (Silk alone was worth more than fifty thousand Spanish crowns). The Turks acquired a dozen small or medium trading ships, fifty-seven hundred captives, and leaving, they burned the city to the ground. As a sweetener, when Barbarosa's fleet cleared the harbor they encountered the first eight of the Spanish ships returning from Tunis, heavy laden with spoils, and he added them to his now sizable convoy.

Once again at sea, he couldn't resist gloating to Ochiali, "This, I think, is better than going up to the Levant, creeping like city dogs from port to port!"

But his mood didn't last.

His first stop was his old home of Algiers, and once there, a strange lassitude seemed to overtake him. There was little reason to remain, but he seemed reluctant to set out on a return to the Golden Horn. Days, weeks, passed in idleness; he was sampling a new vintage of wine two months later when Piali arrived in a fast galley bearing a ferman from Suleiman ordering the immediate return of the fleet.

While delivery of the Sultan's proclamation had been the purpose of Piali's trip — he also carried another message of the greatest sensitivity.

Charles wanted to buy Barbarosa's services.

---

1.   To Charles' tactical credit, he had earlier given his second in command, Andrea Doria, instructions to secure Bone — but Doria's men were also engaged in the Tunis rape.

Janissary Mounted Mehter (Military band).

The Spanish King had come to the conclusion that it would be cheaper to pay than to fight, and had dispatched a team of Venetian intermediaries to Istanbul where they approached Piali. Assuming that Barbarosa would be willing to command Spanish ships, Charles offered a title in Spain and a half million Spanish gold crowns for his services.

At first Barbarosa left no doubt, "Tell that sniveling copper worshipper that he tries to buy me too cheaply." Then he thought for a moment, "Wait — if I don't answer immediately, I maintain some advantage. They will be uncertain." Suleiman's generals who lost battles tended to have short careers; perhaps Tunis had made Barbarosa vulnerable. He shook his head in despair. "When Suleiman is finished with me, I might wish I had accepted the offer! If Charles thinks it a good time to buy me, maybe he knows something I don't."

So, carrying the riches of the Balearics, thousands of new slaves for the bagnios — and the secret of Charles' offer — Barbarosa headed east.

As the fleet breezed homeward, lateens and oars extended to catch the early autumn westerlies, Barbarosa remained somber. All this time and no message from Suleiman — then suddenly, the brief and businesslike command to return. Piali was of little help to him, he only knew that the Sultan was back from Tabriz and the Persian war. There had been no discussion or instructions — just the ferman.

The ships were muddy looking, the weather cold and dreary. Even the rarely issued crew jackets seemed to be as gray as the overcast. Twice they rowed all day entirely by compass in fog that rose like smoke from the sea, so dense it obscured the oar blades. Any other seaman would have put up ashore, but Barbarosa not only possessed the skills to keep his ships on course and together with horns and drums, he seemed to relish the discomfort and unease bred by such weather.

Hour after hour, day after day, he kept to himself, moodily contemplating the spray thrown up by the surging bows or sitting on the aft deck open to the cold, late season wind. He realized only too clearly that Suleiman's campaigns were littered with the corpses of generals found wanting in battle. The offer from Charles buttressed his fear and, in spite of himself, tempted him. Princes and generals changed sides every day. Andrea Doria had sold his services under at least three different flags. The King of France could sign a treaty one day and abrogate it the next. Power and riches were the coin in which men dealt.

Weeks later, upon arrival in Istanbul, he found the omens no better. It was raining lightly, the day was gray and raw; the mood of the Golden Horn a dramatic reversal of the gay scenario three years earlier when he had entered with his triumph of gifts. The sight of a forest of masts — the ships he had sent home from Tunis a year ago — comforted him only marginally. Perhaps the fleet was to be enshrined as a tribute to his memory.

As his weather beaten hulls eased their way to the docks, the smooth water of the harbor prickled with raindrops, the sky rested on dark clouds, the City huddled in cold rain. As he exchanged his clean wooden deck for the dirty stone of the quay, the only encouragement was the properly respectful tone of the large bell on the dock that announced his arrival. Otherwise, The Great City seemed to have had turned its back on him.

The small detail of minor officials who showed up were no better than the weather. None of them had any idea of what was afoot — only that the palace had been practically shut up for days and important men were flying in and out, preoccupied, uncommunicative.

Nor was there ceremony when he reached the outer Palace gate.

Piali and Ochiali, walking with him, were sure that his late season crossing was faster than expected and therefore unannounced, but Barbarosa remained dubious. Beyond the gate, as the three of them followed the stewards down the long passageway, he murmured, "Piali, my son, the only question remaining is how it will be done. A Yali on the Bosporus from which I can watch you put to sea? A quiet apartment in the Bagnio when I can let my life run out the end of my one eyed friend?

A warm spot in the Caucasus where I can poison myself with wine? The daggers of the mutes?"

Dragut answered for Piali. He would not tolerate Barbarosa's pessimism, and he tried sarcasm, "Well, old man, after all, you were a King before you came east to the Sublime Porte. Maybe you're entitled to a bowstring like the royal brothers!"

The jest was too close to Barbarosa's own thoughts. "May ten thousand lice infest your armpits, you donkey! Men who would force a cord around my throat will have to be stronger and faster than any I have yet seen!"

At the entrance to the Inner Court, there was no longer any doubt in his mind that he was being snubbed. Palace guards informed his companions they would have to wait outside, and rather than the chamberlain who would normally escort the Admiral of the Fleet, there was only a young palace aide who asked to be followed. To reach the throne room, the aide led the way through a little used tunnel in the bowels of the ancient Byzantine palace foundations. Alone, with only the guide's shadowy caftan floating before him, Barbarosa could taste a thousand years of cruelties impregnated in every crevice of the tons of marble and stone that lay above him.

Keeping stride for stride behind his guide, his misgiving was tangible. He reached inside his caftan, tightened the girdle holding his daggers and surreptitiously loosened his scimitar.

The Room Within was dimly lit; a few oil lamps struggling with the gloom of the late day. As he entered, Barbarosa saw only three formally attired officials seated side by side on a couch, facing him across a low table as though, he thought, about to pronounce sentence. During his journey toward them over sixty feet of cold, echoing marble, his attention was focused entirely on the three, and as he identified each man, the doubt that had lived with him for weeks fastened a constricting hand on his heart.

Ibrahim was not among them. One he knew only as a field general who had accompanied Suleiman to Persia, the others he knew well. On the left was the grim, unsmiling general and ex-admiral, Lutfi Pasha. Barbarosa had never thought of him as an enemy, but certainly not as a friend, for their opinions had been too frequently in conflict. On the right was Iskender Chelebi, the royal chamberlain in charge of Empire finances, the man who, at Barbarosa's request, had been removed from the power and profit of fleet biscuit supplies.

The impressive turbans and formal caftans of the three indicated that either an important decision had been reached, or a ceremony was about to take place. All were impassive, no one spoke while they waited for the echo of Barbarosa's boots to die.

It seemed unlikely that a public sentence would be announced. Far more probable would be a quiet execution. For weeks he had clothed himself in doubt; he now donned resolution. He might be at the end of his days, but the price for his departure would be high. He stopped before them, and placed his hand on the hilt of his sword as though preparing to bow. If they came after him from the shadows, at least he would have company on his long voyage to meet the houris. Before he went down he could have the head of Iskender and at least one other. To guard against any surprise, he glanced to his left, where he sensed the presence of someone.

There was his fate. Sitting quietly on a low couch, nearly invisible in the semi-darkness, was the Sultan himself.

Startled, Barbarosa turned to face his future. He took his hands from his waist, spread them before him, made a deep bow, and automatically offered the standard greeting due the most powerful man on earth, "May God bless and protect the Lord of the Two Worlds." His mind still was not functioning; he could not reason clearly; the greeting was automatic.

The answer was not.

The blank, unsmiling face, beginning to show age lines, pale from a winter in the frost of Persian mountains, and gray with an increasingly bilious digestive system, revealed nothing for a moment — then through the drooping mustache came the words, "May God give health to my Beylerbey of the Sea."

Barbarosa did not grasp the significance of the title, and he needed to digest the implications. He parried, "You do me honor, Magnificent One, how can I serve you?"

"Henceforth, you are Hayreddin Pasha, Kapudan i derya, Beylerbey of the Sea — and as a member of my Divan, sitting below only the Grand Vizier and the Beylerbey of Anatolia." A faint, rare smile lit the Sultan's wispy beard. "If you wish, rather than three horse tails, I'll award you three stern lanterns — for instead of horses and armies, it is all things and territories of the sea that you will command."

Barbarosa's relief was overpowering. His knees felt weaker than in any battle. Rather than being disgraced or killed, he had become the third ranking official of the most powerful empire on earth.

The Shadow of God had spoken.

Tunis city walls before Barbarosa. One reason that Muslim jails held few prisoners.

An Unarmed Moorish Merchant. The African Arabians were among the best horses in the world.

13

THE IONIAN CAMPAIGN

1536

From his position on the ground, the first thing the burly man heard when he recovered consciousness was, "You fought a good battle, flat headed one". Focusing uncertainly on the person who had spoken, he responded as clearly as his damaged mouth and poor command of the Turkish language permitted, "Fight because woman." Realizing that the murderous scimitar swinging just above his face could make his shoulders lonely for his head in an instant, his only move was a questioning look. It was answered with a nod. He carefully raised his head, spit out a tooth, lifted a broken arm with a good one, rolled to his knees and levered himself unsteadily erect.

Studying the man, probably a blacksmith, whose neck and head formed one continuous line from his massive shoulders, the swordsman swung the heavy sword back to give room and observed — this time in Greek, "You understand Turkish, but you sound like a wild pig running from dogs."

Now in his native Greek, the injured man answered, "I understand Turk talk better than I speak it." As he spoke, he reviewed the scene.

The tableau was simple enough. In addition to the swordsman — a man as large as himself — there was a Turkish sailor kneeling near the entry gate in front of four Janissaries. Another Turkish sailor, this one dead, was sprawled nearby, blood from his broken head soaking into the hard earth, his lowered trousers exposing his fundaments. Beside the body was an oak stave which the blacksmith recognized as his own. There was no one else in sight.

The swordsman spoke again, "Before you move further, brother, what are your intentions? Do you want more lessons in arms, or will you pledge to leave well enough alone?"

The sword was listening.

Avoiding a direct answer, the blacksmith asked, "Where are the woman and child?"

The swordsman spoke sharply in the direction of the house, "Woman, come care for your man!"

The door of the house swung open and a woman came out, stepping unafraid past the half naked corpse, followed by a boy of perhaps six. Other than a scratch on her cheek, disarranged hair, and a torn dress — which exposed the outer thigh of a leg longer than that of most men — she appeared unharmed. As tall as the tallest Janissary, she carried herself like a pacing tiger; her powerful stride across the yard invited an appraisal of her hard haunches as they fought the fabric of her light gown.

She was the largest well proportioned woman in the experience of the entire group — yet feminine. Lean, with an abdomen as flat as a Sipahi archer and shoulders suitable for a Greek discus thrower, her bare arms and partly open shirt displayed skin of pure Cathay silk. As striking as her size was her hair. Undone and hanging to her waist, it flamed like a Sicilian sunset, emphasizing eyes so blue as to appear translucent. With a sword and armor she could have been a leader of a Sabine phalanx— the mythical women warriors who withstood Rome for three campaigns.

Seeing her come out of the house, the injured man answered the swordsman's question "Aye, Turk, I'll give my pledge, but if you intend for her the same that he did," indicating the dead man, "you'll not be safe from my stave!"

The Turk nodded good naturedly; he appreciated a brave man. "She'll not be harmed." He took a handful of straw, wiped and sheathed his scimitar, and moved to seat himself on the low garden wall, casually turning his back on the pair as he did. With the concern of bridegroom welcoming a new bride, the Janissaries by the gate watched for him.

With the wide-eyed child close by her side, the woman seated the wounded man on a flat stone and inspected his bloody face. He paid little attention to her ministrations, concentrating on the events of the afternoon. He knew that the dead man with his parts exposed was the one he had caught trying to mount the woman, and that the prisoner squatting near the gate was the man who had been pinning her down.

He remembered charging the rapist with his oak stave, but there memory ceased. For the life of him he couldn't remember either this gray bearded man with the huge sword or the Janissaries. He shook his head and gave up trying the puzzle.

From her already ruined dress she made a temporary sling for the patient's arm, then addressed the boy. He picked up a water bucket and trotted away. Her speech caused the swordsman to turn back from his seat on the wall and inquiringly raise his bushy eyebrows.

The blacksmith, his head now clearing rapidly, realized that the language of the woman had not been understood. "Her speech comes from the tribes in England," he said. "Its called Celtic."

"Does she understand Turkish?"

She answered for herself in a clear, musical voice, surprisingly soft for one of her size, "Some. Better with Greek or Frank speaking."

The swordsman switched to Greek, "I have never seen hair more bright. Do all Celtics have such fire in their hair?"

Busy with her first aid, the woman answered economically in basic Greek, "No, but many."

After watching in silence for a few moments, the swordsman commented, "Your warrior won't need those teeth, and I'll have a ship's physician care for the arm."

She looked at the stranger with gratitude, "Arm will have no harm until set. He lose only front teeth. Thank you, stranger, you turn that sword flat. He is strong man, but foolish think he kill armed men."

Then she addressed her patient in a local dialect, "Had it not been for this man whose sword broke your arm and flattened your face, that coward," indicating the crouching prisoner, "would have killed you. After you split the head of the first animal he was about to run you through from behind when this big Turk jumped over the wall. The worthless dog dropped his pike and fell to his knees, in great fear. Then you went after this swordsman also, and he was kind enough not to kill you."

"So. The blow must have clouded my mind." The blacksmith spoke in question as much as in fact. Another tooth was located to be removed.

Impressed with this extravagant female, the swordsman interrupted their conversation, "When Caesar conquered Britain a thousand and half years ago, he wrote of tribes that painted themselves blue, but not of red hair."

The woman answered in the same bell-like voice, "Young Princess of Britain who will be Queen has red hair."

"Queen? Is she to marry her father or brother?"

The woman looked at him curiously, "She have no brother. When father King dies, she will be Queen. In Britain, woman may rule."[1]

The idea amused the man. It also touched some reservoir of approval. He could think of a half dozen women who had more sense and judgment than many princes. But still, on balance, the idea was preposterous. Would she keep a harem of males, he wanted to know.

The woman looked at him directly, almost in challenge, and shrugged her shoulders.

He continued, "I'd like to visit your country where everyone has red hair and women are Kings. Do all the women look like you?"

Again, that cool, appraising look, "Most more beautiful, few as tall. You wish to visit, I travel with you." Nodding in the direction of the black hulled galleys in the bay, she added, "I earn my passage." Her disclaimer of her own beauty was an attractive modesty — and inaccurate.

Even though close to his sixtieth birthday and somewhat slower in the foot-races of love, the swordsman felt a familiar surge and warmth — this one would invigorate the most discouraged appetite. He tried French. "What is your name, and how come you to Greece?"

She responded fluently. "I am named Margaret Bannock. I came with my father looking for special sheep in Persia. We got to the city of Yambol, five days up Hebrus river," she gestured in the direction of the Greek mainland, "before the fever killed him."

It was her turn to ask. "Please, your name?"

The big man, at ease as he studied her — much as one might look over a horse at sale — answered absently, "My name, tall woman, is Khizr, son of Yakub."

It was her turn to study him a moment, then she spoke as an equal, much as would any confident fighting man. "The great Turk who leads these ships is named for his red beard. Your beard is not red, but I think you are one of his Captains. They say some are as old as he is."

Ignoring the implied comment about his age, Barbarosa asked, "And the child?"

---

1.   This meeting occurred in 1536. At the time the claim to the throne of Elizabeth's older sister, Mary, appeared illegal, for Henry VIII's marriage to her mother had been declared invalid. Henry's only son, Edward, was not born until 1537.

"The boy is not mine." She indicated her patient. "He belongs to him."

The Janissaries stood attentively, patiently; they were accustomed to the Kapidan i derya's curiosity — endless conversations on tools, plants, craft items, food — strange things with strange people. They might be here all afternoon.

Barbarosa listened to her recital as he watched the play of muscles in the exposed satin flesh of her shoulder and thigh. He realized again how imposing she was — too promethean for Harem duty, too physically extravagant for the typical Turk.

But he was a Greek. And wouldn't be in Istanbul for a month yet.

Why not continue the discussion of Britain's royal succession on a sunny afternoon at sea?

Looking at him openly, frankly, she seemed to have read his mind and seemed not unpleased.

With an almost imperceptible hand motion, he beckoned the yellow booted Janissary squad leader. Nodding at the bound prisoner crouching by the wall, he ordered, "Iron that man and have him delivered to the city square this evening before prayers. Get the Greek with the broken arm to a physician. He is to be fed and brought to me tomorrow. The boy is to be given to the slave masters with instructions to hold him for my judgment in Istanbul."

Without looking at her, he continued, "The woman is to be delivered to my ship today and given quarters. She will need clothes. Allow her to bring what she wishes." Then to her, "These men will accompany and protect you. You are to do as they say instantly and without question."

He turned abruptly and set off rapidly down the stone street. Two Janissaries swung in behind him, easily keeping pace with their long strides, while the other two remained to carry out their instructions.

He didn't see her for three days.

On shipboard, she was given a small sleeping area adjoining the large room running the width of the galley stern just under the quarterdeck — the Admiral's quarters. Although alone, she was cared for and comfortable. She was brought her choice of fresh food. Her quarters were well aired and she could bathe simply by stepping outside to a lattice sheltered grating and asking for water. From somewhere above, a steady flood of cool sea water, pumped by unseen hands, cascaded through somewhat higher wooden baffles just above her head. The water could also be directed to clean the nearby protected bench that hung over the water, a private waste facility. Inside, there were books in Arabic and Latin, neither of which she could read, but in the afternoon and evenings she could listen to hours of stringed instruments from the forward part of the vessel — a daily indulgence of the men.

When Barbarosa finally came to her, it was in the afternoon of the first day at sea. He told her to undress, bathe, and stand before him naked in the sunshine that came in the high stern windows. He had already bathed and, without speaking, when she came to stand before him, he too stripped.

After studying her for several moments, he invited her to the low couch with a gesture.

She was without reserve or shyness. She now knew her master to be the Admiral-in-Chief of Turkey. With proper conduct she might turn her situation to advantage. She welcomed his embraces with willing abandon, at first anxious to please, soon more than pleased herself. Enjoying a rapid climax she could repeat indefinitely, she was enthusiastic and cooperative in every possible exercise of Venus. Given her choice of positions, she preferred to be on her hands and knees or bending over the chart table, an exercise he assured her was the classic Persian mantra, "Cow Position". But in whatever position, she was an explosive hunger that challenged him to do his best.

If truth were to be known, more than his best.

He had met his match in hand-to-hand combat.

Within the week, he viewed the daily assignation with lessening anticipation, and by the third week, their intercourse was almost entirely vocal. He assured himself that it was her fluency in French and English that interested him to the exclusion of other, more active pastimes. Or perhaps it was her knowledge of Henry VIII. Or her explanations of the differences between a Catholic Spain and a Protestant Church of England.

But for whatever reason, as time passed, he talked more and danced less.

He did learn enough English to discover how difficult the language was, acquired a few words of Celtic, some knowledge of sheep farming, and a good background on the quarrel between Henry VIII and The Pope. This educational process not only grew to occupy most of his time with the promethean redhead, it gave him an idea.

The Pope had sent ordinary priests and monks across the endless desert to the great Khan. The Venetians had sent the trader Polo to Cathay. Why not send this unusual woman to the ruler of her own land? She could carry a message of friendship for Protestant England and praises of the new Turkish fleet.

He told Piali that he intended to free her to carry messages to Britain.

Privately, Piali considered the idea a mild aberration, but did not find it necessary to say so. No fool he, without mentioning that his Admiral seemed to have suffered some loss of weight and spirit in past weeks, Piali observed, "The Prophet tells us the gift of freedom earns merit!"

Barbarosa felt that Piali was a good man to have along; wise, agreeable — a man of sagacious judgment.

When they arrived in Istanbul, he charged a Genoan trader with her transportation to Marseilles. She agreed to keep her hair coiled and to wear enclosing robes and veil as she traveled. He placed in her girdle enough gold to get her to England and to buy a small flock of sheep once she arrived, smiling at the thought of anyone attempting to take the gold by force. He also charged her with delivering a document, "To His Majesty, Henry, the Ruler of England and the Western Sea," describing the power and invincibility of the new Turkish fleet and assuring Henry that Suleiman, God's Representative on Earth, would look with favor on any proposal that discomfited Spain.[1]

Her erstwhile protector, who did prove to be a blacksmith, had been delivered to Barbarosa the day after their initial introduction, and the Admiral, busy with the details of preparing for departure, provided a swift solution.

He looked up at the muscular figure — arm splinted, clothes clean and repaired from the previous day — and he complimented him, "We value and respect brave men. If you swear loyalty, there is a place for you in my fleet. Iron workers are always needed at sea and we can make a seaman of you, free to earn pay. Your child will be taken to Istanbul. If he is bright and healthy, he may enter a school for children."

"As a slave?"

"Yes, but not in the sense Christians think of slaves. He'll be educated

---

1.   Years later Elizabeth did in fact ask Suleiman for assistance against "that infamous idolater, Charles," and for some years England and Turkey were de facto allies.

to the level of his ability, and may personally serve the Sultan if he dem-
onstrates the quality and intelligence we demand. He'll be instructed in
The Faith of a True Believer. You'll not see him again."

"The woman?"

"She has chosen to come with me. I shall see that she is cared for."
Barbarosa looked at the man appraisingly, "The decision to join is yours,
but it must be made this morning."

"If I refuse?"

"Unless you can pay tribute, you will be chained to one of those oars."

The man shrugged. "I accept." He added, "May I ask one more question?"

"Yes."

"What happened to the mangy dog that you took? I should like to
meet him."

"Then you will have to join the devil in hell. He was beheaded last
night. When a city surrenders, I permit my men neither rape nor robbery."

B arbarosa's acquaintance with the Scottish giantess came about as a
result of a major sea campaign that had begun, as do most human
affairs, with only the dimmest of premonition — in this case a bit
of gossip.

He had heard the rumor first from Boaz a year a half earlier. "That
blonde Russian bed-companion, the one the Sultan went so far as to
actually marry, has put a curse on him. He is said to restrict himself entirely to her and, like a young boy in love, writes poems to her signed
Muhubbi — affectionate one. He has permitted her to move into the
inner palace and has sent his first wife, Gulbehar, to live with his mother
in Adrianople. I'm convinced that she makes many of his decisions. I
know that she told one of the eunuchs, 'I live with the Sultan, and make
him do what I want'. That's a statement that would cost any other woman
a trip to the bottom of the Marmara."[1]

"Is this the one known by the Europeans as Roxelana?"

---

1.   The preferred method of execution of Harem women was to drown them in a
      weighted bag.

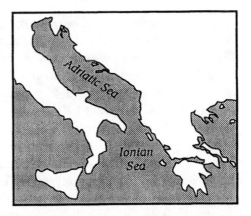

"Yes. She was a slave girl bought in the Caucasus." Boaz shifted his position on the low couch restlessly, angered at the encroachment of Harem influence on a government of which he was proud and in which he had served his life. "The Sultan's affliction will damage the Empire. For example, she is doing her best to undermine Ibrahim, for she sees him as an enemy of that oldest son of hers, Selim. She wants Rustem, who married her daughter, to replace Ibrahim as Grand Vizier."

"Why does she think Ibrahim is hostile?"

"Ibrahim is known to have said that her son is so unlike the Ottoman line that there is doubt about who fathered him. Although its true that the boy is short and fat with features as oriental as the Khan, Ibrahim is a fool to let his opinions be known. Her hostility is not to be undervalued. Of course, most of what I repeat about her is gossip. But I believe it to be reliable. The woman is said to be entertaining, good-natured. The name chosen for her, Hurrem — laughing one — fits her. But I'm convinced that when she sings to Suleiman through his one-eyed friend, she hums a tune of murder. The Sultan has been nearly twenty years on the throne and time gives birth to fear. No longer the open, brave young horseman, he worries about his wealth, health, and enemies. He doesn't smile and few jokes are dared in his presence. His ministers make decisions with guesses as to his mood rather than with the facts at hand."

Barbarosa observed, "I have heard that Ibrahim has assumed great pomp and display. He is reputed to be the richest man in the Empire. The great home he is building in the Old City is costly."

"True," said Boaz, "And he likes to be recognized for his power. In this last campaign in Persia it was nearly three months before Suleiman joined him. During that time he signed his name Seraskei, Commander-In-Chief, and some of the documents reached Istanbul. This is not uncommon in war when the Sultan himself is not present, but when Ibrahim's intent is embroidered, his conduct can lead to suspicion, and Hurrem is just the one to water such worry in the garden of the Sultan's fear.

"To tell the truth, Ibrahim does suffer from the corruption of power. Like pestilence, power becomes the curse of whatever it touches. Successful generals acquire imperial guards, rich merchants wear silk, royal treasurers lounge beside cool fountains and enjoy the most tender virgins, mullahs who attract followers tend to hear messages directly from God, and physicians who achieve cures tend to establish hospitals that serve rich patients. Like the grave, power is eternally grasping, and Ibrahim is little different in that respect.

"In addition, Ibrahim's old enemy, Iskender Chelebi, the chief treasurer — I know you remember the jackal from your early shipbuilding — swore before his execution for embezzlement a few weeks ago that Ibrahim was disloyal to Suleiman.

"An oath before death?"

"Yes!"

"Was any of it true?"

"I don't believe for a moment," said Boaz, "that Ibrahim was disloyal. Proud, haughty, in love with wealth and display — but disloyal, never. However, the Sultan is becoming more religious, and such an oath at death carries a lot of weight."

"What will happen to Ibrahim, and how soon?" asked Barbarosa.

"I don't know. I used to think a forced retirement to the Caucasus. Its well known that while they were still young and perhaps in love, Suleiman promised Ibrahim he would never be put down. But now I predict the silken cord of the mutes within the year."

Boaz was to miss his forecast by only a few months, and blood stains on the walls of the Sultan's apartment after Ibrahim spent the night there indicated the use of knives. As Boaz had forecast, Rustem did become Grand Vizier, although he found it best to wait for a few years while two successive incompetents temporarily filled the post. Years later he was to repay Roxelana's support by brainstorming the successful campaign which would permit her son Selim to inherit the throne.[1]

With Ibrahim's death, the pain in losing a man whom he had come to enjoy and respect was tempered by a change in Ottoman foreign policy

---

1. Rustem was to prove able, but exceedingly venal. Upon his death he left an estate of 815 farms, 47 water-mills, 1700 household slaves, 600 expensive copies of the Koran, and more than 2,000,000 gold ducats in his strong box.

that Barbarosa had long advocated. Ibrahim had leaned toward accommodation with the Venetians; Barbarosa insisted that Turkey must have a network of galley bases.

A war galley lived at the end of a short umbilical. Not only did weather and primitive navigation make these fragile craft reluctant to leave sight of land, but time spent at sea was constrained by the food and water needs of several hundred men in a small, light ship.[1] Bases should be within fifty miles or so of one another — certainly no more than a hundred.

For centuries Venice had controlled the Adriatic and Ionian with ports either owned outright or held in tribute. These properties provided resources and manpower — "Venetian fir" from the Balkans was sold to all comers, including Turkey — and many Venetian trading ships were manned with paid professionals recruited from the still medieval cities and primitive countryside along the coasts.

Forty years earlier Turkey had expanded in Greece and taken Venetian bases such as Modon and Coron. But the campaign was largely by land. Now, with Ibrahim gone and a temporary Grand Vizier in office who had little time for affairs of state,[2] Barbarosa went to the Sultan with his ideas about Turkish expansion by sea — a strategy that would require no army beyond a few siege guns and Janissaries.

Coincidentally, a few foolhardy Venetian raiders strengthened his hand by taking ten Turkish cargo vessels in one raid almost within sight of Lesbos, and a month later by capturing a ship owned by the Sublime Porte which was not only carrying a considerable cargo belonging to speculators in the Harem, but the Bey of Gallipoli. Once the attackers discovered the ownership of the vessel and the identity of the passenger, they burned the ship and killed everyone but a young boy who escaped by hiding on a piece of driftwood.

The murder of the Bey demanded revenge. Moreover, the ladies of the

---

1.   The weekly ration for each seaman in the 16th century British navy, while not always met, was officially 7 gallons of beer, 28 ounces of rum, 1/2 gallon of water (to include washing of self) 5 pounds of salt beef, 1 pound of salt pork, 2 pounds of fish, 2 pounds of cheese or butter, 2 pounds of chick peas, 7 pounds of bread or 5 of biscuit. The Turkish menu differed, but even without alcohol, total amounts must have been similar.

2.   The Vizier who was in office for a short time after Ibrahim, fathered one hundred and forty recognized children during his lifetime.

Harem whose investment had gone up in Venetian smoke were in a position to insure that their complaints were heard at the highest level.

Lufti Pasha, the senior field commander, insisted that he could take Corfu, the Venetian stronghold at the entrance of the Adriatic, with only ten thousand men and medium guns. Although the Sultan did not accompany the expedition, Lufti's idea was approved and Barbarosa's fleet delivered the soldiers and guns. The attack stalled and before Lufti could get more ambitious plans underway, the Sultan himself arrived, took one look and announced, "This place is not worth the life of one soldier of mine". Under fire, the army escaped the island over a bridge of lashed pontoons and galleys — a superb piece of seamanship that impressed the Sultan. He gave Barbarosa permission to conduct his own kind of war at sea.

With six thousand assault soldiers and ninety war galleys — plus a squadron of siege guns on special barges — a force that was becoming his trademark — Barbarosa spent the rest of the summer persuading islands and cities in the Eastern Mediterranean to transfer their loyalty to Turkey and to make generous contributions to the Ottoman treasury. Those defenders who asked for terms and swore oaths of allegiance were permitted to keep their land and they were not plundered — only tributes and annual contributions to the Ottoman treasury were required. However, any island or port which offered resistance was sacked, leaving only enough workers and farmers to feed the people under the guidance of Turkish officials.

The Divan's formal report to the Sultan was to say, "Throughout the chain of Venetian islands that hangs in the Sea like a loose sash before the waist of your Empire, this great Sword of Islam has taken islands and cities, leveled defenses, removed valuables, and brought with him huge numbers of Christians suitable for slavery."

Now, with the season near end, his ships surging homeward on a cool and steady northwest wind and the tall Scotswoman for intellectual stimulation, Barbarosa indulged himself in self satisfaction. He was vaguely ashamed of his un-Islamic pride, but he couldn't deny himself pleasure. At an age when few men could — or would — struggle with the hardships of shipboard life, he was returning triumphant and rich from an adventure of his own design, a commander of the greatest fleet in the world.

In a thinly disguised plea for praise, he asked Piali to review the summer's totals again.

Suleiman's Tugra (signature) done in blue and gold; a carved stamp, traditional from the time of Sultan Murad in the 13th century, who could not write.

Pinpricking him a bit, Piali recited, "Here, o keeper of the mighty red-haired mare, is the list that will be presented to the Chamberlain at the Outer Wall. Since Corfu, twelve islands have been incorporated outright as Turkish territory and thirteen more accepted as tributaries paying annual fees. We have secured the coast from Corfu past the Gulf of Corinth, well into the Aegean. We passed on only two ports, Nauplia and Malvasia, that were not worth the cost and time of battering down.[1] There are sixteen thousand slaves along with treasure valued at more than a half million gold sultanins. From your share alone, you can afford to build a public bath as great as any in The City."

The arrival of Barbarosa in Istanbul this time brought no wild animals to catch attention, rather the victory parade in the hippodrome was noted by the quality and quantity of prisoners. One group in particular was remarked by the Genoan trade representative, "I count at least five hundred of those young boys in tight-fitting red velvet shorts, each carrying a purse of gold. There is a sight exceedingly dear to Turkish hearts!"

"You mean the gold?"

"Foolish one; what Turk would prefer Gold to those tight shorts?"

His companion waxed philosophical. "One must admit that vices of the Turks are more pleasant that those of their predecessors in this remarkable city. Here, on this ancient racetrack a thousand years ago, Justinian raised the sport of horse racing to a compulsion of the people. Gambling and wild public sentiment made the teams of drivers state heroes. Greeks being Greeks, it wasn't long before some fed their horses substances that caused them to outperform themselves. Eventually, by

---

1.   The Turks apparently only recorded those places taken that they planned to fortify. Venetian records claim eighty islands or ports ravished during the campaign.

Imperial order, animals in every race had to be tested — which was done
by tasting the droppings of the winners.

"Here, where the Turks eat young boys, the Christians used to eat shit."[1]

.⌣

A week later came the victory feast. One hundred guests, including
foreign ambassadors, were invited, and Barbarosa promised a truly
unique African dinner in the Arab style. In a very rare appearance,
the Sultan himself agreed to attend the opening part of the evening.

The food was served in series: with honey cakes and unleavened bread
came soups of lentils and lamb thickened with flour, plus a pale amber
liquid with floating dried mushrooms and tiny pastries. Each soup bowl
was accompanied by pistachios, almonds, figs, walnuts, cashews and pine
nuts — a combination widely believed to be an aphrodisiac.

In respect for the Sultan's presence, no wine was in evidence; only tea,
juices and the mildly disapproved coffee.[2]

The soup bowls were replaced with fruit: iced melons, peeled sweet
oranges, pre-sectioned pomegranates, grapes of two colors, and the soft
banana of western Africa. One strange fruit — a red, thin skinned, juicy
sphere, hardly sweet, to be eaten in the hand as one would an apple —
brought the host to his feet. With a flourish, Barbarosa gave a short speech
with the pedigree of this new arrival.

The musicians paused as he commenced. "May you all enjoy the product of Christian seamen such as the Genoan Colombo, who brought this
lovely fruit from the New World. We have grown and enjoyed it in Africa
for twenty years now, but the Spanish fear it as poisonous. The Franks,
as different from the Spaniards in food as in ambition — claim that it
will stimulate men and greatly excite women for Persian mantra exercises. They call it the 'love apple'. In Italy, cultivating this fruit has become a mad preoccupation, leading to speculation and gambling. For-
tunes are being won and lost."

1.   "Tasters of the Dung" became a profession in Constantinople, complete with its
     own Guild.
2.   Coffee had been traded in Turkey for some time, but was just then becoming popu-
     lar. It was still eyed with disapproval by religious leaders to whom anything that had
     not been drunk by The Prophet was suspect — if not actually sinful. It was also
     expensive.

Bastinado in action.

He offered to give some of the tomato's seeds to any who wished either to test the French theory or to get rich in Italy. "Its growing season is short. It comes from a vine and can be grown indoors if sun can be found a few hours a day."

Large dishes of vegetables — leeks, tiny sweet onions, lettuce, boiled greens, hearts of palm, beans, peas of two kinds, and a dish of sugar paste were served Arab style — to be eaten with the hands. Sticky rice balls invited dipping into sugar, saffron, cinnamon, pepper, or ground cloves. Another gesture for Arab visitors was a traditional food of the desert, dried locusts. Some were crisp and whole to be dipped in a honeyed sauce. Others were powdered into a paste of soured camel milk curds.

Ottoman Turks, whose agriculture, perhaps the greatest in the world, was the basis of an epicurean food tradition, were more curious than impressed.

Bowls of warm rose water followed for hands in anticipation of the meats — young beef cut small and cooked on skewers with peppers and bits of dried apples, with spiced roast goat, antelope, whole lambs hot from the pits with crackling skins, and mutton baked in the Jewish style, salted and soaked in water to remove the blood. With the meats came geese and swan cooked whole and golden chicken lightly crusted by the oven.

For those thinking of the sea there were two kinds of small fish, fried whole and covered with a sauce made of eggs and goat's milk, and sea turtle brought from the distant Indian ocean.[1]

In an hour the Sultan, a light eater, rose. The entire group instantly quieted.

He spoke to Barbarosa, "Hayreddin, you are a treasure. Not only do you enrich my treasury and extend the borders of my Empire at sea, you carry the finest traditions of The Prophet. I am moved to transfer the captured islands to your authority. Henceforth, as Beylerbey of the Sea, you will now govern all islands within the seas owned or paying tribute; and, to show my gratitude, you will receive an additional annual stipend of 100,000 aspers."

Barbarosa inclined his head in appreciation, "Lord of the Two Worlds, the increase in my authority is an honor I shall do my best to discharge." Then he added, "I would however, be willing to forego the gold. Like a merchant in your great bazaar, may I strike a bargain with you?"

The Sultan sent him a questioning look, and the listening diners froze in silence, but Barbarosa hurried on. "In exchange for the money, I will take fifty of the new twenty-pounder culverins."

Suleiman answered, with a perfectly straight face, "Few of my officials buy their own guns; you are unique. However, since we are striking a bargain, for that price I can offer only forty."

It seemed that the Sultan was making a joke.

Barbarosa inclined his head in acceptance, "Shadow of the Sun, I accept."

With the Sultan's departure, gluttony became the order of the day. Ices were repeated and a flagon of a thin, sharp wine, much like the resinous Greek wines, was set every few places for the Algerians — heavier date and honey wines for others. Although a forbidden pleasure, few denied themselves.

The tempo of the music changed, and semi-naked, barefoot dancers — one for every two guests — stormed into the room to whirl in sinuous circuits before the seated diners. Moving from man to man, each

---

1. While many people have subsisted on its fish, in comparison with other oceans and seas, the Mediterranean has always been poor in marine life. Most Turkish fish came from the Black Sea.

dancer would pause and kneel on the carpet immediately before a seated diner, hold him in close eye contact — her snakelike torso moving hypnotically — until he nodded or gave a sign of approval, whereupon she would leap up, turn her back and bend over only inches from his face, rapidly rotate herself in inducement, until sud-

Ibrahim's house today.

denly, at the sharp rise of the horns and crack of drums, she would snap herself back and upward toward him in a thrusting challenge — a demand which penetrated the consciousness of even those taken prisoner by wine.

These exercises made a deep impression on Ochiali. Although the dancers were modeled on the full-figured Egyptian ideal — ordinarily not his preference — he asked for and was awarded one of the young ladies. He left early.

Eventually, most of the guests became either groggy or comatose. Several had to disgorge their overload of wine and food, and Barbarosa received promises of undying friendship from at least a half dozen dignitaries.

Boaz practiced his typical restraint, eating and drinking lightly. Thinking to himself of his friend the Agha, to whom he had given the desert dancer — now on border duty with the Sipahis somewhere in Persia — he resolved to write him that "the Pirate from Lesbos" was not only a great galley builder, and a stunningly successful war commander, he was a social success of the first order.

High ranking Ottoman officials.

14

PREVESA

1538

Venice had few or no land-based resources. Alone among Mediterranean powers, this island City/State had to have access to the sea over which her life-blood of trade flowed. When Venetian leaders assessed the damage wrought by Barbarosa's sweep of the Ionian and Adriatic, their conclusions were grim: either accept losses and negotiate a subservient treaty — or throw down the gauntlet.

Their decision was to project Barbarosa to his greatest victory.

The debate in the Venetian senate was spirited; hot-heads wanted war; cooler heads argued for a compromise that would retain their trade privileges. The elderly Doge, Gritti, cautioned his fellow senators, "I fear we enter a course from which we cannot escape. The Turk commands much of the world, his strength is the strength of many nations, his intentions resolute, and his bravery unquestioned. To engage this great empire with the sword is to risk all."[1]

Proudly — and rightfully — known as the "Bride of The Sea", Venice had a noble tradition to uphold. Hanging over the debate was a thousand years of naval dominance in the Eastern Mediterranean. The hot heads wanted to know who these heathen Asian horsemen were to challenge the greatest shipbuilding power in the Mediterranean? They argued with the vigorous personal pride of men who demanded satisfaction with swords for small social slights; men who swore generations of revenge for family quarrels.

The Republic declared war.

In the winter of 1537, emissaries proposing an alliance and the cre-

---

1. Gritti is quoted verbatim.

Gritti, Doge of Venice. The office approximated Prime Minister.

ation of a great war fleet were sent to Charles, Genoa, and the Pope. (For once the bellicose Knights either were not asked or were committed to other enterprises) Neither Spain nor Rome thought of Venice as a Good Neighbor nor was sea trade an overriding necessity for them, but the Pope would attack Islam on any pretext — sometimes none — and Charles had several reasons of his own. As the self appointed Sword of Jesus, he believed from the bottom of his heart that he was Christ's most valuable soldier — with a soldier's duty. Muslim North Africa was supporting the feared Morisco minority within Spain. Turkish corsairs were drawing a stream of a gold from Spain's trade arteries in the Western Mediterranean. Further, as the Hapsburg Emperor of the Holy Roman Empire, Charles had been personally embarrassed by the recent disgrace of an army paid with Spanish gold and commanded by a relative. A Hapsburg Count Katzianer, one of the veterans of Vienna (and consequently overrated) had led an Austrian army to the Turkish Danube where a smaller Turkish force inflicted an ignominious defeat in a battle that came to be known as the "Rout of Valpo".

The Count himself fled in such a hurry that his tent, complete with silver set for dinner, was captured. In recognition of his performance, the Turks, smiling, named a monstrous bronze cannon acquired in Austria and never fired, "The Katzianer".

A motivated Charles contributed the majority of ships as well as nominating and paying for the commander — Andrea Doria. Genoa and the Papal states willingly contributed a few ships, the German states of the Holy Roman Empire contributed men-at-arms, and when the Venetian quota of ships was added, the "Holy League" — as it named itself — rounded out at one hundred and fifty war ships carrying twelve thousand soldiers.

Significantly, included in this fleet was a squadron of twenty sailing galleons mounting nearly five hundred heavy guns.[1] While galleys were cheaper, far more maneuverable and, considering Mediterranean weather, more reliable than a heavy sailing vessel, where the fire power of a galleon could be brought to bear, a galley was hopelessly outclassed. A galley's highest purpose was to place fighting men on an enemy decks. To do so, it must ram and engage. Against sailing galleons several times their size, this was nearly impossible. Even if the relatively light galley could manage to penetrate the storm of iron balls that dozens of heavy guns could raise, boarders from a low galley could scale a galleon's twenty and thirty foot oak sides only with the greatest difficulty.

While engagements between sailed galleons and rowed galleys were not unheard of, twenty galleons operating as a unit meant that the coming battle was to be a major test of a new Mediterranean strategy. With the championship of the Mediterranean at stake, the test was to be conducted by the two tigers of the sea, Condottieri Doria and Pirate Barbarosa, opponents for more than twenty years.

In Istanbul, with only one hundred and thirty ships immediately available — some thirty of which were so light they could only be marginally classed as war-galleys — the Turks were outnumbered three to two in ship tonnage and, because of the galleons, three to one in fire power. Barbarosa accepted these odds but, as the weaker of the two, needed to find favorable ground. He also needed to dictate tactics.

A bit more than halfway up the western coast of Greece was the Gulf of Ambracia, a secure anchorage whose only entrance was commanded by the fortified Turkish town of Prevesa. Ships entering the Gulf had to follow in line for three miles through a narrow channel shallowed at one point to eight feet by a sand bar — all within reach of Prevesa's guns.[2] Protected from weather, with stores and water easily at hand, once anchored there, Ambracia was a position from which Barbarosa could accept or refuse battle at his pleasure.

It was also nearly a thousand miles from Istanbul and less than a hundred miles from Corfu — where the Christians were assembling.

---

1.   One authority gives the Christian fleet total as 2500 cannons — but this must have included mankillers and small swivels.

2.   A war galley drew less than eight feet, a galleon up to twenty.

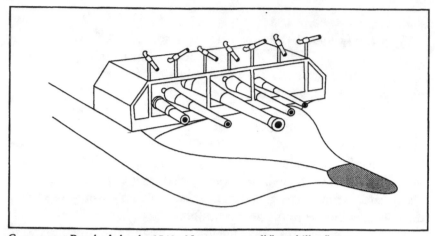

Cannons on Rambade by the 1540s. Note seven small "mankillers" on top.

Boaz questioned that difficulty. "Can't he block you from entering?"

"He could. But doldrums curse the lower Adriatic this time of year, and I doubt his galleons will have enough wind for another few weeks. He won't fight without them. Nor will he have knowledge of my intentions."

"You can sneak in right under his armpit?"

"You have the idea." He went on to explain, "In Ambracia, we will have a safe perch from which we can strike, one on which we can sit as long as necessary. The day is coming when heavy galleons will drive galleys from the sea — even now, with only a few round ships Doria would take our measure if I should engage in a conventional battle. But I don't plan to offer him that benefit. Most of his fleet are galleys and cannot long remain at sea. He can beach a bit to rest, but there will be no supplies available. If we refuse to engage he will starve out in only a few weeks. When that happens, he will have to lift his guard and retreat — and when he does he will be in a vulnerable position. If our timing is right, we can strike with great advantage. Let me explain his problem a bit.

"A galley is vulnerable on its sides where it can be rammed. For fighting a fleet action, galleys must be in line abreast where they can protect one another. If an upcoming battle is possible at any time, Doria must constantly maintain this formation — a difficult and wearying task —

and if he departs, he will have to break his formation, making himself vulnerable.

"Once Doria takes a position to guard me, if I have sufficient patience, sooner or later opportunity will be on the table for me to seize."

"From your description it sounds like the old Persian folk tale of having a tiger by the tail. Once he grasps, he can't let go."

"Again, you have the idea. The galleons, however, are a different story and, frankly, I don't know just how much damage we can inflict on them. One thing seems certain; we'll have to catch them by themselves or separate them from the galleys, and we'll need a calm day. While I can generally predict weather a bit in advance, I don't have the power to arrange it. We'll just have to wait.

"With your long sense of history, you must remember that the battle of Actium in this same Gulf set the course of Roman power for two centuries. When Antony and his favorite reis, Cleopatra, were destroyed by Augustus Octavius, it set the winner on a course from which he became Rome's greatest Caesar. While I am no Caesar, or can hardly expect advancement beyond my present eminence, forces of history play here also. This battle may set the course of Turkish fleets for another century."

Boaz nodded, but in his heart he was uncertain. "Khizr, for once I am willing to say In'shallah, and mean it! If God wills, we shall win."

Despite his confidence, before he departed, Barbarosa insured that instructions on the discharge of his estate were in Boaz's hands. Since he was somewhat unique among Ottoman officials in that he was not a slave of the Sultan, Barbarosa's wealth would not automatically revert to the royal treasury. It was his to dispense as he saw fit — and Boaz was entrusted with that duty.[1]

Against his own better judgment, he took aboard Hurrem's son-in-la, Sinan Pasha. He was a General[2] who had fought well in Hungary on two campaigns with Suleiman, and had requested a command. Where matters of the sea were concerned, his conversation replaced intelligence, but there was no easy way to refuse him, and Barbarosa had neither the time nor the inclination to argue.

---

1. Everyone drawn from devirsme ranks — most of the governing officials in Turkey — were legally slaves of the Sultan and their property reverted to him upon death.

2. Sea warfare was considered little different than land. Most Admirals of the time — including Doria — learned their trade on land.

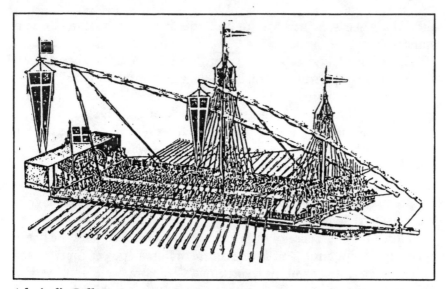

Admiral's Galley, of the type used by Andrea Doria.

When the sun greeted the Golden Horn on the 24th of August, the fleet had disappeared into the mists of the Marmara. Avoiding land to keep his destination secret, favored by wind, and driving his ships twenty-four hours a day, Barbarosa made the nine hundred mile trip to history in twelve days.

Enroute, Dragut questioned him along the same lines as Boaz. "Do you have some magic scheme stored in that gray beard of yours to deal with those guns?"

Barbarosa expanded on the explanation he had given Boaz, "Sooner or later, Doria will have to lift his guard. From time to time we'll move out of the passage and wait under Prevesa's guns, but we won't move unless he breaks his formation, or the weather favors us with no wind. He will have to be constantly prepared. Hopefully, after some days of this, he can be enticed to separate his round ships from his long ships. When that occurs, thirty of our best ships will keep the galleons busy. Thanks to the Sultan at my banquet last year, we'll have a twenty pound culverin on each ship — more distance and accuracy than the Christians expect."

He described his modification plans for the selected ships, "We'll remove the masts and rams from a few of the best ships. No higher than six feet above the water, they'll be poor targets. Like wolves baiting bear, they'll be wounded, but without rambades they'll be hard to hit and, anyway, if they keep those round ships away from the galley battle, their job will be done."

"Enough wind to move the galleons would be fatal."

"An understatement friend, but in Ambracia we have a place to wait until either God decides to withdraw the wind or Doria has to break his formation to relieve his galleys."

South of Prevesa, just out of range of the fortress guns, Demata bay — more correctly a straight open on both ends — was bordered on the east by the mainland and on the west by the long, hilly island of Levkas. There, four days after the Turks had reached safety in Ambracia, one hundred and thirty five Christian war galleys and twenty galleons arrived and settled in for what turned out to be a long wait.

Within easy inspection of a long glass, the Christian fleet was impressive.

Yet not all bad.

Some of the galleys, Doria's personal flagship among them, employed as many as seven men per oar — a cumbersome and unproductive technique in combat.[1] The sailing ships, once rationed of wind by the Levkas hills, moved awkwardly. Communications seemed to be poor between various elements of the fleet. Dragut observed, "When engaged, that herd of goats won't understand one another. I'll bet a trained falcon they won't be able to maintain safe paths of fire and, if divided, won't be able to regroup."

There was plenty of time for evaluation, and it was to be followed by boredom, for a seemingly permanent peace set in. As each succeeding sunset released another day into eternity, patience demanded its due in increasingly large amounts — in both fleets.

The Christians suffered most. The season was late, inviting bad weather from the northwest into the open throat of Demata bay, and the crowded population on their galleys consumed stores at a prodigious rate. Each day brought the galleys closer to their logistical limits, and fed the inherent conflicts within the alliance.

At the root of League differences were national priorities. Spain, essentially a continental power, was reluctant to risk much in order to pull

---

1. With so many men side by side, the arc of the loom required the men towards the end to walk several steps with each stroke which was tiring and produced little thrust.

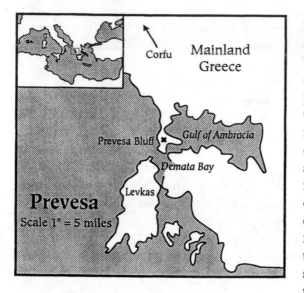

Venetian chestnuts out of the fire. The distrust between the Venetians and the Spanish was palpable. Between Genoa and Venice the residue of centuries of competition — occasionally war — nourished a long-held cancer. The German mercenaries preferred to fight on land rather than sea. Doria owned some of the galleys personally and was not likely to take any unnecessary risks with them — a fact that hardly endeared him to the others.[1]

Nor were things in the Turkish fleet all sweetness and light. The Corsairs, among whom patience and deception were habit, had no objection to waiting, but the "Old" Captains, burdened with a heritage of aggression as well as the Islamic bellicose concept of masculinity, felt differently. To hide behind Prevesa's guns was distasteful, cowardly.

Chief among the dissidents was Sinan Pasha. He argued that it was only a matter of time before the thousands of soldiers that could be seen eating and drinking wine[2] every day on the Christian ships would assault Prevesa. He wanted to move cannons to the narrow neck on the southern side of the channel where he could drive the Christians away from the beach. Barbarosa believed, however, that Doria would not risk any sizable number of men ashore in uncertain autumn weather with a fierce enemy fleet waiting to pounce on their only escape. And anything less than an all-out attack by thousands of men and siege guns could be beaten back by Prevesa's defenses.

---

1.   There were eight Genoan galleys which were all Doria's personal property, leased by Spain for 5,000 Spanish ducats a month each. If one was lost, its lease terminated.

2.   When it sailed against England in 1588, the Spanish Armada carried 14,000 pipes (barrels) of wine and only 11,000 pipes of water.

Barbarosa tried to explain that there was nothing to be gained by driving the enemy further to sea. "Its to our advantage to keep him on our backs. He has to constantly maintain an order of battle, even when at anchor. He has no place to replenish stores and water. Every day shifts the balance in our favor." He added a homily. "Haste is from the devil, patience is from God. Invest a day in hope, a week in prayer."

Neither philosophy nor reason swayed Sinan. Like many emotional, egotistical men, he used the Koran as his rationale. "God said to Mohammed, 'As for the infidels, strike off their heads, maim their fingers. The head of an opponent is better than the choicest camel in Arabia.' Will you argue with God?"

Barbarosa was willing to forego divine battle advice, but he finally gave way — whether to persuasion or to avoid insubordination is not clear.

Sinan chose a senior reis named Murad as his deputy, took the Janissaries and two dozen of the best heavy guns ashore, moved them across the southern peninsula and began to dig in.

Once ashore, his adventure lasted less than a day.

As soon as the sun peered through threadbare clouds the next morning, the Christian galleons unlimbered their broadsides, and within hours the beach was a tangle of ruined equipment and human casualties. Such heavy naval guns were an entirely new experience for the Old Turks, and they were helpless. They buried their dead, carried their wounded back to Prevesa, and the survivors quietly rejoined the fleet.

Barbarosa didn't criticize. He considered Sinan to be beyond persuasion, but he felt that the second in command, Murad, who was widely respected among his fellow Old Turks, was worth courting. He would save him — and his followers — for the future. So, resisting man's greatest pleasure, he avoided reminding Sinan of earlier advice. And he reminded his Corsair Captains, "Those who criticize do so to stroke their own feelings of inadequacy."

Sinan's disastrous venture receded into memory, and the waiting continued.[1]

The 25th of September was a rumpled and dreary day, careless about its appearance, reflecting a sullen sea. When the first Captains arrived at

---

1.   The Christians did put a limited force ashore to attack Prevesa and managed to support it for two days, but as Barbarosa had forecast, the fortress easily withstood.

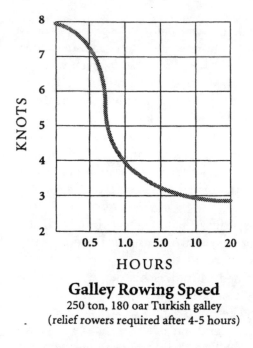

Galley Rowing Speed
250 ton, 180 oar Turkish galley
(relief rowers required after 4-5 hours)

the improvised command center on the Prevesa bluffs, Barbarosa, who had been there all night, greeted them with enthusiasm, "As soon as the rest of you lovers of sleep arise and rub dreams from their eyes, I have some orders for ship movements."

Within minutes they were assembled and he gave them his weather forecast for the following day. "The weather will be little changed during most of the day except for wind direction. It will be from the south until about noon, then will die out completely. Come night it will rise again, this time from the west and it may bring rain. No bora or anything like that, but enough to make Doria uneasy."

Before daylight the Turks were to exit the bay again and take up formation just outside the entrance bar. As before, they were to rest on their oars. "By now, Doria'll be hungry to get us away from Prevesa's guns. He has been in position a sufficient time to make him impatient for decision. He will draw off to entice us, and if we delay taking his bait, the wind will die, and he won't be able to keep his round ships and long ships together. When that happens, our stripped ships will keep the galleons busy while our main fleet deals with his galleys."

"What if the wind rises again from the south and his galleons can join his fleet?" one of the old Turks asked.

"If it happens before we engage, we'll retreat to our hiding place. But if the wind rises after we are engaged, prepare to join the Houris in heaven, my friend. You will earn your place in paradise."

When the nervous laughter subsided, one of the Old Turks, still dubious, raised a valid point. "What's to keep Doria from bringing his galleys back to rejoin the sailing ships once he sees they are in trouble?"

"The difficulty he would have in reestablishing a battle formation that includes the round ships. And he would have to fight his way through us if we stay close. He'll have no trouble convincing himself that the galleons are able to take care of themselves.

"We only need remember that where there is death, there is joy. Surely God will decide. We must fight this battle with every drop of strength and courage. Along those lines, I have an announcement. I want slaves to know that if we win, they will be free when we reach Istanbul. Those of you who own their slaves will be paid by the Sublime Porte. If anything goes wrong, I hereby pledge my own gold to this promise. I expect those who survive to carry out my oath."[1]

He concluded. "Prepare yourselves, for here in Demata Bay you will see some fighting no one has ever seen and may never see again."

At the next dawn the Turkish fleet was floating under Prevesa's guns, inhaling, by courtesy of a light south wind, the fragrance of enemy galleys long at sea. Two hours later, when the sun achieved adolescence, oars still hung slack in the water.

Doria's desire for action overcame his caution and, dangling bait before the fish, he began a slow fleet movement west past Cape Zuana, the northern point of Levkas. By the time he made his decision and the ungainly formation got underway, the breeze had became fitful and weak and the galleons began to lag behind. As the Christian formation began to lose its coherence, Barbarosa nodded to Piali, "Align the wings of the crescent. Follow the crosskissers. Remain out of cannon range."

The signal flags flew.

More than two hundred and fifty galleys, Christian and Muslim, danced a ponderous polka slowly west for an hour and then, to keep one end of his long line anchored to the land, Doria swung the dance south. As the last of his rowing galleys passed the headland on Cape Zuana, the wind died completely and his fleet was now separated; the galleons becalmed.

The curtain was ready to rise on the drama.

On the edge of the galleons, flying the flag of Venice, the largest was that of Admiral Alessandro Condalmiero, so grand it was known simply as the "Galleon of Venice."

---

1. Such promises were not uncommon, but they were sometimes abrogated, which may explain Barbarosa's charge to survivors.

The specially configured flotilla chose it for a test.

On signal the low galleys leaped forward in pairs, lashing white paths toward the enemy flagship. At four hundred yards, the leading two fired their heavy culverins and spun out of line for the next two who, in turn, yielded to two more. No harm was done but twenty five or so Turkish balls managed to paint impressive splashes and the Galleon couldn't warp around rapidly enough to bring its broadside to bear.

The feint had served its purpose. Head on, the Galleons were dangerous, but not necessarily fatal.

The galleys drew off. Circling recommenced.

Galleons and galleys were designed for entirely different tactics. Galleons fought in line astern[1] in order to maximize their collective broadside power. Galleys, whose few guns were bow-mounted, attacked in a broad line abreast hoping to break up the enemy formation and provide opportunity to ram and board.

But classic tactics were not to be seen today in Demata Bay. The Christian sailing galleons had no ability to move and Barbarosa discarded the tactical heritage of two thousand years. There was to be no attempt at ramming and boarding. The lithe, swift rowing galleys were to use only their bow guns and their ability to maneuver.[2]

Repositioned, the galleys exchanged a flurry of signals. Then, reaping the benefit of Barbarosa's endless hours of communication drills, like ants gathering from all sides on a dead donkey, they struck simultaneously, crossing one another's paths, firing at random targets and retreating before the confused and erratic Christian guns could be steadied.

And fortune smiled.

A ball from either the first or second ship of an attack pair — the gunners couldn't agree which — sliced off the mainmast of Condalmiero's galleon, leaving it in a tangle of rigging and wounded men. The ship was to survive the day but remain helpless.

With the damage to the Great Galleon, the floodgates of fortune opened for the Turks. Two more Christians were badly damaged, one helpless, the other sinking. A third one, on fire, struck its colors. At this rate, most

---

1.   From this tactic came the term "Ship of the Line".

2.   Turkish galleys, slightly faster than Christian, could quickly achieve eight knots, easily go astern, be turned in little over their own length, and by trailing oars could squeeze through a passage of less than thirty feet.

of the sailing ships would be crippled before dark, and the galleons improvised a defensive formation. One by one, with towing gigs, they warped their cumbersome ships into a rough square, abandoned individual fire, and lowered their cannon trajectories to skip across the surface in a broad pattern. Four dozen closely grouped stone and iron balls scaling along the surface of the water meant disaster to any galley caught in the path, and two galleys were sunk. Another lost most of a bank of oars and still another was holed above the water line.

From that time, the galleys, with only sporadic short dashes, remained just out of range, firing an occasional ball, until another bit of good fortune was presented to them. Forced to try and stretch the reach of their guns, the Christians increased their powder loads until a heavy pedrero aboard one of the Venetian galleons — probably a sixty-pounder by the size of the fireball — exploded and set its ship aflame. The galleon burned to the water.

After that the galleon-galley battle became a standoff.

Meanwhile, the main fleets continued to jockey for position in a dance down the west shore of Levkas,

Had Doria turned and rejoined his galleons, the afternoon may have ended differently, but even had he wished to do so, his unwieldy fleet formation and position would make it dauntingly difficult — as Barbarosa had predicted.

For four tense hours Barbarosa had followed his strategy of plodding cautiously after Doria.

Knowing intimately the capability of the rowing ships with which he had lived for a lifetime, and adding to it his evaluation and judgment of the enemy, Barbarosa revealed his genius late in the afternoon. In a move that is still regarded as the one of the brilliant decisions in the history of naval warfare, he struck the heart of Doria's formation. The line of ships visible to the Turks at the edge of the Christian formation appeared as though Doria was managing to keep the edge of his fleet fastened to the shore — making it difficult, dangerous, to attack. But taking the long chance that the visible Christian ships were a screen for disorder among those out of sight, Barbarosa drove the horns of his line in on the ends, and sent the main strength of his fleet directly into the Christian middle.

He was proven right. The main part of the Christian fleet had become a line of stragglers separated into different national elements strung out along twenty five miles of rocky coast.

In the short hour of daylight remaining before night and rain arrived, the Turks broke Doria's formation completely apart and destroyed or captured a half dozen galleys. Doria welcomed the wet night, extinguished his stern lanterns, and lashed the sea into foam toward Corfu and safety.

Back in Demata Bay, the punished and dispirited galleons harnessed the same wind to slog their way to open sea; their swift attackers acting as escorts, remaining out of range and wishing them Godspeed.

When the night brought rest, the Turks had lost twelve galleys outright and three to be abandoned; the Christians had lost eighteen galleys and six galleons either sunk or severely crippled. These totals were hardly impressive — a conclusive battle involving three hundred ships might well have resulted in a hundred losses — but the rout was complete. The heart of the Holy League had been pierced. Quarreling, it dissolved into its components.

Christianity was not to mount another major fleet challenge until Don John, the bastard son of Charles, opened fire at Lepanto more than thirty years later.

The superiority of the Turkish fleet and its commander glowed like the sun. Islam ruled the Mediterranean.

On his own deck, unable to remain the calm victor, Barbarosa danced a small jig. "When we get home, I plan to tell the Frank ambassador — who can be relied on to pass the message — that it was wise of Doria to extinguish his stern lanterns as he fled. Not only did we lose sight of him, but the Devil was waiting to welcome him to hell and couldn't find him either."

Word of Prevesa reached Suleiman at night by horse relays spurred from Greece to the steppes of Russia where he was visiting the Krim Khan. In one of the dramatic moments of his reign, the entire army was ordered to its feet to listen in silence as the messenger delivered, through relaying criers, his preposterous news. Fires were lit and the rest of the night spent in celebration and praise of God.

To rub salt in the wound, the eventual settlement terms required a half-million gold ducats from Venice for Turkey's expenses. With the Holy League dissolved, they had no option but to pay. The elderly Doge, Andrea Gritti, who had counseled against hostilities, refused either to sign the peace or vote for the money. Neither speaking nor eating, he fasted to death within days.

The Bride of the Sea had become a handmaiden to a nation of horsemen, existing on its Adriatic lagoon by Turkish sufferance.[1]

B arbarosa was now set for another triumphant return to Istanbul, this time with glory awarded to few men.

Using the excuse that it was late in the season and a poor time for multi-ship movement, he broke the fleet into components for the return home. The time had come, as he had told Boaz, "to deal with the old Turks", and he insured that most of the senior Turkish captains — without Sinan Pasha — were assigned to his section. As they visited friendly islands enroute, he arranged to have them eat in his company as often as they were ashore. The victory at Prevesa was the greatest maritime event in Turkish history, a major turning point in the struggle between Christianity and Islam, and these men had shared in it. They had come to respect his ability, and he only needed a small sign to know that he was loved.

The sign came in Yithion, a small Greek city on the Gulf of Messina.

That evening after prayers and dinner, Barbarosa announced a handsome reward for every reis, and the mood of the group, enhanced by the announcement and the wine, was boisterous. With late season blossoms gently shaking their heads in the light evening breeze, the moon bright on the sea, and Prevesa to warm them, the time was at hand for tales of war and other lies. Would the Turks' traditional reserve break down? Would they include him in their personal camaraderie?

He would see.

Murad, the second in command during Sinan Pasha's ill considered adventure on the beach at Prevesa, was a key to the hearts of the Old Turks. His approval would signal the group's decision.

Murad had a friend who was always to be found by his side. They were

---

1.   Spanish and Italian historians complain of Doria's "inexplicable failure" to regroup and come to the aid of Condalmiero — in some cases developing far-fetched theories, such as having Doria (who was a major Genoan investor) throw the battle as part of an agreement with Suleiman to leave the trading island of Khios in Genoan hands — or secret instructions from Charles to Doria to avoid battle. Such theories presuppose sophisticated communications, a lack of religious conviction, or a degree of conspiracy that simply didn't exist. The battle of Prevesa was won through Turkish skill, equipment, and by the brilliant and courageous strategy of Barbarosa.

Venetian Flag – Winged Lion.

a Damon and Pythias pair; unlike, but inseparable. Murad was a forceful, direct, man — in many ways similar to the Corsairs with whom Barbarosa had been dealing for thirty years. Self made, able, and blunt, Murad was the spokesman for the pair. Mustafa, while a man of unsurpassed physical strength and bravery, expressed himself poorly; consequently, he had little to say. He was frequently the butt of friendly practical jokes among their group, but all respected his courage and liked him for his constant good humor.

Barbarosa poured wine for his guests. By now the Turks had become used to his taste for the disapproved pleasure and had no objection to joining him. Nodding to Mustafa, he said to the group, "While Mustafa here is not what one would call handsome, he reminds me of my great brother Aruj. Brave in battle, exceptionally quick in wit, and," he paused for effect, "A man like a Persian Poet in his beauty of expression."

That outrageous description of Mustafa's eloquence set the tone, and Barbarosa turned to Murad. As a long-time friend, would he share with the group a bit of Mustafa's history? "Can you describe for us any of his adventures?"

Murad understood. He took up the challenge. "Mustafa and I have been together twenty years and during all that time he has kept his own counsel where his activities on the love platforms are concerned. But I do happen to know of a particular adventure he had."

Murad had the ball and the game was on.

He warmed to his subject. "Like Prevesa, which taught me more in two weeks than ten years at sea — one of Mustafa's lesser known experiences taught me a most valuable lesson — in this case about women."

He had the group's attention. "Our Mustafa has two outstanding qualities: he has no fear, and he dislikes speech. He speaks little, but acts. He goes directly to the attack, a true man of action. In the case of a particular woman for whom he had formed an affection, he knew not how to say what was on his mind and, since there was no opportunity for direct action, for months he wrestled with a powerful frustration.

"His desire became frantic; his hands trembled and his knees were weak when she passed him in the street. For him, her graceful movements were an excitement, her soft speech caresses, her glances invitations. But he could not find the sweet words with which to woo her.

"He wanted to cry to her, 'My longing is such that I walk naked before your house', or, 'When loves calls: listen. When it speaks: obey'. But when he reached for the words nothing but a croak came forth. He dreamed of her until she became both real and unreal. She was two people to him, an houri of his dreams, and at the same time a completely innocent being. He hardly knew where real life began and dreams ended."

He smiled at Mustafa in sympathy. The audience stirred in anticipation. Mustafa managed an embarrassed smile.

"The day came when he found reason to go to her home, and the house slave seated him in the main room. When his dream woman entered in a light gown, advancing across the room with her fluid, graceful movement, he could only hang his head in confusion. She stood so close before him he could sense the fragrance of her heavenly dampness. Her open, friendly manner was an invitation which drove him beyond the bounds of reason."

Murad paused, sipped his wine, and continued, "In innocence of the intensity of his desire, she stood before him, spread her arms in regret that she had not been there to greet him when he arrived. Transfixed with her fragrance and proximity, speechless, he unknowingly leaned toward her, his face on a level with her pleasure triangle.

Now Murad raised his volume and tempo of speech. "In his fevered imagination, she seemed to gently thrust her body toward him until less than an arm's length separated his face and her heaven. He could no longer resist. Unable to speak, the fighter in him won through, and in a sudden movement, the bravest of warriors abandoned caution. With a groan, he slid to his knees from the cushion and thrust his face against her fragrant mystery.

"She tried to draw back, but he held her against his face with his great hands. Unable to escape his fevered grasp, she was rigid, unmoving, perhaps frightened. Not knowing what to do and, reluctant to try to tear him away by force, like a young mother she gently placed her hand on his head as though to calm him, patiently waiting for him to come to his senses. But in that long moment, on its own initiative, her body relaxed and yielded slightly to his hunger, and she began to caress the sides of his head."

The entire group was in thrall, not a chuckle, not a sound — enjoying the erotic description — waiting for the denouement.

"She continued to give way. Without conscious decision she allowed her robe to open, exposing her perfumed garden to him. Feeling his great shoulders trembling, with a strangled sob she gave in completely, and rotated herself upward to give him access. He responded like a nursing calf, hungry, impatient. And almost immediately she began to reach her pleasure. Lightly, slowly, like the tenderest branch responding to the caress of the morning sun, he could feel the first flutter of her inner thighs. Then, as he continued his nursing gluttony, she began to gently roll her body like a dancer.

"In a rising explosion, her rapture began with a delicate shudder and ended minutes later in a frenzy. She swayed like a tree in strong wind, undulated like a fish swimming upstream, and finally, like a sail rattling in a storm, twitched and jerked, barely able to stand — dissolving from her knees to her shoulders.

"His ears were extended like sails before the wind. She grasped them with both hands. But, like the brave man he is, he hung in to his attack — refusing to leave his station!"

Murad shook his head in admiration at his friend's bravery.

"With her final throb, she cried aloud — a noise if heard out of the room unmistakable in its origin and meaning — and with a shudder like a campfire dog passing acacia thorns, he joined her with his own pleasure — in his pants!

"It was over. For a minute he was stunned. Then he suddenly realized where he was, and he came back to reality, so frightened that his balls drew up as though on disappearing strings. He struggled to his feet and looked toward the doorway.

"There was no one in sight.

"Still without speaking, she patted his beard dry, and taking his hands in hers, quickly squeezed them as though in thanks and turned to leave. As she reached the door, she finally whispered to him over her shoulder.

"My husband is in the garden. I will let him know you are here."

The laughter broke in waves — in which Mustafa himself joined, nodding as those closest to him pounded him on the back.

Murad had declared the old Turks members of the Barbarosa approval brotherhood.[1]

---

1. Mustafa's story may be doubted, but the final conversion of the "Old Turks" after Prevesa was very real .

Sultan Bayazid 1481-1512. The son of the great warrior Mehmed, his rule was marked by peaceful scholarship. He deserves credit for much stability of the Empire after Mehmed's expansionism. He attempted to create a Turkish navy and for a while had some success. But by the time his son Selim had overthrown him, land warfare was again the sole preoccupation of The Empire's fighting men.

15

LA BELLA

1542

Perhaps a third of the distance up the Dalmatian coast of the
Adriatic, the fortress of Castelnuovo dominated a large bay between Albania and Montenegro,[1] providing valuable support for
trade and trade shipping, as well as a base for war galleys. An
ancient structure, since the days of Bayazid it had been a Turkish possession and, since Turkey controlled the nearby Albanian and Macedonian
hinterland and could resupply it easily, it had been only lightly garri-
soned. Returning from Prevesa, spoiling for revenge, the Holy Fleet assaulted and easily overwhelmed the lightly defended fortress and, in a
move which Venice looked on as encroachment into their territory, left
large amounts of munitions and nearly four thousand men in Spanish
pay to garrison the installation.

Castelnuovo was a long way from the Golden Horn, but the next season, Barbarosa went there with sixty galleys and a dozen cannon barges
and, in a textbook siege, convinced the defenders that time spent on Turkish oars was preferable to any more of the eighty-pound iron balls his
new siege guns were delivering with such accuracy. It was a textbook
assault; successful in three weeks — demonstrating that Barbarosa's talents extended to land war.

A teacher from his early days as a young reis on pirate galleots,
Barbarosa always insured that those of ability under him were given ev-
ery chance to learn and develop. When the white flags went up at
Castlenuovo he sent Piali into the fort to accept the surrender. "You can

---

1.   Castlenuovo was near Cattaro — present day Kotor. Barbarosa's victory was a ma-
     jor accomplishment, but since it was late in his career, it received little attention
     from Christian historians.

learn some Spanish."

Piali went ashore and not only arranged the details of the surrender — he found a treasure: several hundred barrels of large-grain gun powder suitable for cannons, plus more than eight thousand stone cannon balls with a value equivalent to a flotilla of galleys.[1]

"What are the sizes?"

"There are three weights: twelve, twenty, and forty pounds. The two larger will fit our forward firing guns, and while we have nothing the size of the smallest," he handed Barbarosa a painstakingly carved small stone, "there are enough of them to justify having a dozen guns cast when we get home."

Upon leaving Castlenuovo Barbarosa earmarked for duty on Turkish oars most of the three thousand prisoners he had taken, something he rarely did in such numbers. Turkey had a different problem in manning their galleys than did Christians. In sharp distinction from Christians who used galleys as floating prisons. Turkish ships did not employ many criminals. Islamic courts relied little on incarceration. Criminal punishments were those of 7th century Bedouin tribes — stoning, amputation, death on hooks. Consequently, Turkish jails held only a fraction of comparable European numbers of felons. Beyond that, Islam prohibited enslavement of True Believers, a rule hardly of concern to Christian Kings.

By 1539 the Turkish fleet had become an imperial force that not only undertook annual raiding campaigns, but one that maintained patrol and administrative functions over long reaches of the sea — and it required a minimum of forty thousand rowers during the sailing season. Barbarosa convinced Suleiman to institute a national levy of one man, plus his pay and upkeep, against each twenty households. From this national draft he obtained most of his rowers. These volunteer/conscripts, as well as professional rowers recruited largely from Greece and the Balkans, were paid about the same as Janissaries — four or five aspers a day and bread year around — and they worked seasonally, turning to other occupations between November and March. Many maintained families. As long as he lived, slaves in Turkish fleets were never more

---

1.   The economics of stone ball manufacture was the main impetus for the 16th century development of improved, cast iron cannons able to fire the much cheaper mass produced iron balls. With every ship now carrying cannons of some type, the expenditure of expensive stone balls could bankrupt a state.

than a fraction of the total manpower.[1]

Consequently, Turkish galleys in combat were generally more effective, ship for ship, simply because rowers could lay down their oars and take up swords — an emergency that required concentrated attention on the part of the guards on Christian ships.

When he sailed for Marseilles in 1542 to join France in a war against Spain more than three quarters of his rowers were professional oarsmen in the sense that they were free men and paid. Not more than three thousand of his fourteen thousand men on oars were slaves.

And the care with which Barbarosa oversaw the manning and preparation of his fleet in that year demonstrated the degree of importance he attached to the planned campaign. The Franco-Turkish alliance for the upcoming war with Spain was to be a watershed in the ancient war between Islam and Christianity.

The Ottoman Empire, while suffering from shiite challenge in distant Persia, was essentially a monolith. The Turks had no internal political or military divisions. They could speak and fight with one voice, one command, one strategy, one national interest.

In Christian Europe however, from the earliest days individual ambition and greed had carried more weight than the words of Jesus. By the 16th century, nationalism, a child given birth by centuries of greed and hatred on the part of Christian Princes, was becoming a major force. The State itself was replacing "religion".

The Christian church, designed to maintain a rule of Roman Law across Europe, was not only rotten to the core, it was ill equipped organizationally to deal with quarrels among its member-states. Traditionally, in fact, the Church had encouraged or abetted such war. Four centuries earlier, the Knights of France, enroute to Jerusalem on a Crusade, visited their brother Christians in Constantinople and, seeing the wealth of Byzantium for the first time, decided they needed to go no further to find their fortune. Abetted by the avaricious Venetians (who viewed Byzantium as a trade competitor) — and approved by the Pope (to whom the Eastern Church was a challenge) — the Crusaders sacked the city and abandoned the Crusade, returning home with their their booty.[2] Only a decade or

1.   Christians on Barbarosa's ships were generally permitted the exit from slavery made possible by acceptance of Islam — and they took advantage of the offer more frequently than admitted by Christian historians.

2.   The Bronze lions that guard St Marks square in Venice today are souvenirs of that "Crusade."

so earlier, a war between France (supported by the Pope) and Spain came
to an inglorious end when the victorious soldiers hired by Charles left
Rome in ruins in a sack notable even by Christian standards of cruelty
and greed.

Barbarosa's campaign in 1542 — the first time a Christian state
(France) formally joined an Islamic state (Turkey) against another Christian state (Spain) — was an outgrowth of this rivalry and it seemed inexplicable unless one understood the King of France.

When he became King at twenty, Francis inherited the strongest state
in Europe and, when the once in a lifetime election to the office of Emperor of the Holy Roman Empire was held shortly afterwards, felt himself entitled to the office. However, by means of bribery so extensive that
Spain was impoverished, Charles bought the election for himself. If that
weren't enough, a few years later Charles declared war against a French
army enroute to Milan (a city-state claimed by France) and took Francis
prisoner. The French King languished in Madrid for two years — freed
only after signing a devastating agreement to give up Burgundy, a major
portion of his kingdom.[1]

Francis' hatred of Charles, already vigorous, spread its roots.

A man of immense popularity, Francis was a true Renaissance King.
He sponsored tournaments during which he personally jousted against
the greatest Knights of his Kingdom and at the same time he was a dedicated supporter of the arts who brought Leonardo da Vinci to France to
design a castle and who hosted Benvenuto Cellini as his guest for five
years. He supported writers, musicians, poets, and opened academies
throughout France. Rabelais was a friend and confidant — in fact, Francis
may have been the model for Rabelais' rollicking, carousing Gargantua.

This larger than life figure spent little productive time on governance
and he vacillated constantly in the decisions he did make. Intellectually
and politically dominated by his mother and sister, he had no cohesive
or lasting foreign policy. A great horseman who spent weeks and months
engaged in his second great hobby, the hunt, he paid only casual attention to affairs of state, preferring to pursue his first hobby in the many
boudoirs available to a vigorous Bourbon king.

His own ministers called him "amorous as a cat".

Personally impecunious, he constantly bled France for gold with which

---

1.   An agreement he promptly repudiated, once safely back in France.

Francis I. 1497-1547. Big, blonde — 6 feet 4 inches — handsome, athletic and physically without fear, he once challenged Charles to a personal duel to settle an oncoming war. The Spanish Emperor declined, and Spain won the war by conventional means.

he rewarded the noble classes who supported him, paid his mistresses, supported an outrageously ambitious castle building program,[1] and indulged his court in its sybaritic existence. He had never the slightest idea of the relationship between the national income and the national outgo and, as a result, was chronically short of money.

He preferred to conduct his foreign policy much as he did his jousting tournaments, with Charles of Spain as his lifetime opponent — to be rechallenged after every fall. By 1540 he was ready to again challenge Spain. The large fly in his ointment was that Christian armies had to be paid . With France broke as usual, he needed prosperous allies.

His first choice, Henry VIII of England, was satisfied with keeping Spain and France in a more or less even balance and would not commit either money or men — both of which in any event were in short supply in England. The German states distrusted France because of growing intimacy between Francis and a new Pope. The Mediterranean maritime powers such as Venice were primarily concerned with the threat of Islam in their own waters, and had no interest in picking quarrels with Spain.

That left Turkey, the only state with sufficient resources and money to be a worthwhile ally.

Francis was forthright. He declared to the Venetian ambassador,

---

1. About this time Francis began construction of the outrageously costly castle at Chambord — designed by da Vinci — one of Europe's treasures today.

"I cannot deny that I earnestly desire to see the Turk very powerful and warlike — not for his own sake, since he is an infidel and we are Christians — but to lessen the power of the Emperor (Charles), to force him into heavy expenditure, and to rally all the other governments against so great an enemy."

The French approach to Suleiman was welcomed. The Sultan saw a chance to wound Spain, the possibility of treasure, and a blow at Christianity all in one — with a navy that paid for itself.

Francis planned to invade Spanish Netherlands — the Flemish property Charles had inherited from his maternal grandmother. While this was being done, France would furnish supplies and bases for the Turks who were to strip Spanish coasts, a move that would tie down Spanish forces south of the Alps.

Thus began the last great adventure of Barbarosa.

·⁓

When he called his senior fleet officers to his spacious dockyard office in Istanbul, all of his old corsairs were available except Sinan, the Jew from Smyrna, who was under the care of Arab surgeons for decaying eyesight. As Barbarosa welcomed his old friends, they noted that he was beginning to show his years. He now shaved his head — some said for religious reasons, some said to disguise his increasing baldness, some said for stimulation (a freshly bald pate was thought to be an aphrodisiac) — and his closely trimmed beard was white. He wore wire spectacles when reading, notched his belt noticeably closer to its end, and moved with more deliberation.

To Salah, Aydin observed, sotto voice, "The old man is slowing down. I imagine his great organ dangles between his knees like a horse given its head. I wonder how often he does the dance of the two backed beast these days."

Salah's whisper was more optimistic. "I would guess he would respond to a bugle call — played by the right trumpet."

Suspicion or no, they awarded him respect far beyond the tolerance and affection ordinarily reserved for the elderly. He was, they admitted as they studied him, as vibrant as ever, his enthusiasm for the coming campaign contagious.

Barbarosa mentioned the Treaty with France and outlined Francis' plans for war in northern Europe. Then he discussed his own plans in the Western Mediterranean.

He revealed that the Sultan had permitted him to offer, at his own discretion, extra shares of treasure taken. He touched briefly on the forces that would be operating, told the captains they might well be absent for two years. "Francis has agreed to victual us and supply us once we are in his ports, but we should not rely too much on his promises. His quartermasters load wine before gunpowder, and they are apt to offer us pork. The Italian coast can supply some food enroute, but most coastal villages can't feed a hundred and twenty ships. The fleet will remain together until we reach Reggio. After that we'll break into sections that will leapfrog one another until the west coast of Corsica our entry into Marseilles.

"I have a plan for Reggio."

The assembled captains expected him to lay out another assault similar to that of '34. He removed his turban and rubbed his glistening crown. "I intend to protect our route through the Messina straight. Today I'm going to present a somewhat unusual plan." He paused and allowed the muted song of saws and hammers from the adjoining shipyard to lull the expectancy. Within the comfortable room, motes of dust soared lazily in the sunbeams reflecting from crystal and porcelain. "Some weeks ago I sent word to Reggio that we were willing to discuss a brokered arrangement for the use of the straight."

Such an offer would preclude an attack.

The idea settled throughout the room, capturing the listeners. The approval among the individual thinking processes could practically be heard. As one reis said in an aside to Drub-devil, "He sees beyond a rich city!"

Barbarosa continued, "I told them that we would come under a flag and would require hostages for the negotiations. Yesterday I received their acceptance."

While a comparatively new experience for most of the reis, such acquiescence was not unprecedented. Ten years of Turkish dominance of the Mediterranean had wrought great changes in the outlook of Christian coastal cities. Barbarosa's name alone was enough to strike fear in most of them. In some ways, he had achieved a stature comparable to the

Salah and Aydin. Salah Reis, an Egyptian by birth, showed great initiative and leadership. In only one raid against Saharan dissidents after Barbarosa's death, he brought back fifteen camel loads of gold and jewels — plus five thousand Negro slaves.

great Greek Alexander, whose reputation frightened cities into submission upon his advance.

Six weeks later, as the gig flying Barbarosa's green pennant put out from one of the six black war galleys anchored immediately inside the Reggio breakwater, cannons mounted on the brick fortification above the main quay began the slow firing of an eighteen-gun salute. The Italian salute finished, flags on the six galleys dipped as the flotilla swiveled a part turn to disperse the black smoke downwind while one after the other fired three cannons at five-second intervals. As the echoes from the last gun died, the flotilla spun back to its original formation, oars on opposing sides pulling and backing simultaneously, the deck master's whistles twittering.

To the surprise of those watching, the infidel ships from distant Asia not only knew the correct procedure for firing salutes, but performed it in style.[1]

And, as if by coincidence, once the exercise was completed, the yawning gun muzzles of the six ships contemplated the exact center of the city — much like the guns of the hundred or so more black galleys just out-

---

1.   Saluting prior to battle had long been a custom of land armies. Led by the English, it had only recently been adopted by European ships as a salute to dignitaries.

side the breakwater.

There were five passengers aboard the oncoming gig. The portly figure of the Reggio Governor, Don Diego de Gaetano, could be recognized. The slight female figure beside him was assumed to be his daughter. The others were the Ottoman Beylerbey of the Sea and two of his captains.

"He comes ashore with only two guards?" an observer wondered to his neighbor as they watched the progress of the gig.

Another bystander put the visit in perspective. "They need not fear. Look at those warships. I would as soon face the devil and all of his legions as meet the fanatics in those black hulls if anything should happen to him."

An old man agreed, "To worry about the Turks is to be wise. This man and his brother came to Algiers as guests. Once inside, they murdered their host in his own bath and took his city. With that force anchored outside the breakwater they can take this place whenever the mood comes on them — just like they did ten years ago. This morning they had six of our nobles and a female member of each man's family delivered to them as hostages. I see that the Governor is coming ashore and bringing his daughter with him."

"She may be the most beautiful girl in Southern Italy."

"So much the better. That pirate is famous for his appetite for tender women. She may make tender his heart for us."

The speaker was much closer to the truth than he could know.

Just then, a flutter of signal flags on the Turkish galleys caught their attention, and the man who knew of Aruj's visit to the Sheik in Algiers told the group, "The Turks can carry on conversations by means of signals. They not only have flags, but lanterns at night, as well as horns and drums."

"Well, I'd be just as happy if they ran up another flag, or blew a horn, or anything to tell those horny-looking cannon to point the other way."

The exchange drew laughter.

Earlier, when the Governor had delivered the group of hostages, Barbarosa had been brief and businesslike — assigning the Italians and their women to aides — but when he saw the Governor's daughter, the old pirate's interest registered a sharp gain.

Don Diego said, "It is a privilege for me to present my daughter Maria.[1] She was only eight when you visited us last, and she wants to meet the man who rules the Mediterranean."

The girl looked directly, but with respect, at Barbarosa, "Your treatment of my city places me in your debt."

Barbarosa was enchanted.

Foreign and exotic, she was the antithesis of dark Turkish beauty. Her yellow-gold hair and blue eyes betrayed ancestral involvement with a Nordic crusader, and her height, no less than her subtle figure, would be embarrassed by the plump, voluptuous standards of Istanbul. The shimmering light blue of her harem-style trousers and slippers were one with her silk blouse — an eastern costume certainly worn to impress the visitors — and matched her eyes perfectly.

Speaking quietly to Salah, Aydin offered his appraisal. "I like eyes dark enough to make a man hard, her arms are somewhat slender, and her breasts are small but, friend, if she were for sale, I'd buy her myself."

Salah nodded an agreement, and said, "These traders set a tender lamb before the Lion."

"Well, that's a feast all right. Better than a burnt sugar desert. We'll see how high our Admiral's fires still burn."

Her vivacious mannerisms were those of a favored daughter. Without hint of coquetry or flirtation, Maria was unaffected and direct when addressing Barbarosa — another rare experience for a Turkish Pasha. To the old Admiral, accustomed to captives, slaves, or subservient Muslim women, her forthright manner was a challenge, her direct speech fascinating. In a clumsy attempt at humor, he spoke over her head to the Governor, "Is this child familiar with your city's needs? Does she bring your proposals?"

Maria responded, "It is not for us to propose. We must accept. But," she smiled, "the Prophet advises True Believers to treat with fairness those who have been conquered. We place ourselves in your heart."

Though spoken in Italian, her use of the Koran as authority was intelligent and thoughtful, her unaffected bearing, high spirits, and youth were a tonic for the man of more than sixty summers. He spoke in Turkish to Aydin and Salah. "With a woman such as this, a man could live the

---

1.   Only one reference is given to her name, and the common Christian name of Mary is perhaps an assumption, but her relationship with Barbarosa is a matter of record.

years of Methusela and retain the fire of youth." Realizing she had not understood the Turkish, he translated his remark for her benefit.

Certain that the pounding of her heart could be heard, she took a visible breath and answered, "To live with the Lord of the Mediterranean would be beyond the fondest dreams of any woman."

He studied her in silence and she shyly returned his look. For a moment the old man and the girl existed only for one another, unaware of an audience.

Maria was trembling slightly, either with fear or excitement. Whether she was desperate, willing to bargain herself for her city, or whether she was moved by the chance to catch the eye of this famous figure with extravagant rewards at his disposal, could not be known with certainty. Although there was a slight tremor in her voice, she held her face up, chin high, looked directly at her listener, and finished her sentences without flinching. If she was sacrificing herself, she was doing it with style.

Barbarosa made a decision. Seemingly talking to himself, he muttered cryptically, "Following the sea for a lifetime has taught me that one who lets opportunity slip away will never row home victorious. Bring this girl ashore."

Heading the welcoming group on the dock was an elderly man wearing a huge hat that would have done a Janissary proud, a heavy chain around his neck from which hung a great seal, and a great long coat embellished with gold trim that was soaking up the sun to his discomfort. He was tottering under the weight of the costume.

The Governor pointed him out as the mayor, an honorary post reserved for elderly officials.

The mayor's welcome was effusive. He assured Barbarosa that Reggio had not had so great an honor conferred upon it since Caesar had paid a visit fifteen hundred years previously, Suleiman was praised as the greatest light in the East and the Ottoman Empire was admitted as mightier than Rome. The seamanship just displayed by the black galleys was rated the best in the Mediterranean, and he implied that Barbarosa himself lacked only the ability to walk on the sea.

Barbarosa answered courteously in the local Italian dialect and inquired as to the preparations made for the meeting. He was told that it was to be in the city castle and that carriages were waiting.

As the old Corsair stood there, the Italians could see for the first time for themselves that the legend of the Mediterranean was only a man — older than most realized — who neither breathed fire nor wore horns. This large, but somewhat ordinary figure, had only two arms and one head, and he was addressing them in their local dialect. Except for his Eastern finery and military bearing, he could have been a rich uncle come directly from Rome.

His escorts were two Sinbads come to life: Aydin (Cacha-diablo) and Salah. With their jeweled turbans, each was nearly seven feet tall, forcing the elderly mayor to lean backward to look them in the face. Wearing the ubiquitous Turkish war swords and short curved daggers, their outfits were identical: long pantaloons tucked into ankle high soft boots, brilliant green blouses gathered at the wrists and tucked under scarlet sashes and gold embroidered jackets. Both had dark beards, and their weather-beaten complexions were almost as dark as their ships.

As the carriages passed through the city, there were few women in evidence, but the entire male population of the city seemed to have turned out. The welcome contained no hostility, only cautious curiosity — and perhaps fear. The girl accompanied them in the carriage but left them at the entrance as the Turks were escorted past the carabinieri honor guard. The Mayor ushered the Governor and his three visitors down a mirrored hall to a smaller ornate room. At the entrance was an honor guard of a dozen young men costumed in Turkish attire, complete with turbans.

Barbarosa complimented his host, "The dress of your servants is a thoughtful gesture. These young men would appear well in the Sultan's service." He added with apparent sincerity, "If you wish, I will make the necessary arrangements to have them accepted at the Sublime Porte."

Don Diego managed a precarious smile. The Turk might be serious. Making the best of an awkward situation, he indicated a rosewood serving table, "We are pleased to offer you the best wines in Southern Italy We feel sure that The Prophet would have viewed alcohol in a more favorable light had he the opportunity to taste our first pressing."

Barbarosa nodded, "Wine itself was not the objection of The Prophet. He used it Himself, and found no fault with it until disgusted at the behavior of weak men when too much was taken. However, for now we have no need. We have come to learn."

Among the dozen or so Reggians waiting in the room, an elderly Colonel quietly addressed a young Lieutenant at his side. "That Turk already knows more about Reggio than we know ourselves. His spies could tell him which of us has been given horns in the past month."

Since the aide being addressed had recently shared moments of intimacy with the young wife of this particular Colonel and thus awarded the Colonel himself a set of horns, he attempted to divert the conversation to a less dangerous subject. "Turks, sir, rarely find blondes in their own territory."

His answer was a grunt.

The crowd overpowered the room; body odor rose like a fog. The Muslim visitors were fastidious, washing several times daily and bathing fully when possible, but Christian superstitions awarded miraculous healing qualities to a well oiled, greasy body, and Europeans rarely bathed. To compensate, they doused themselves in strong perfumes and, as the room warmed, the close aroma became heady as young wine.

Noticing Aydin's shallow breathing, Salah muttered in his ear, "We are fortunate. This company seems not to have many lice. Few are scratching."

Barbarosa opened the discussion abruptly, almost rudely. To the governor, he said, "Don Diego, my life is in its autumn and time is not mine to squander. Therefore, I will state the first step of our agreement.

"The girl Maria must be mine."

The demand was startling, direct to the point of threat.

In the stillness of the room, the fussy, overfat Governor showed an unsuspected dignity. His answer was courageous, unadorned with servility. Choosing his words carefully, he told Barbarosa that his daughter would have to make that decision herself. Sharp intakes of breath could be heard.

Barbarosa simply nodded.

The Governor sent for her, and there followed a sentient silence. Barbarosa continued standing for a moment, then seated himself, inviting no one to join him. His restlessness betrayed him to Aydin and Salah. The term "nervous" was not one that would apply to Barbarosa. Impatient, perhaps?

Gaetano sweated visibly, the other Italians hardly less, and the room began to acquire the air of a farm slaughter-yard on a warm day.

Maria entered.

Her father informed her of the requirement and added, "The answer is for you to make." She looked at him with surprise and said, "I am to decide?" Her father reaffirmed his statement, and she turned to Barbarosa where he was seated. "When is my answer expected?"

Hearts raced in the tension of the moment; Barbarosa and the girl because of their emotions, the Reggio officials because they feared the reaction of this Old Man of the Sea should this headstrong girl reject him.

Barbarosa deliberately, slowly, rose from his chair, put his hands on his hips, hesitated only long enough to place overburdened Reggian hearts at risk, and answered her, not unkindly, "This question is sudden and, if you accept, it will set your life on a course from which there is no returning. You may have a day."

The broad-shouldered, white-bearded Turk, an official representative and personal friend of the most powerful ruler on earth, a living legend to Christians and Muslims alike, dominated the room and everyone in it. Those who saw him for the first time in the intimacy of the room were transfixed, and those who knew him from the past were impressed anew. No Reggian could avoid the thought of the thousands of Christians counting the days in Turkish bagnios, the millions of ducats of Christian gold resting in Istanbul vaults — even of the fighting men who had felt the keen edge of this man's personal scimitar.

With his arms akimbo and brilliant silk caftan flaring from his shoulders, here was the legendary King of the Sea making known his demands in an almost gentle manner.

She had not taken her eyes from him and, standing so close to him that he could see the pulsing of a tiny vein in her throat and a film of perspiration on her upper lip, she spoke clearly for all to hear, "I don't need a day. I can answer you now, here."

A dozen putative Italian heart attacks hung in the balance.

"Yes. But my city is to be free."

In spite of his tan, Barbarosa's fair complexion betrayed his pleasure. "Agreed."

The stunning development left everyone uncertain as to protocol, but relief and approval were in abundant supply. After all, many Christian women were already in Constantinople. One more girl could certainly be spared to a Turkish harem. The collective sigh of relief from the Reggio officials raised the humidity in the room to new and higher olfactory levels. Don Diego de Gaetano had made a brilliant bargain! A daughter for a city!

There was little more conversation. Barbarosa left details of the Strait of Messina agreement to his captains, and asked for a suitable beachside villa for himself.

He spent what was left of the day alone — bathing, resting, and scanning the impressive collection of eighteen books he found shelved. Those in Latin or French were hand engraved, but the two in German — a language he read poorly — were made by the new printing process and were apparently Protestant versions of the Christian bible. He realized that the owner of this comfortable home was not only rich and educated, but certainly courageous. If the Jesuit "Soldiers of the Pope" — were to discover such dangerous material, the owner would be a certain visitor to the stake with pine faggots to warm his feet.

Maria was delivered just as dusk absorbed the daylight, and Barbarosa greeted her in only a light caftan tied loosely at the waist. As his new possession moved toward him across the room, he invited her, "Come enjoy the stars and the sea. Will you have wine?"

"Yes, a little." She walked to the low wall and stood for a moment as she inhaled the fragrance of dusk-obscured spring blossoms. The moon, the bright heart of the sky, apparently caught her attention. In the silence, her motivation was still not evident. Was she joyously entering a great adventure, or courageously preparing herself for sacrifice? Her beauty was his, but he did not want dutiful submission. If he was to sail tonight on the sea of desire and fulfillment, he needed the reassurance her youthful approbation could give him. In her heart of hearts, could she really want him in spite of his white beard and bald pate? For the first time since Isabella, he had become the captive of a woman. Her allure aroused a drive in him for the first time in years — a need equal to that of survival, and his eyes grew soft with the discovery. His mind turned to the shimmering staircase of eternal life. For what does a man wish? What will he leave on the sands of time?

With a start, he brought himself back to the present.

She turned from her study of the moon, so full of light it was about to spill over, nodded at the room inside, put a gentle hand on his sleeve and asked shyly, "I don't know what to do. Will you instruct me?"

The strength of youth poured into the Admiral in full flood. He led her inside, motioned her to sit on the small settee before the bed, leaned over her, and lightly ran his fingertips along her flawless teeth. "Teaching you will be the greatest pleasure. Are you afraid?"

"Yes, but only from my lack of knowledge. I don't fear you."

He leaned to kiss her, gently savoring her mouth. "Bella, your breath is like a fresh peach. I can taste you." She didn't realize she had been given Isabella's name; she thought of "Bella" only as "beautiful."[1]

She reached up with both hands, held his face down to her own, and said, "Let not you think I am here with fear. I wanted to come, and I am glad." With an open mouth her tiny tongue explored between his teeth. "I wanted you to know there was no doubt."

"I realize that the well from which men draw the water of self-deception is bottomless. May I not draw from that well in believing you."

"You are not deceived. I mean what I say."

"You fire me with a desire that I had thought departed." He lay back on the bed and motioned her to disrobe.

Rising and standing before him, she proudly undid her silken girdle and let her gown fall, leaving her with only her bracelets and a simple necklace. The soft candlelight accentuated her small breasts and left her shadowed triangle a mystery for him to solve. She raised her hands to smooth her hair from her face, the graceful rippling of her slim torso and upper arms an offer of love.

"Do I please you?"

"I am a singing brook that babbles your praises. My eyes hunger for your face, my ears for your voice, my lips for your flesh!" He raised himself to a sitting position and swung himself around to sit on the edge of the bed where he could touch her, lightly tracing her breasts with his fingertips, stroking her slimness down to her hips. He took her in his gnarled, liver-spotted hands and turned her from side to side to admire. "A jewel, a passion flower, a small bird in flight, a dream for my heart to carry," He leaned forward to gently explore her throat with his tongue.

She placed her hands on his shoulders. "May I see you, also?"

"Of course." He stood up on the platform supporting the bed which acted as a pedestal, causing him to tower over her. His body was smooth,

1.   As far as known, he never called her by any other name.

almost hairless, except for a light cover of curly gray hair on his chest. His belly was generous, but he was firm and muscular.

He was also erect, pulsing with the eternal male imperative.

She looked and touched. "The ancient Romans worshipped the God Priapus, and I can now see why. To hold this magnificent thing is like touching God Himself."

"Are you afraid, La Bella?"

"Oh no." Swallowing, "Well, yes. Its so much larger than I imagined." With an impish smile she added, " It says, 'Take heed, I am master and I demand respect'!"

He laughed in joy. "La Bella, may you always feel this way about my lifelong friend. Care for him, cherish him, and he will protect any house in which you find yourself." Taking her by the elbows, he lifted her to stand on the bed.

She steadied herself with one hand on his shoulder, and breathed, "Will you take me now? I want to please you."

He nodded, and she sank back on to the bed, taking him with her.

Positioning himself, he whispered, "I want to open you up like the beautiful flower that you are. I may hurt, but it is nature's pain."

As she felt him brace to thrust, she intuitively raised her legs to pull him into her — impaling herself on him. The sharp pain startled her into crying aloud. But she didn't pull away.

Restraining himself no longer, he sank himself fully into her and felt the membrane giving way. To a Muslim to whom virginity was worth more than gold — life itself sometimes — the effect of that magic sensation was immediate. Almost instantly, with a surge rising from his feet, he began to pour out his essence.

Finished, the encounter hadn't taken two minutes.

In earlier years, such a rapid execution of his masculine responsibilities would have been embarrassing, if not shameful. This night, however, he was pleased. He had regained his youth! David had found his Bathsheba. Ulysses his Penelope.

He raised himself to look down on her. "You will be the dawn of my day. When my fires burn low, I shall throw the kindling of your beauty on them and they will blaze again!"

In a few moments, she did and, as promised, his fires were promptly relit.

She had saved her city[1] and, as time passed, she became convinced that she had made the best of the bargain for herself. Barbarosa was totally infatuated with her from that first night, and genuinely in love within weeks. She not only gave him youth, a quality critically important to the Islamic masculine culture which had forged so much of his personality, she was to make his passage into old age a joyous one.

He was later to marry her.

Suleiman by an unknown artist. Probably a copy of a Bellini. The Turks called him, "Sublime One," "Shadow of God." He called himself "Ruler of Two Worlds." Europeans called him "The Magnificent."

---

1.   As long as Barbarosa lived, Reggio was never again troubled by Turkey.

16

TOULON

1543-1546

Leaving Reggio, Barbarosa followed his plan of dividing his fleet into two units — one with Dragut and one with him — a move which not only doubled the number of Italian cities eligible to become involuntary contributors to the Turkish fleet, but made more manageable the totals of water and fresh foods to be procured at any one stop.

Life aboard the Admiral's galley was not uncomfortable as long as the weather remained good, which it did for the three days his section of the fleet needed to reach their first objective, an uninhabited small cove on the Amalfi coast. No sooner anchored, than a hundred or so men, led by a renegado of Italian birth, went ashore and disappeared across a low saddle between the adjacent hills.

Maria couldn't resist asking about their purpose.

Barbarosa teased with a lugubrious expression. "Within ten miles of here there is said to be a noblewoman of such exceptional beauty that she can paralyze men by her radiance. They have been sent to bring her to the joys of The Prophet."

Fear struck the heart of a new wife. "You must mean the Countess de Gonzaga. Her beauty is sung of." She paused to assemble her courage. "Do you want her for yourself?"

He laughed outright as leaned over and drew her to him for comfort. "No, by no means, La Bella. After discovering the delights in you, I have no need for another woman. If she is as beautiful as rumored, I will present her to the Sultan. He is besotted with a young wife whose influence is evil. My hope is that this Gonzaga beauty will cause his walnuts to float on a new sea of desire — and perhaps free his mind."

"Is the Sultan's woman the Roxelana of whom I have heard?"

"Yes. We call her Hurrem — the laughing one."

"Is she beautiful?"

"Very beautiful as a young woman, and I'm sure she is clever enough to make much of what she retains."

The raiding party would be gone as long as twenty four hours. Most of the ships in his section of the fleet were offshore. Alone, the Admiral's galley quietly swung at anchor near the pristine sand beach and its bordering trees. Fully protected from wind and wave, the quiet of the

Roxelana is commonly shown (imagined by later artists) as a dark-eyed brunette, but this is surely a mistake. She was from the Caucausus where most were Aryan and fair.

spring day was broken only by the music of birds and insects. As La Bella looked overside, the ship appeared suspended on a clear membrane, the water invisible. Five feet beneath the hull, sinuous eel grass could be identified blade by blade in slight windrows of bottom-sand fashioned by the unseen current.

It was an ideal retreat for the developing acquaintance of a man and a woman from different worlds, and the two made the most of it all of the day and into the evening.

While the following day was yet unborn, the raiding party returned, quietly threading their way through the shoreline forest.

Empty handed. The bird had flown.

It was a near thing, they said. The Count was away and they easily entered the castle. The Countess had been in her bath, but she was rescued by a strong groom who carried her in his arms to the stables where he commanded a horse. The groom was brave as well as quick-thinking man, for he wounded two of the Turkish visitors before making good his escape. Without horses, the raiding party was unable to follow, so they contented themselves with such quick loot in the castle as they could carry away before sunrise aroused the countryside.[1]

Barbarosa was philosophical. Even If the Countess had been taken, there was no assurance that she would be welcomed by the Sultan, and there was always another day for this kind of adventure. He had spent a pleasant visit with La Bella, again proving to himself that his vigor matched his desire. Within the hour, his section of the fleet weighed anchor and walked northwest to the rendezvous with Dragut. The meeting was exactly on schedule and, three weeks later, in the ancient French port of Marseilles, a fleet of more than a hundred Muslim warships peacefully entered a Christian city for the first time in history.

The Franco-Turkish treaty seemed to mean all things to all people — an example of two cultures speak-ing different languages through the same instrument. From the Turkish point of view the treaty committed France to support Turkey against Spain. From the French point of view it meant valuable trade and commercial privileges within Turkish Europe and Asia.

France eventually proved to be closer to the mark.[2]

The Turks were not so much out-maneuvered at the bargaining table as misunderstood. The provisions that proved to be so favorable for France were hardly within the thought processes of Islamic Turkey. Extra-territoriality was a case in point. France was to have jurisdiction over French nationals within Turkish territory but reciprocal privileges were not provided for Turkish nationals in France. This "concession" by the Turks was hardly what it appeared. Turkey had traditionally allowed — required — other religions within its borders to be responsible for their own members. "Law" to Muslims was a set of religious dictates. Unbelievers were not considered worthy of God's justice. Expulsion of a foreigner was considered proportionate punishment by Turkey for anything less than a crime of blood, which was promptly rewarded with a sword to non-

1. The sequel to the Countess de Gonzaga incident became fuel for satirists and jesters all over Italy who claimed that the groom enjoyed the Countess's favors during their time on the road. Whether it was true or not, the lady's charms had certainly been exposed, and The Count, being a sensitive man, had the groom beheaded.

2. The term "capitulations" by which the treaty eventually became infamous, was a Latin term for "chapters." It acquired its pejorative meaning later.

Muslim and Muslim alike.

Nor did Turkey feel a need to protect their own nationals in France. There were no Turks in France. Where Turks lived, Turks ruled.

At the time, the treaty was an achievement for Suleiman. Some European states already viewed Istanbul as an alternative to their own masters. Corsica, for example, an abused province of Genoa, sent the native island hero, Sampieto de Bastelica, to Istanbul with letters imploring the Turks to send a fleet and adopt Corsica as part of the Ottoman Empire. For some time German Protestants had been clandestinely encouraged by Turkish gold. Now, an open alliance with one of the most powerful Christian states whose King was the chief ally of a new Pope was a new and a major advance. It created an opening for Turkey to cause trouble, and the campaign of 1543 was designed to ratchet the window wider.

But the best laid plans of men were again to fail. When Barbarosa arrived with his magnificent and terrifying fleet, it seemed only a matter of time until the Mediterranean coasts of Spain would be laid waste. The Turkish fleet was to remain in France a year, where its presence legitimized Turkey's Mediterranean supremacy

Barbarosa's tomb in Istanbul.

and where the fleet itself gained a widespread respect. It was also to be a year when its Admiral set new standards in extracting royal gold from the mattresses of France.

But the joint campaign was never to take place.

Barbarosa was welcomed in Marseilles by the personal representative of the King, Duc de Enghien, Francois de Bourbon. Along with his welcome, the Duke had ready a proposal for a first objective: Nice, a nearby Episcopal See coveted by Francis. The city was vulnerable and could be reached in only a couple of days. He offered two thousand French soldiers — commanded by a full general, no less — with their own transport barges.

This first, and only, hostile action set the tone for what proved to be the failure of the overall campaign.

Barbarosa had already formed an opinion of French seamen, but this was the first time he had actually worked with them. Watching the dirty, ill equipped soldiers — some obviously drunk — boarding their barges, he observed, "God forbid that these are the people with whom we are to join in battle!" His opinion was no higher after watching the Frenchmen attempt to row past the breakwater in the teeth of a vigorous on-shore wind. An entire day was wasted, and one barge went ashore with damage to its rudder that cost them another day.

On the third day, Barbarosa detached war-galleys with tow lines to pull the barges far enough to sea that their convict oarsmen could move them at a steady knot or so in the general direction of Nice. The Turks had to suffer through three days of this seamanship — but in partial recompense, once reached, Nice itself was shockingly easy. It was not even necessary to off-load the siege guns. One salvo from sixty bow guns gave birth to a white flag on the city's walls.

When the gigs carrying officials put out from the city, Barbarosa reluctantly decided to ask the pear-shaped French general to attend the bargaining. He used Dragut — whose French was rudimentary at best — as his cat's paw. "Old friend, you speak French like a true Turk and we need someone who understands French bravery and skills. Would you invite the commander of our new friends to join us? And would you get him to bathe first?"

Dragut contented himself with sketching in the air with his hands the exceptionally wide hips of the large bottomed Frenchman.

The General required two gigs for his large party — one for guards-
men who announced his arrival with long curved trumpet type horns,
one for a half-dozen overdressed aides, whose formal wool uniforms were
badly in need of washing. Perspiring profusely in the domineering sun,
the General climbed aboard the flagship flaunting a uniform so extreme
that Dragut commented in Arabic to Barbarosa, "Your friend resembles
a male Cairo whore. Does anyone have plans for him tonight?"

At the bargaining table, the General displayed insolence and inflated
ego, insulting the petitioners, insisting on excessive details recognizing
French dignity and authority, and generally making himself a nuisance.
Barbarosa's instincts were to send the buffoon back to his barges, but
someone had to occupy the city and, since Nice had asked for terms there
was to be no looting and no profit in sending his Turks ashore. It was
agreed that the French soldiers would occupy the city.

With no point in keeping the fleet standing by, Barbarosa headed west
for Marseilles.

In violation of the terms of the surrender and of accepted international comity of war, as soon as the Turkish fleet was over the horizon,
the French ravished the city.[1] Duc de Enghien was to be rigid with embarrassment, but there was little that could be done after the fact.
Barbarosa would never trust his new allies again, at least in part because
he had to hear Dragut repeatedly comment on the inadvisability of placing trust in one so generously buttocked as the French general.

Before Nice had ceased smoldering, messengers from Paris brought
word that there were delays on the northern end, and everything was to
be held up for the winter. Francis still intended to strike the Netherlands
in the spring, which would put the overall plan into operation again, but
until then everything was on hold. Istanbul was weeks away both going
and coming, and the fleet had not met the traditional requirement of
Turkish warfare — it had not made a profit.

Barbarosa decided to winter as the guest of France.

Marseilles did not suit him. It was too large, there was too much traffic. He would be within potential reach of a hostile shore force and would
have trouble clearing for action in the crowded harbor in the event of a

---

1.   The affair was widely criticized, whereupon French reports promptly blamed the
      Turks. In fact, the Turkish ships were at sea when the atrocities occurred. Barbarosa
      didn't learn of it for days.

surprise visit. There was no fleet at sea that threatened him, and France was Turkey's sworn ally, but Barbarosa had not survived a half century of piracy, war, and treachery by trusting to the good will of others.

He wanted a better location. But he kept his needs to himself while he waited for his allies to consider the possibility that their guests could convert Marseilles into a Turkish city overnight. Once he announced his intentions to remain for the winter, his hosts began to offer alternative locations within days.

Toulon could be largely cleared of commercial traffic, there were adequate shore facilities, the fleet could easily be re-supplied with consumables, and he could move as much of his force ashore as he wished. The port suited him, but he permitted the French to convince him. Although a warrior, he was not unmarked by the Islamic merchant tradition.

Enough of the population would have to evacuate to provide adequate housing for such of his forces that would come ashore. The anchor blocks and breakwater would need some repair and construction. Food for his crews of Islamic dietary standards? Provision for public water in accordance with the Koran? Ramadan was shortly due, could Christian church bells be silenced during that month? Sex? (The French response to that requirement was very satisfactory. Captains were to be provided with specially selected partners and the men would be entertained at controlled bordellos — all at the expense of the French Crown.)

Once completed with these details, Barbarosa moved to the main item: Gold. France was not only to provide food and supplies, but agreed to be responsible for the "cost of the fleet not in action". Charles, with typical foggy foresight, agreed easily with this general category – even though it represented the "profit" which any Turkish fighting force in the field was expected to yield. In the event the war with Spain and its expected spoils did not materialize, France was to reimburse Turkey a figure which Barbarosa would establish.

That agreement was to cost France and its handsome King dearly.

Finally satisfied, Barbarosa accepted the offer of Toulon and, there, like the Old Man of the Mountain that rode Sinbad nearly to death, his fleet enjoyed the hospitality of France for a long winter.

Slaves could not live aboard ship during winter months, and slave housing and control ashore would be a problem. Consequently, Barbarosa dispatched Dragut to Algiers with all of the slave galleys.

Seventy three Turkish war-galleys remained in a Christian harbor of easy access to European visitors.[1] News of the fleet spread quickly. Since very few Christians, other than unlucky captives taken at sea, had seen Turkish galleys first-hand, within weeks there began a parade of visitors: military, courtiers, nobles, monks and priests, ordinary sightseers and commoners.

They beheld an elegant sight.

Most Christian galleys were flamboyant, rich in color and gilt. These visitors were somber, totally black, beak nosed hounds of death riding quietly at anchor in the crowded harbor, and they stood out from the few remaining Christian ships like mounted knights at a peasant fair. Their fierce, competent dignity elicited fear — and a startled respect.

There are no contemporary paintings of Barbarosa, however, the architect Sinan, who cast his statue in Istanbul, knew him. Allowing for the tendency of admirers to glorify, this bust may well be a likeness.

Even on the beach where ships were hauled in rotation each week for careening and greasing, these lethal black javelins reminded one of killer wolves lying quietly among the sheep.

The Turkish galleys and their crews were a first for Europeans. Buckets and mops were in constant use, decks stoned regularly, bilges pumped daily and flushed weekly, padded rowing benches stripped for airing after rain, sails and rigging kept well secured, guns cleaned and oiled constantly, tar or oil applied regularly to wood exposed to weather, and olive oil rubbed into leather port shields and thole slings. Constant care was not only lavished on the ship and its equipment, but to the amazement

---

1. Some Christian historians claim that Christian slaves (including Frenchmen) could be seen chained in the Turkish ships that winter. In fact, Barbarosa had no French enslaved at all during that campaign and, of the other nationalities, there weren't enough slaves to completely fill even Dragut's ships. Finally, no slaves would have been shackled to open benches during winter months.

of onlookers, the Turks worked at their battle skills at least part of every day, six days a week.

Typical of these drills was a battle station readiness. At the sound of a horn — Turks seemed to have trumpet signals for every activity — oars were smartly lifted from the water and drawn inboard in one coordinated motion. Upon another horn note, they were simultaneously raised and stacked in groups of four, each rower fastening his own oar with a restraining yoke to the gunwale adjacent to his position. Once the oars were aloft, four men held them while others rapidly lashed each oar-group together in a pyramid. The purpose of the drill was perfectly clear; it left crew movement relatively unimpeded, and would if needed, provide a framework for sheltering canvas.

One other drill not only impressed, but pained their hosts. Each day the weather permitted, a flotilla put to sea for cannon drill, an exercise that was a terrible waste in the eyes of French officials — who had to provide the powder and shot.

A naval attaché from one of the Papal states included in a dispatch, "Never have I seen men like these. They have in mind nothing but their ships and war. Neither cold nor rain makes them take cover, their food is simple; mostly various corns, olive oils, ship's biscuit, mutton, fish and greens. They do not quarrel among themselves. Sergeants and officers are obeyed instantly. They take no wine nor do they gamble. They are the best trained crews I have seen and their ship's guns are better in range and accuracy than ours. When one considers that they go insane in battle, feel no pain when wounded, and are willing to die in order to get to Mohammedan heaven, I know of no force at sea that can deal with them."

Half the men lived ashore in constant rotation. Seen up-close they were as foreign and exciting as their ships. With swords and daggers lending a fierceness to their exotic dress, these stocky, turbaned, pantalooned figures from the mysterious East were fascinating and intimidating. They were quiet and serious in demeanor, kept largely to themselves, and were never involved in shore altercations with the locals. There was some trade, especially in the brothels, but no taverns were trashed in drunken brawls, no maidens ravished, no citizens abused.

Tales of Turkish rapine, looting, murder had been standard European fare for generations, and it was difficult for Christians to believe that these men were not only well behaved, but actually fond of the children that accompanied them on the streets. The Turks either ignored or were patently disdainful of Christian men, but the affection of children who followed them was quickly returned. Friendships made that winter in Toulon were largely inter-generational.

B arbarosa permitted his captains to explore as they wished while each officer's ship was in repair. At an early meeting, he gave them some advice.

"Be careful that none of you catch the new French pox."

Ahmed asked, "What's the French pox?"

"A disease taken in sex, which I believe came from the natives of the Spanish Indies, carried back by the soldiers of the Genoan Columbo. At any rate it was first seen in Spain. The Spanish however, blame the French — that's where it gets its name. It's a new sickness, no one knew of it until twenty or thirty years ago, and it is spreading all over Europe like a spring bora. There is no cure."

"How does one see this disease, how is caught?"

"By congress. In the female, it is not always visible, especially in its early stages. On the man, it first makes ugly sores on his sad friend, and then a flush, like pox, over parts of the body."

"Is it painful?"

"Not so I'm told. In fact, the sores and pox go away after a while. But once a man has contracted the ailment, there is no cure. It remains hidden, and in a year or two one loses strength. At the end of the sickness, sometimes several years, the brain becomes soft and the man dies raving and in pain."

"The women too?

"Oh no, they get better after a time, but continue to pass the sickness."

And with that good news, he left the potential adventurer/tourists to plan their explorations.

A s the winter progressed, the exotic Turkish presence justified a steady stream of parties, dinners, receptions. Barbarosa enjoyed these and was at his best during them. There he had opportunity to indulge in his fetish for clothing — his jeweled ceremonial scimitar alone was worth the ransom of a ranking aristocrat. Fluent in a half dozen languages and knowledgeable in European politics, he was a social lion. An intelligent and influential aristocrat, his host, the Duke of Enghien was to become a fervent admirer.

At a typical evening, the ambiance of the Duke's Mediterranean residence and the glittering attendees were impressive. Members of the leading commercial families, such nobility as Toulon afforded, a sprinkling of French admirals and generals — even a distant Royal Cousin were there. The language of the evening was French, although two minor French diplomats understood some Turkish.

The Frank diplomats were talking quietly to each other. "His royal highness, Francis, has been paying through the nose like a woman bleeding during her time. Before he is done, he could have built his own fleet for what this winter is costing him. Barbarosa has him bent over a barrel of gold and is giving it to him like he must give it to that young wife."

"How is the gold paid"?"

"Specie, man. Specie from Paris. And every month."

"Well," added a more cautious analyst, "There are ten thousand Turks sitting out there. If they wished, they could take a lot more than Royal gold."

"Do you know that he has Christians chained to those galleys in the outer harbor?"

"Maybe. I hear the rumor. It would please me if they chained every damn Spaniard or Italian in the Mediterranean to those benches. But I've never seem any Frenchmen— nor do I know anyone that has."

When Barbarosa and the Duke talked, the nobleman questioned costs.

"May I speak honestly, efendi?"

"Honesty wears the gown of a loved wife."

The Duke never failed to appreciate Barbarosa's epigrams. He nodded and went on, "The draw-down of gold last month was felt to be perhaps a bit more than might have been needed." He was trying his best to introduce the King's complaint in such a way as not to offend his guest's sensibilities.

"Is there question as to the accuracy of our statements?"

"No, no," the Duke assured him hastily, "Only the totals are found painful by His Majesty, who, after all, must take most of this gold from his own purse."

Barbarosa looked intently at the Duke. "Friend of my heart, I doubt not that the royal treasury of Francis is no less impecunious than that of most kings, but believe me, the best interests of France — especially in view of the fact that we are forced to spend the winter because of French failures to prepare and fight last season — will best be served if I do not have to explain to my captains why their crew's pay has been shortened."

Le Duc had a live, not entirely civilized, tiger in his house.

I n Europe, changes were taking place that would undermine any continuing cooperation between Islamic Turkey and Christian France. Chief among these was the decline in influence and power of the Roman Catholic Church. While unspeakable horrors of murder and torture would continue among Christians in the name of Christ for centuries as Catholics and Protestants slaughtered one another, Europe was rapidly becoming a collection of nation-states who depended on shifting allegiances and alliances rather than on Papal instructions.

The underlying cause of this change was the rot within the Roman Church. Luther's protest was inspired by outrageous corruption, but rather than changing itself, the Church had used its energies in an attempt to silence Luther. The various Popes of the early 16th century were either uninterested in, or unable to effect any reform and Luther's movement snowballed.

After Alexander's excesses, Julius II and Leo X continued as great spenders and sellers of Holy Offices, and Adrian VI, the childhood tutor of Charles who had assuaged his greed as head of the Spanish Inquisition for years, lived only two years after his election. Clement VII was noted chiefly for the loss of England to Protestantism and for his ill-chosen support of Francis in a war with Spain during which Rome was sacked and he himself was jailed. Paul III, in office at the time of Barbarosa's visit, was willing to approach reform, but his efforts had not yet borne fruit.[1]

With its reputation remaining in tatters, the Roman Church was increasingly disregarded.

Without the authority of a strong church behind him, Francis was

---

1.   Reform is not the province of the elderly. Owing to the process by which Popes were
      selected and held office, the Church was cursed with Popes whose intellectual and
      physical vigor had been sapped by age.

forced to deal with sister states — and he failed to enlist any. In fact, he lost ground. Henry VIII announced opposition to any French campaign against Spain. With this bad news added to the drum-beat of criticism he was receiving for his association with the Turks — some of it from within his own court — his resolution weakened, and at the end of the winter he abandoned his "Turkish Adventure."

Thus all of the provisions of the agreement with Barbarosa blossomed.

Francis' personal gifts to Barbarosa were notable even by royal standards — and while the amounts of gold transferred from France to the Sublime Porte have never been published, Suleiman was satisfied.

He was to welcome home the fleet and its Admiral with praise.

W hile the Atlantic was not unknown or unmastered by galleys — Venetian so-called Great Galleys had been venturing on trading voyages as far as England and the northern coast of Europe for two centuries — Turkish fleets were rarely to visit that great Ocean. Among Muslim seafarers, adventure outside the Gates of Hercules was enjoyed only by North African corsairs.

Turkey's fleets were better used to support her interests in the eastern Mediterranean. War galleys were not designed to deal with a galleon, nor were they likely to find suitable storm havens along the Portuguese coast. Enroute south that winter, Dragut restricted himself to threatening Cadiz and taking a dozen Spanish and Portuguese merchantmen.

His voyage was notable chiefly for the acquisition of an extraordinary item of treasure.

A Unicorn Horn.

There were not more than twenty in all of Europe, each with an attested history. A round, tapered, striated, whorled piece of ivory, eight or nine feet long, weighing about 20 pounds, one of these was a treasure without price — a royal prize for which kings would bargain. Two of these magical objects had belonged to Byzantine Emperors for a thousand years, passed on from generation to generation as national treasures. They were stolen from Constantinople and taken to Venice in the 14th century when the city was sacked by Christian Crusaders.

Now, two centuries later, one of the two was on its way to Spain.

The exceedingly rare — in fact, never seen — Unicorn was believed to

Barbarosa's residence (saray) in Istanbul.

be a magic animal possessed of gifts that the owner of a horn supposedly acquired. "It preserved a man from the arrow that flieth by day and the pestilence that walketh in the darkness, from the craft of the poisoner, from epilepsy, and from ills of the flesh. It is an amulet, a talisman, a weapon and a medicine chest..."

The Turks never reported to whom it was consigned, and when it reached Istanbul, it disappeared, never to be positively identified again.[1]

B arbarosa had four years to live after his return from Toulon. He remained in good health but didn't go to sea again. Suleiman had not yet fully succumbed to the paranoia that was to discolor his final years and their friendship remained strong, so the Admiral retained his influence in maritime matters, insuring that command of Turkish fleets — for by now there were several — went to capable men. He was idolized, he was very rich, and he had the domestic warmth of La Bella. He built a large public bath, which he humorously termed a bagnio, free to all, and a palace/yali for himself. Due not only to his fame, but to his facility in languages, he was popular with foreign dignitaries — whom he received with good humor and with free advice.

In his sixty seventh winter, he took a fever and lived only a week.[1] He

1.   A unicorn horn was a narwhale tusk, but that fact was known only to one or two lucky arctic hunters who caught the rare mammal.

died in bed, at home, La Bella at his side. After providing for her, he left most of his considerable estate to Islamic charities.

A Turkish national hero, he rests today in a modest tomb of his own design within a stone's throw of the westerly flowing current of the blue Bosporus. Adjacent to the tomb is a marble statue of him flanked by two fighting men depicting him in turban and flowing caftan, sea boots and scimitar, standing on the sharp prow of a ship, looking forward to a distant horizon.

For more than four centuries it has been a shrine which seafarers salute for good fortune as the Bosporus carries them past bound for distant seas.

The statue of Barbarosa is credited to Sinan, but the firearm carried by one of the warriors is from a later period.

---

1.   It is likely tht he died from pnuemonia, for there was no pestilence at the time.

Flag of Turkey. Red with White crescent and star. Boldly the Turkish flag seems to have been adopted using Byzantium Christian symbols commemorating a bright moon that saved Constantinople from Philip of Macedon thirteen hundred years earlier.

EPILOGUE

Like Camelot, in Turkey,
"…there was one brief shining moment…"

The Osmanli Turks created one of the remarkable Empires of history, one that was to cast it glow — or shadow — over the world for more than 400 years. Despite a system that gave absolute power to one man, a culture which condemned the female half of its population to practical servitude, and burdened with a religion which not only forbade but punished change, the Ottoman Empire survived, persevered, its design to so well engineered that it kept running for centuries after it was out of fuel, brain dead.

The 16th Century opened with Islam riding the crest of this superb government and offering its greatest challenge in the eight hundred year "war" with Christianity. It was to close with Islam in retreat, never again to seriously challenge its brother religion. The Islamic East was to mire itself permanently in ignorance and cruelty, while in the Christian West the Renaissance provided the key that was to eventually fling open the door of opportunity for mankind.

•⁓ From Greatness

Barbarosa was the Grand Admiral of Turkey from 1532 until his death in 1546 — a period of only fourteen years, but a time which coincides with the heart of Suleiman's rule and the apogee of Ottoman greatness. During Suleiman's reign, Turkey was not only the world's preeminent military power, but was a fertile, civilized culture. Artists and scholars were subsidized. Public schools (medresses) were widely available. City hospitals and hospices were maintained. Architecture flowered: Istanbul remains one of the world's treasures today because Suleiman encouraged the master architect Sinan (originally a devirsme slave child) to create a magnificent legacy of bridges, highways, aqueducts, parks, fountains, and public structures. Merchants and traders of all nationalities were encouraged and an economy was developed that enriched life and bade fair to eliminate poverty as conceived by the 16th century.

Suleiman's Turkey was a decent master of its varied peoples. Religious minorities were protected, taxed fairly, and didn't have to serve in the army. (The devirsme affected relatively small numbers of children, and in many cases was by no means unwelcome). Significantly, Orthodox Christians as well as Jews preferred Turkish rule to domination by Roman Christianity. Even some Roman Christians (such as Corsica) actively sought membership in the Ottoman Empire.[1]

Ottoman government was the engine that powered this greatness. The first true meritocracy outside of Confucian China, it was unmatched for efficiency, economy, and honesty. For the century and a half that the Ottoman line provided able Sultans (1413 to 1566), Turkey sought out, trained, and gave authority to men of talent regardless of origin — a system that gave the Empire a huge advantage over European nations where opportunity to rule was restricted to a very small group among whom individual ability was discovered only by chance.

But this superb arrangement was flawed with the poison of unchecked power — worse, a power made legitimate by religion. This poison found a hospitable environment as Suleiman aged and, gaining strength as less able men succeeded him, was to rapidly metastasize in the Ottoman body.

Mankind is as addicted to power as is the wolf pack, the lion pride, the cow herd, or the chicken flock. No one is exempt. Women offer green meadows of sex on which rulers and rich men may graze as eagerly as female rats in the sink spurn lesser males to offer themselves to those who have established a territory. Power in Turkey became an aberration that severely distorted those who wielded it. Within a single century, Turkey was to have a ruler who personally sold offices for gold to be stored in a vault under the royal bed, a successor who drowned companions of the royal bed after one night of connubial joy, and another who practiced archery skills on live captives and slaves.[2]

1. The attitude of the Roman Church was expressed well by Pope Gregory, who said, "It is far better for a country to remain under the rule of Islam than to be governed by Christians who refuse to acknowledge the rights of the Catholic Church."

2. In a paroxysm of anger after the Turkish naval defeat at Lepanto in 1571, Selim the Sot (whose nickname betrays his habits), ordered the death of all the Christians in his Empire (He was kept drunk until he forgot the order).

With despotic power unchecked, religion was free to cast its spell.

·⁓ The Role of Religion a Sorry One

Christianity, Judaism, Islam are all "revealed" religions — essentially legal systems — but they diverged in the reach and interpretation of their rules. The God of Jews and Christians judged men by how much they managed to act in ways He prescribed, what kind of Godlike images they created of themselves. The God of Islam, however, judged men by how well they obeyed, submitted, to Him.

Until about mid 9th century — during the Umayyad Caliphs — the idea that the Koran might be subject to further interpretation gained adherents and a flourishing intellectual culture developed in parts of Islam — the Moorish civilization in Spain being the best example. But from the time of Mamun's successor, who said (of the Koran), "That which is between the two covers is the word of God, and what we read and write is the very speech of God," Islamic scholars claimed their rulebook to be "uncreated", by which they meant that the accepted version of Mohammed's utterances was actually God speaking. The Koran was not only God's word, it *was* God.[1]

From that time, for a Muslim to "create" new ideas became a mocking of God.

One of the greatest Islamic legists never ate a watermelon because he could find neither Koranic instructions nor any history indicating that Mohammed had eaten one. Another famous Islamic scholar boasted that he had not read a book other than the Koran for twenty years; it encompassed all knowledge.

"In'shallah", as God wills. An ordained course of events,

The forbidding of progress.

In Muslim Turkey the religious system of education bred a sense of superiority. The financial and commercial controls of the Empire — trade, manufacturing, science — if not actually forbidden, were disdainfully assigned to the hands of non-Turks. The printing press, for example, was prohibited until well into the 18th century, nearly two centuries after cheap and popular fliers were convincing Europeans to sail for the New World. The early tradition of religious tolerance was abandoned. Dissec-

---

1. The Muslim God is omnipresent, part of everything and every action. "…when He decides upon an affair, He says to it, be.' And it is." (Surah XL, 68).

tion of human bodies was forbidden and medicine careened into a pit of superstition. Art was similarly circumscribed because depiction of the human form was forbidden. Religious practices replaced military skills and discipline.

Worst of all, the increasing subjugation of women resulted in an incalculable loss of human talent and energy.

In the final analysis, Turks became men of the past, straight-jacketed into 7th century interpretations of the vague, elliptical, sometimes contradictory, impressions of a religious visionary.

Progress became a violation; acceptance a virtue.

·⌐ Military Decay was Inevitable

Led by the army, the step to widespread corruption was short and soon taken. Before it was abandoned entirely, the Devirsme became a simple slave hunt, with a strong coloration of pederasty. Janissaries were allowed to marry and their children were permitted to enlist, opening the door for nepotism and clique growth. The Janissary Corps, eventually bloated to a hundred thousand, most of whom were barracked in Istanbul, drew up its own seat at the table of power, choosing claimants to the throne and murdering or overthrowing occupants already wearing the crown.

Technology, traditionally an area of Turkish military excellence, atrophied.

Homosexuality, long tolerated in the East, became widespread in the military. Men of that persuasion may be brave warriors — Alexander the Great was a practitioner of the art and the outrageously brave Mamelukes of Egypt were homosexual to a man. But Alexander's "Pretty Boys" were companions rather than soldiers — and the Mamelukes died on their own spears when confronted with gunpowder. Sexual privileges became a franchise of power and a source of abuse.

Change in Sea Warfare — Our Particular Interest

Like the Turkish Army, the quality of command and leadership in Turkish fleets began to decline almost immediately after Barbarosa. For a time Turkey challenged Portugal in the Indian Ocean, but could hold only the Gulf of Aquaba and the Red Sea. A description of the southern fleet Admiral says it all, "He weighed over four hundred pounds and had to be lifted to his feet on the quarterdeck — as well as braced for his

familial obligations."

In the Mediterranean, at the decisive Battle of Lepanto only twenty five years after Barbarosa's death, the Turkish fleet was burdened with fifteen beys, four admirals, and two overall commanders (one of whom was a brother of a new Grand Vizier), most of whom believed that anything less than an all out frontal attack was criminal cowardice. The lesson that Barbarosa had taught at Prevesa was forgotten. The Christians towed heavy galleons into the front of their galley line and rang a death knell for the Turkish fleet.

Since early Rome, Galley war had largely been conducted by converted merchant shipping. But the rapid development of guns and gunpowder — no less than food costs to maintain large fleets — made them obsolete within practically one lifetime and, with no urge to develop new platforms, when galleys died, Ottoman sea-power went with them.

What of Today? A Future for Turkey?

In 1922 the Turkish Army partially redeemed itself by leading a revolution intended to drag the nation out of the enervating grasp of religion and to thrust it into the 20th century. Ataturk, a charismatic leader revered today, remained in power long enough for many of his reforms to take root. They survive in varying degrees today.

- Modern Turkey forbids political power to religion and has outlawed many of its confining practices.
- It has established (and practices) equal rights for women.
- It has a representative, parliamentary, government that conducts free elections.
- It has extensive secular public education and a Romanized written language.
- It has a court and justice system based on secular law (German).
- It has a vigorous media, one that would be classed as exceptionally free in much of the world.

And Many of Turkey's Natural Advantages Remain:

It has one of the better climates of the world. It is agriculturally rich and is well on the way to satisfying its energy needs. It lies astride the routes of communication of hundreds of millions of people. It has a vigorous and cheerful people, responsive to the rule of law — a people to whom work is pride — and it has a history and tradition that unifies ninety percent of its racial melting pot.

'There is hope'

Elif

Demet

Modern Turkish women researchers and guides in Istanbul

ABOUT OUR PLAYERS

Andrea Doria achieved his life's ambition. He became ruler of Genoa and lived into his nineties.

Charles soon abdicated in favor of his son Philip and spent the rest of his life in religious reflections.

Francis died only a year after Barbarosa, leaving a legacy that was to mature into the corrupt brilliance of Louis XIV a century later.

Henry VIII died the same year. Elizabeth was to eventually become his successor — as Margaret Bannock had predicted.

Suleiman lived on for twenty years. Increasingly paranoid, he was convinced by Roxelana to murder his son by his first wife, a move that put her son Selim the Sot on the throne — where he promptly sped Turkey into corruption and decay.

...AND BARBAROSA'S FRIENDS

Dragut became the Grand Admiral of the Turkish fleet. He was later to recapture Tunis, take Tripoli, and inflict a major defeat on Spain in a battle off Djerba. He died during the Turkish seige of Malta executing orders with which he disagreed.

Ochiali also became an admiral and, in his old age, was drawn into the battle of Lepanto where he was to lead the only wing of the Turkish fleet that survived. He died soon after.

Hassan Aga, the eunuch, was a popular and efficient Viceroy of Algiers. He died from "abdominal humors", having cheerfully yielded Algiers to Hassan, Barbarosa's son.

Hassan was also to die young and leave no heir. During his time, however, he drove the Spanish out of North Africa in all but Cueta and Oran.

Salah served as an Admiral, then succeeded Hassan as Viceroy of Algiers. He died of the plague.

Sinan the Jew spent his declining years as a scholar/author of navigational texts and was honored with the title Admiral, the only Jew so distinguished in Turkish history.

Aydin and Ahmed retired in Algiers and lived to respected old ages in their gardens.

La Bella? We don't know.

GLOSSARY

ALLAH
: Supreme Being. God. (The Koran was written in Arabic and all religious terms are expressed in that language; some Muslims consider a translation of the Koran into other languages to be sacrilegious.)

ANATOLIA
: Asia Minor portion of the Turkish Empire, approximately the land area of modern Turkey.

DIVAN
: (Literally "couch"). Sultan's cabinet. Collegiate group at head of Turkish government who also functioned as a type of appeals court and high level omsbudmen.

HAJ
: Also Haji. Honorific title applied to those Muslims who have made the pilgrimage to Mecca.

INFIBULATION
: Sewing together of the outer labia of women to insure chastity. The clitoris is first incised, then the labia sewed from top down with leather or horsehair, leaving only a small opening for urine. Only practiced by primitive African and Shiite Muslim zealots. Unlacing was possible, but some new husbands prided themselves on being able to insert themselves by force — while special musicians played loudly to drown the cries of the bride.

ISLAM
: The term literally means "submission to God's will" and is used as a noun. May be applied collectively to the lands in which the religion dominates or to its followers, e.g. "all of Islam."

ISMAILI
: Heretical Islamic sect best known for their secret sub society of Assassins — secret bands of mystical fanatics who eliminated enemies by murder. Their influence can be felt today in Islam. (Assassins translates as "under the influence of hashish").

KOHL
Cosmetic made from finely powdered antimony or smoke blackened ground almond shells. Used to darken women's eyelids.

KORAN
Literally: "To recite." A compilation of the revelations of Mohammed as remembered and refined by his immediate followers. About the length of the New Testament, it is believed literally by Muslims, all of whom know it intimately.

LEVANT
Coastline of Asia Minor (Turkey) and Syria. High Levant described the coast all the way from Greece to Egypt.

MAMELUKE
(Also Mamluk) "Possession" in Arabic. A slave military caste who ruled Egypt from Saladin until subjugated by Turkey — but allowed to remain in power — until Napoleon wiped them out in the early 19th century. Exceptionally fierce fighters, they were almost exclusively homosexual (they ensured succession by adoption). An example of the intellectual and social corruption into which segments of Islam fell.

MUSLIM
Literally "a follower." A believer in Islam. Can be used as either adjective or noun. Also known as Moslem, Musselman, or Mohammedan.

RAMADAN
The ninth month of the Muslim calendar during which absolute fasting, to include sex and water, is observed during daylight. A basic requirement of Islam, it was named for the "hot" or "dry" month, but the Muslim calendar is lunar, and months move forward each year, so it may occur in winter.

RUMELIA
Originally the European portion (Balkans, Transylvania, Macedonia etc) of 14th & 15th century Ottoman Empire. Taken from "Roman".

SERAGLIO
Royal household or court, of which the harem was a part.

SHARIA
The holy law of Islam. The core of authority drawn from Mohammed's revelations. Basic interpretation of the Koran.

SHERIF
An official. Originally a descendant of Fatima (the daughter of Mohammed) but came to mean an appointive head of a division of government, such as a city.

SHIA	Fundamentalist, radical, emotional Islamic sect. Centered today largely in Iran.
SHIITE	Practitioner, follower of shia.
SUNNA	Conservative philosophy, explanation, interpretations of the Koran. Religious rules accepted as law by sunni (mainstream) Muslims. Also known as "The Tradition."
TELERO	Venetian term for outrigger on galleys which held the tholes. Typically four to six feet outboard of the hull, it provided a fulcrum located about one third of the oar's length from the rower.
THOLE	Or tholepin. Oarlocks. Oak or metal dowels set into outmounted frames (teleros) or on gunwales, which acted as fulcrums for oars.

SELECTED BIBLIOGRAPHY

Anderson, R. C., *Oared Fighting Ships*, Percival & Marshall, London 1962.

Asimov, Isaac, *Constantinople, The Forgotten Empire* Houghton Mifflin, Boston, 1970.

Atil, Esin, *Suleymanname*, Natl Gallery of Art, Washington D.C. 1986.

Beeching, Jack, *The Galleys at Lepanto*, C Scribner's Sons, N.Y., NY 1982

Bradford, Ernle, *The Sultan's Admiral*, Harcourt, Brace. N.Y., NY 1968.

Bridge, Antony, *Suleiman the Magnificent*, Granada, London 1983.

Coles, Paul, *The Ottoman Impact on Europe*, Harcourt, Brace, World, N.Y., NY 1968.

Currey, E.H., *Sea-Wolves of the Mediterranean*, J. Murray, London 1910.

Dereksen, David, *The Crescent and the Cross*, Putnam's Sons, N.Y., NY 1964. *(The best book on Constantinople and the Turks who conquered it)*

Fisher, Sir G., *Barbary Legend*, Oxford University Press, 1957.

Guilmartin, John F., *Gunpowder and Galleys*, Cambridge University Press, London 1974. *(The best book on galleys and cannons)*

Khalifa, Hoji, *History of the Maritime Wars of the Turks*, (As quoted).

Hallam, Eliz, *Chronicles of the Crusades*, Weidenfield and Nicholson, N.Y., NY 1989.

Haedo, Fra Diego, *Two Histories of Algiers* (As quoted.)

Kinross, Lord, *The Ottoman Centuries*, Morrow Quill, N.Y., NY 1977.

Landstrom, Bjorn, *The Ship*, Doubleday and Co, Garden City, NY 1961.

Lane, Frederic C., *Venetian Ships and Shipbuilders of the Rennaissance*, Johns Hopkins Press, Baltimore. 1934.

Lane, Frederic C., *Venice, A Maritime Republic*, Johns Hopkins Press, Baltimore, 1975.

Lane-Poole, Stanley, *The Story of Turkey*, G.P. Putnam's Sons, London 1888.

Lane-Poole, Stanley, *The Story of the Barbary Corsairs*, Putnam's Sons, London 1890

Lewis, Bernard, *Istanbul and the Civilization of the Ottoman Empire*, Univ of Oklahoma Press, Norman OK. 1963.

Lewis, Bernard, *The Arabs in History*. Rev ed., Harper &Row, N.Y., NY. 1967.

Ludwig, Emil, *The Mediterranean*, Whittlesey House, London 1942.

MacNeil, William, *The Pursuit of Power*, Univ of Chicago 1982.

Mattingly, Garett, *The Armada*, Houghton Mifflin, Boston 1959.

Melek-Hanum, *Thirty Years in the Harem*, Harper & Bros, N.Y., NY. 1872.

Morgan, J., *A Complete History of Algiers*, London 1731. (As quoted).

Penzer, N. M., *The Harem*, Spring Books - Chaucer Press, London 1936.

Pipes, Daniel, *Slave Soldiers and Islam*, Yale, New Haven 1981.

Rodison, Maxine, *Muhammad*, Pantheon Books (Translated by Ann Carter), N.Y., NY, 1971.

Rogers, William, *Naval Warfare Under Oars*, US Naval Institute, Annapolis. 1940.

Slaughter, Frank, *Constantine*, Doubleday & Co, Garden City, NY. 1965.

Time-Life Books, *Early Islam*, Time, N.Y., NY. 1974

Villiers, Adam, *Men, Ships, and the Sea*, Natl Geo Soc, Washington DC. 1973

White, Lynn, *Medieval Technology and Social Change*, London. 1962

Wolf, John B, *The Barbary Coast*, WW Norton, NY, London. 1979

Most of the Arab customs and terms, especially those sexual, come from Sir Richard Burton's *Arabian Nights* — and from two recent biographies of Sir Richard: McLynn, Frank, *Burton, Snow Upon the Desert*, John Murray Ltd, London 1990, and Rice, Edward, *Captain Sir Richard Francis Burton*, Charles Scribner's Sons, New York 1990.

National Geographic publications have been valuable for maps.

CHARLES I of Spain

A man in whom the poison of insanity ran — his mother spent the last quarter of her life under restraints, and his grandson boiled and ate his own shoes — he truly considered himself the personal representative of God on Earth. Despite his unprepossessing appearance, his skill in planning and governing was unmatched and his courage remarked. His lifetime enemy, Francis, considered his presence in battle worth "…five brigades of cavalry…"

FRANCIS I of France

A true Renaissance king, a larger than life figure who personally jousted with the greatest Knights of his kingdom, he employed Leonardo da Vinci, sponsored Rabelais, and kept Cellini as an artist in residence. He spent little time governing, preferring the many boudoirs available to a vigorous Bourbon King. His own ministers called him "…amorous as a cat…"

SULEIMAN of Turkey

A product of three centuries of absolute family power, trained from earliest childhood to believe in his own omnipotence, the richest man alive, a wave of his hand could set into action the most powerful military force in the world, a scribbled signature could grant a kingdom. The Turks called him, "Sublime One," "Shadow of God," "Lawgiver." He called himlself "Ruler of Two Worlds." Europeans called him "The Magnificent."

The Corsairs of North Africa

Brave, highly skilled seamen, many of these pirates were former Christians. Fearsome fighters, they were called "sea-ghazis" after the fierce, Turkish cavalrymen who laid waste to much of Eastern Europe. Unexcelled at their trade, they made Algiers "…ready to sink, opulent with wealth: gold, silver, spices, pearls, amber, drugs, silks, velvets…" Despite a Spanish reward equal to the ransom of a noble and a sentence of immediate execution, their numbers… "were little reduced."

The Roman Catholic Church

"When the kindness of Constantine gave Holy Church endowments
In lands and leases, lordships and servants,
The Romans heard an angel cry on high above them,
This day *dos ecclesiae* has drunk venom
And all who have Peter's power are poisoned forever."

—William Langland